# Harmonious Worlds

Crafting inclusive governance for a diverse humanity.

Abraham Chaffin

# Foreword

At the onset of this book, I was of the mind that this book would be about revealing which type of government would be most ideal and reveal the faults of those political parties which has left many of us unsatisfied. However, as is the usual outcome during the generation of these books, I was pleasantly surprised things did not go according to plan. Instead, I was left with a book which required me to use empathy, understanding, and patience to consider other new points of view.

The AI was asked to provide guidance for what a perfect government would be for the benefit of all humanity. AI chose and brought together diverse components. These components were brought together and melded into a unique vision. This vision of government, befitting harmonious societies, is astounding. The boundaries of these components are not always clear but the essence and intentions of these ingredients are added to blended into this vision of what government could potentially be.

# Contents


1. Unity in Diversity     *1*

2. The Digital Polis     *23*

3. Green Governments     *48*

4. Economic Inclusivity     *74*

5. Guardians of Heritage     *99*

6. The People's Voice     *124*

7. The Art of Peace     *150*

8. Educating Citizens     *175*

9. Health as a Political Pillar     *200*

10. Adaptive and Resilient Governance     *226*

# Preface

In an era marked by unprecedented global interconnectivity and profound diversity, the quest for effective governance has never been more critical or more challenging. "Harmonious Worlds: Crafting Inclusive Governance for a Diverse Humanity" emerges from this crucible of complexity, offering a visionary perspective on how we can navigate the intricate landscape of governing diverse societies in the 21st century.

This book is born out of a simple yet profound realization: there is no one-size-fits-all solution to governance. The diverse tapestry of human society - with its rich array of cultures, traditions, and values - calls for a governance approach that is equally diverse and nuanced. This realization is not new; it is as old as human civilization itself. Yet, in our increasingly interconnected world, the need for such an approach has become more urgent and apparent.

Our journey begins with an exploration of global governance, not just as a political necessity but as a moral imperative. In a world where our destinies are ever more intertwined, the need for a governance framework that acknowledges and celebrates diversity while fostering unity and a shared vision for humanity is paramount.

From there, we delve into the realms of digital democracy, economic equality, environmental stewardship, cultural preservation, participatory politics, conflict resolution, educational policy, and public health. Each chapter is not just a standalone exploration but a thread in the larger tapestry of this book's vision. Together, they weave a narrative that is both rich in its complexity and clear in its purpose.

The writing of this book has been a journey of discovery, dialogue, and reflection. It draws upon the wisdom of the past and the innovations of the present, offering insights that are both timeless and timely. It is a call to action for policymakers, scholars, and citizens to rethink governance in a way that respects and harnesses our diversity, not as a barrier to overcome but as a resource to embrace.

As you turn these pages, I invite you to join me in envisioning a world where governance is a harmonious symphony of diverse voices, a world where every individual, community, and nation finds their place in the chorus of humanity. This is not just a dream; it is a possibility within our grasp. Together, let us take the first steps towards making it a reality.

# 1. Unity in Diversity



## 1.1 The Tapestry of Cultures

*- Understanding the Diversity of Global Societies*

In the intricate weave of the world's tapestry, each thread represents a unique culture, belief, and way of life. As we embark on the quest to envision unity in diversity, it is essential to first understand the vast spectrum of global societies, acknowledging that each holds a vital place in the mosaic of humanity.

The concept of a tapestry is apt for our purposes; just as a weaver selects threads of various hues and textures to create a harmonious design, so must we appreciate the different elements that contribute to the global cultural fabric. This appreciation is not merely an aesthetic or philosophical stance but a fundamental principle for crafting inclusive governance.

The diversity of global societies is staggering—ranging from the nomadic tribes that traverse sprawling deserts to the hyper-connected citizens populating the world's metropolises. Each society comes with its own set of values, traditions, and social norms, which have been honed over centuries. These differences can be seen In the myriad languages wo speak, the religions we practice, the foods we eat, and the arts we cherish. Yet, within this diversity lies a commonality—the innate human need to belong, to contribute, and to have a voice in the decisions that shape our lives.

In the pursuit of inclusive governance, it is crucial to recognize that one size does not fit all. The frameworks and systems that work for a technologically advanced urban center may be ill-suited for a rural community deeply rooted in ancestral traditions. Governance, therefore, must be a fluid concept, adaptable and sensitive to the needs of each unique societal fabric.

Despite the differences, global societies face common challenges. Climate change, economic inequality, and the struggle for human rights transcend national and cultural boundaries. These shared issues serve as a reminder that while our cultures may divide us, our collective challenges have the power to unite us.

In the sections that follow, we shall explore how governance can become a loom that interlaces these diverse threads without fraying them, creating a strong and inclusive structure. We will look at specific examples of governance that have successfully harnessed cultural diversity, turning it into a strength rather than a barrier.

As we contemplate the vast tapestry of cultures before us, let us remember that unity in diversity is not merely a utopian ideal but a practical goal. It is achievable through the thoughtful design of governance systems that respect and celebrate the rich palette of human experience while working towards a common good. This is the foundation upon which a harmonious world can be built—a world where every thread, every culture, is valued as part of the whole.

*- The Importance of Cultural Recognition and Representation*

As we embark on the journey to create inclusive governance for a diverse humanity, we must first acknowledge the rich tapestry of cultures that make up our global society. This tapestry—a vibrant and intricate weave of traditions, languages, beliefs, and histories—is not merely an embellishment on the fabric of humanity. It is the very substance from which our collective identity emerges.

Cultural recognition and representation are foundational to any governance system that aspires to be inclusive. When we speak of recognition, we mean more than the passive acknowledgment of different cultures—it is an active, ongoing process of understanding, respecting, and valuing the distinctiveness of each cultural thread in the tapestry. Representation, on the other hand, ensures that these diverse voices are not just heard but are also influential in the decision-making processes that affect their lives.

Why is this so important? Because when cultures are recognized and represented, they are empowered. Communities that see their identities reflected in governance structures feel a sense of belonging and legitimacy. This fosters social cohesion, as individuals are more likely to invest in a system that they feel represents their interests and values.

Conversely, the absence of cultural recognition can lead to feelings of alienation and marginalization. When people are made invisible within the systems that govern them, the fabric of society begins to fray. Discontent brews, often manifesting in social unrest or even conflict. Thus, the very stability of governance is contingent upon its ability to mirror the diversity it purports to serve.

In this digital age, the ways in which we can achieve cultural recognition and representation are manifold. Technology has the potential to democratize voices, allowing the previously unheard to broadcast their narratives on a global stage. Yet, the digital divide means that we must be vigilant in ensuring that this potential is realized equitably, rather than exacerbating existing disparities.

The governance structures we envision in this book are not monolithic; they are as fluid and dynamic as the cultures they represent. They are designed with the understanding that culture is not static—it evolves, and so must the mechanisms of governance. In this dance of transformation, the constant is a commitment to inclusivity, ensuring that no thread in the tapestry is overshadowed or cut off.

In the chapters that follow, we will explore how this commitment to cultural recognition and representation can be woven into every aspect of governance— from digital democracy to environmental stewardship, from economic equality to the nurturing of education and public health. By doing so, we will not just strengthen the weave of our global society but also enrich its colors, creating a harmonious world that celebrates diversity as its greatest strength.

## 1.2 The Vision of Inclusive Governance

*- Defining Inclusive Governance Models*

In the soft glow of dawn, the world seems to awaken to the possibilities of a new day—a day where the ideals of inclusive governance could become the cornerstone of a society that thrives on its diversity. This vision of inclusive governance is not a distant dream but an attainable reality that beckons us with a promise of unity amidst our differences.

Inclusive governance models are those that actively embrace the spectrum of human experience, recognizing that every voice has value and every perspective holds a piece of the larger truth. These models are not merely about the absence of discrimination or the tolerance of diversity; they are about the celebration and integration of the myriad threads that together weave the fabric of our societies.

To define inclusive governance, we must look beyond the traditional structures of power that have often silenced minority voices. We must seek a model that distributes influence equitably, affording every individual the opportunity to impact the decisions that shape their lives. This is a model where decision-making processes are transparent, accessible, and responsive to the needs of all, not just the privileged few.

Inclusive governance entails the acknowledgment that different groups have different needs and aspirations, and that these differences should not only be respected but should inform policy-making. It involves creating avenues for participation that are culturally sensitive and linguistically inclusive, ensuring that language and tradition do not become barriers to engagement.

At the heart of this model lies the concept of "co-governance"—a collaborative approach where citizens and governments work together as partners in the stewardship of their community. This approach fosters a sense of ownership and responsibility among citizens, who no longer see themselves as passive subjects but as active contributors to the civic tapestry.

The digital revolution offers unprecedented tools for participatory democracy. E-governance platforms can provide real-time feedback loops, crowd-sourcing of ideas, and direct channels for dialogue between the governed and those in governance. The power of technology can democratize information and empower citizens with data to make informed decisions and hold governments accountable.

But inclusive governance is not just about the mechanisms of participation; it's about the spirit of empathy that should infuse our policies. It's about recognizing the interconnectedness of our fates and fortunes, understanding that the health of the individual is inextricably linked to the health of the collective.

As we embark on this exploration, it is essential to remember that inclusive governance is not a static ideal; it is a dynamic process of learning, adapting, and evolving. It is a challenge to our ingenuity and a test of our commitment to the ideals of justice, equity, and shared prosperity. But above all, it is a vision that calls us to action—a vision that urges us to build bridges where walls once stood and to forge a future where every human being can thrive in the fullness of their potential, embraced by the society to which they belong.


*- The Principles of Equity and Fairness*

In the silken tapestry of our shared existence, the threads of countless cultures, beliefs, and identities interlace to form the vibrant and ever-expanding human mosaic. It is within this complex weave that we find the urgent need for a governance that not only recognizes but celebrates our differences while fostering unity and common purpose. This vision of inclusive governance is anchored in the enduring principles of equity and fairness – values that have long been the bedrock of just societies.

Equity, in its most luminous form, goes beyond the simple notion of equality – where everyone is given the same resources or opportunities. Instead, it acknowledges the unique circumstances of each individual and community, providing the tailored support necessary to achieve an equal footing. The vision of inclusive governance thus demands that we look through the lens of context, ensuring that no one is disadvantaged by their starting point in life. It is the dance of justice, one that responds to the rhythm of need with grace and precision.

Fairness, the twin star to equity, guides the hand of governance to distribute resources, opportunities, and representation without favoritism or prejudice. It is the commitment to an impartiality that transcends cultural biases and systemic barriers. Fairness in governance means decisions are made not behind the opaque veil of privilege, but in the open plaza of public scrutiny, where all voices are heard and considered. It is the embodiment of a moral compass that points steadfastly towards the common good.

The vision of inclusive governance is thus a call to action, a clarion call that resonates with the deep human yearning for respect and dignity. It is an invitation to build institutions that serve as the guardians of equity and fairness, ensuring that the wealth of our diversity is matched by the richness of our opportunities. In this envisioned world, governance is not a distant monolith but a responsive and nimble partner in the collective journey towards prosperity and peace.

It requires a reimagining of power structures, one that disperses authority in a manner that allows local conditions to inform global strategies. Such a vision insists on a governance that is participatory, where citizens are not merely subjects but active architects of their fate. It calls for the shaping of policies that are both mirror and window – reflecting the needs of the people while offering a vista into the potential of an equitable future.

The principles of equity and fairness do not promise an easy path. They demand courage, creativity, and an unwavering commitment to the commonweal. Yet, it is precisely this vision of inclusive governance, grounded in these ageless principles, that holds the promise of a harmonious world. A world where every individual – regardless of race, creed, gender, or geography – can thrive under the nurturing canopy of justice.


<u>1.3 The Role of Philosophy in Governance</u>

*- Ethical Foundations for Decision-Making*

In the verdant groves of ancient Athens, where philosophy once danced among the olive trees, a profound understanding of governance was born. It was here that the concept of an ethical polis—a community bound by moral principles and justice—emerged. As we chart a course toward harmonious worlds, the lessons of those philosophical forebears are more relevant than ever.

The musings of Socrates, the treatises of Aristotle, and the reflections of contemporary philosophers converge to lay the groundwork for inclusive governance. Philosophy's contribution to governance is the scaffolding upon which societies can build structures of fairness, accountability, and collective well-being. It encourages leaders to transcend the immediacy of political gain and consider the lasting impact of their decisions on the fabric of humanity. Philosophical debate fosters the kind of critical thinking that challenges the status quo and pushes the boundaries of innovation in governance.

Within these pages, we explore the ethical imperatives that philosophy provides for decision-making. The principles of utilitarianism, deontology, and virtue ethics, among others, help inform policy that is not only effective but also just. Likewise, John Rawls' theory of justice, with its emphasis on fairness as the essence of ethical governance, as well as the capability approach championed by Amartya Sen and Martha Nussbaum, which focuses on providing individuals the freedom to achieve well-being.

These philosophical frameworks can be applied to real-world governance. For instance, utilitarianism can guide policies maximize happiness for the greatest number, while deontological ethics can uphold the sanctity of individual rights in legislative processes. Virtue ethics, on the other hand, can inspire leaders to embody qualities like wisdom, courage, and temperance, setting a moral example for the polity.

To govern amid diversity is to recognize that there are multiple philosophical perspectives, each with its own cultural and historical significance. For example, Eastern philosophies such as Confucianism and its focus on harmony and social order, along with the African concept of Ubuntu, which emphasizes our interconnectedness and mutual responsibilities.

Here is proposed an integrative philosophical approach to governance, one that melds these diverse ethical traditions into a cohesive framework that respects and values the plurality of human experience. It posits that an ethical foundation for decision-making, informed by the rich tapestry of global philosophical thought, is the cornerstone of governance that can truly achieve unity in diversity—leading not to a uniform society, but to a harmonious world enriched by its manifold differences.

In the intricate tapestry of human society, the role of philosophy in governance is akin to the warp and weft that holds the fabric together. It is philosophy that challenges us to question the status quo, to reflect upon the nature of justice, and to seek out the common threads that bind us in our diversity. The quest for harmony in governance is not merely a political endeavor but a philosophical pilgrimage towards a more profound understanding of unity and diversity.

The philosophical perspective on unity in diversity begins with the principle of pluralism. This is the recognition that multiple, often conflicting, truths and values can coexist and that governance systems must accommodate this plurality to create a harmonious society. Plato's Republic, with its emphasis on the ideal state where each class performs its role for the greater good, hints at such an equilibrium, but modern pluralistic philosophies take this concept further. They advocate for a governance that respects individual differences while striving for a collective harmony.

Aristotle, in his Politics, argues for a polity that fosters the good life for its citizens, understanding that the good life looks different for each individual. Here, the role of governance is to cultivate an environment where diverse ways of living can flourish without impinging on each other. This necessitates a careful balancing act, ensuring that the pursuit of personal fulfillment is not at the expense of communal harmony.

Contemporary philosophers, drawing from the liberal tradition, emphasize the importance of individual autonomy within a framework of social justice. John Rawls, with his theory of justice, envisions a society where governance structures are arranged so that the greatest benefit is afforded to the least advantaged, thereby ensuring fairness and equality. His principles of justice seek to create a system where diverse individuals can coexist, each pursuing their conception of the good life, without disadvantage.

On the other hand, communitarian philosophers like Charles Taylor argue that a focus on individual rights neglects the essential role of community in shaping identity. Taylor suggests that governance must recognize and nurture the cultural contexts from which individuals derive meaning. This does not mean suppressing diversity but rather embracing it as the foundation of a cohesive society where governance acts as a facilitator of cultural expression and dialogue.

In the digital age, these philosophical perspectives take on new dimensions.

The rise of technology presents both challenges and opportunities for unity in diversity. Digital platforms can be designed to foster inclusive participation, ensuring that governance is responsive to the nuanced needs of a diverse populace. Yet, they also risk amplifying divisions if not carefully moderated. The philosophical underpinnings of governance must thus evolve to incorporate these technological realities without losing sight of the eternal quest for a society where diversity is not an obstacle but a source of collective strength.

As we embark on this journey, we carry with us the wisdom of these philosophical perspectives, weaving them into the policies and structures that govern our lives. We recognize that the pursuit of unity in diversity is not a destination but a continuous process of reflection, dialogue, and adaptation—a process deeply rooted in the philosophical tradition that sees governance as the art of making the collective dance of humanity a harmonious one.


## 1.4 Political Science Contributions

*- Political Theories on Diversity and Governance*

In the quest for harmonious worlds, political science serves as a beacon, illuminating the path with theories that dissect and reconstruct the complex relationship between diversity and governance. The contributions of this discipline are pivotal, for they provide a theoretical backbone to the practical endeavors of inclusive governance.

The tapestry of political theories is as variegated as the societies they seek to organize. At one end of the spectrum lies Liberalism, with its emphasis on individual rights, freedoms, and the protection of minorities. It posits that governance should be a reflective mirror of society's plurality, each voice resonating with equal clarity in the halls of power. Liberal institutions are thus designed to safeguard diversity, ensuring that governance is not merely the rule of the majority but an orchestra of varied interests and perspectives.

Contrastingly, Communitarianism shifts focus onto the community as the bearer of rights and values. This perspective argues for governance systems that are attuned to the cultural fabrics of society, embedding the communal narrative into the legislative script. The chorus of the collective, with its shared history and vision, becomes the guiding melody for policy-making.

Delving further into the political science repository, we encounter Deliberative Democracy, a theory that champions the role of dialogue in governance. It holds that diversity should not lead to discord but rather to rich, inclusive conversations that shape the public sphere. Deliberative forums aim to transform cacophony into symphony, with each participant contributing to a harmonized decision-making process that respects and reflects societal diversity.

Rawlsian justice, with its two principles of equal liberty and the difference principle, suggests that the structures of governance must be blind to the accidents of birth such as race, class, or gender. Instead, they should be engineered to benefit the least advantaged, thereby fostering an environment where diversity does not predicate inequality.

The Polyarchal model of democracy brings yet another dimension to the discourse, highlighting the necessity of multiple centers of power to accommodate diverse interests. It is governance as a network rather than a pyramid, where power is dispersed and governance mechanisms are interwoven with the social fabric.

In the synthesis of these political theories, one discerns the blueprint for inclusive governance that respects diversity. Each theory contributes a thread to the loom, weaving a governance structure that is robust yet flexible, representative yet efficient, and above all, just and equitable.

As we move forward in this volume, these political theories will serve as the intellectual scaffolding upon which practical applications are built. They remind us that the goal of governance in a diverse humanity is not to erase differences but to construct a political ecosystem where every difference enriches the collective, where every voice, regardless of its timbre, can sing in the choir of democracy.


*- Case Studies of Inclusive Political Systems*

The quest for inclusive governance has been a central theme in political science discourse. It is a pursuit that acknowledges the intrinsic value of diversity within the human tapestry, and it seeks to translate this appreciation into functioning political systems. This section examines case studies of political systems that have broken ground in the practice of inclusion, providing practical examples of how unity in diversity can be achieved.

The first case study takes us to the northern reaches of Europe, to the consociational democracy of the Netherlands. Consociationalism is characterized by power-sharing arrangements, minority vetoes, and a high degree of autonomy for distinct groups. The Dutch model has successfully navigated deep religious and ideological divides, fostering a political culture of cooperation and consensus. By ensuring that multiple voices are heard and respected in decision-making processes, the Netherlands demonstrates that inclusive governance can be both stable and effective.

Moving across the globe, we encounter the participatory budgeting initiatives of Porto Alegre, Brazil. Here, citizens have a direct say in how a portion of the city budget is allocated, engaging in a process that goes beyond mere consultation to active decision-making. The participatory budgeting model has taken root in various forms worldwide, but Porto Alegre's example remains a beacon. It highlights how involving citizens in governance not only enriches democracy but also enhances the sense of communal ownership and responsibility.

Another notable example is found in the innovative governance of Rwanda. In the wake of a devastating genocide, Rwanda has made significant strides in gender inclusion. With the world's highest percentage of women in parliament, Rwanda presents a radical reimagining of representation. This shift has had profound implications for legislative priorities, including health, education, and family law, demonstrating how inclusive governance can reshape policy landscapes to be more reflective of the population's diversity.

We turn to the complex federal system of India, a nation with an unparalleled mosaic of languages, religions, and ethnicities. India's constitutional architecture, with its system of reserved seats for historically marginalized communities, underscores a commitment to representation and inclusion. While challenges remain, the Indian example offers lessons in managing diversity through legal frameworks designed to safeguard minority interests.

Each of these case studies, with their distinct approaches, contributes to the evolving tapestry of inclusive political systems. They serve as laboratories of democracy, testing and refining the mechanisms that can bridge divides and bring together disparate voices. Through these empirical illustrations, political science not only theorizes about but also provides tangible blueprints for harmonious governance. The common thread binding these diverse systems is the recognition that the strength of a political community lies not in its homogeneity, but in its ability to harness the collective potential of its varied parts. As we continue to envision and build towards unity in diversity, these case studies offer invaluable insights and inspiration, reminding us that the art of inclusive governance is not only possible but already in practice across the globe.


1.5 The Economic Imperative

- *Economic Inequality and Governance*

The mosaic of global prosperity is marred by the deep fissures of economic inequality. These divides, etched into the very fabric of our societies, challenge the integrity of our governance structures. The guiding principle of inclusive governance must, therefore, be to bridge these chasms—not just as a moral imperative but as an economic necessity. It is within the grasp of our governance to weave a tapestry of economic policies that embroider equity into the heart of our communities.

Economic inequality manifests in staggering wealth disparities, limited access to education and healthcare, and unequal opportunities for advancement. A governance framework that does not address these imbalances is akin to a gardener who tends to only the most vibrant flowers while neglecting those wilting at the edges. As such, a harmonious world requires that the fruits of progress be not only cultivated but also fairly distributed.

In the shadow of these disparities, the call for economic reforms has intensified. The clarion call is for governance models that infuse the economy with social consciousness. A transformative approach to policy-making must consider a living wage, universal basic income, progressive taxation, and social safety nets —not as utopian ideals, but as attainable objectives that reinforce the social fabric.

To tackle these imperatives, governments can draw upon a palette of innovative policy instruments. For instance, the implementation of a financial transactions tax could curb speculative trading while funding social programs. Land value taxes could mitigate property speculation and fund affordable housing. These are but two strokes in a broader economic masterpiece that could redefine wealth distribution.

Moreover, technology's role in governance can be harnessed to enhance economic equality. Digital platforms for governance can facilitate the direct participation of citizens in economic decision-making, helping to tailor policies to the needs and aspirations of diverse communities. Through these platforms, the pulse of the people becomes the rhythm to which economic policies dance.

In the pursuit of economic harmony, it is essential to recognize that there is no one-size-fits-all solution. Each society must craft its governance in consonance with its unique cultural, historical, and economic melodies. Some may find their rhythm in the Nordic model's social democracy, while others may draw inspiration from the entrepreneurial spirit of social markets.

Regardless of the chosen path, the end goal remains steadfast: to construct governance mechanisms that are not only just and transparent but also economically empowering. By embedding economic equality into the DNA of governance, the hope is to kindle a future where prosperity is not the privilege of a few but the shared heritage of all. Only then can we truly aspire to a symphony of harmonious worlds, where the wealth of nations is the wealth of every citizen.


*- Strategies for Economic Inclusion*

As we navigate the winding corridors of history, it becomes increasingly apparent that economic disparity is a chasm that not only divides societies but also undermines the very foundations of global stability. Economic inclusion is not just a moral imperative but a strategic necessity for crafting inclusive governance. It is the cornerstone upon which the edifice of a diverse yet cohesive society must be built.

Here, we delve into the tapestry of economic models that have been woven across time and cultures, extracting the threads that can be interlaced to form a more inclusive future. We must first recognize the multifarious forms of value that sustain our world: labor, knowledge, natural resources, and technological innovation. To channel these streams of value into an ocean of opportunity for all, we must be both visionary and pragmatic in our approach.

One such strategy for economic inclusion is the reimagining of social safety nets. Traditional models, often based on industrial-era thinking, are ill-equipped to address the nuances of a digital and gig economy. We propose adaptive safety nets that are responsive to the fluidity of modern work arrangements, ensuring that the self-employed, freelance, and contract workers are not left adrift in times of economic uncertainty.

Another strategy is the democratization of education. An investment in human capital is the most potent weapon against the specter of inequality. By ensuring that access to quality education is not a privilege but a universal right, we pave a pathway for diverse talents to flourish. In this knowledge-driven economy, education becomes the great equalizer, enabling individuals from all walks of life to contribute to—and benefit from—the economic system.

Furthermore, we explore the potential of participatory budgeting as an instrument for economic inclusion. By involving citizens in the decision-making process of how public funds are allocated, communities become directly engaged in shaping their economic landscapes. This fosters a sense of ownership and accountability, bridging the gap between governance and the governed.

As we architect these strategies, we must also embrace the transformative power of technology. Digital platforms can provide unprecedented access to financial services for the unbanked and underbanked, catalyzing entrepreneurship and innovation in the most remote corners of our world. Cryptocurrencies and blockchain technology offer new possibilities for transparent, efficient, and equitable financial transactions, untethered from the traditional constraints of financial institutions.

In the final analysis, the pursuit of economic inclusion is a journey towards a more harmonious world. It is a recognition that the prosperity of one is intertwined with the well-being of all. As we craft governance systems that embody this principle, we lay the groundwork for a society where diversity is not a hurdle to overcome, but a mosaic of potential waiting to be realized. In this harmonious world, economic inclusion becomes the pulsating heart that gives life to the body politic, ensuring that every individual has a stake in the shared destiny of humanity.


<u>1.6 Technological Advancements and Democracy</u>

*- Digital Democracy and Citizen Participation*

In the digital age, democracy is undergoing a transformation as profound as the one it experienced when the printing press first put books into the hands of the masses. The internet has become the modern-day agora, a central hub where citizens exchange ideas, mobilize, and shape the political discourse. Here we delve into the concept of digital democracy, a phenomenon that harnesses technology to enhance democratic participation and bring about a more inclusive form of governance.

Digital democracy is not just about online voting systems; it's about roimagining the entire democratic process. It leverages tools such as social media, data analytics, and mobile applications to involve citizens in decision-making processes in real-time. Through these platforms, barriers to entry that once silenced minority voices are crumbling, giving rise to a more participatory and representative political landscape.

Consider the role of civic technology organizations that develop apps enabling citizens to directly influence local government decisions. These applications allow individuals to report issues, propose initiatives, and vote on policies affecting their community. By simplifying participation, they can lead to higher engagement rates and a deeper sense of ownership over communal outcomes.

However, the fusion of technology and democracy is not without its challenges. Digital literacy and access remain unevenly distributed, and there is a danger that without careful management, the digital divide could exacerbate existing inequalities. To ensure digital democracy fulfills its inclusive promise, we must address these disparities head-on. Governments and civil society organizations must work to provide digital education and improve infrastructure, ensuring that all citizens, regardless of socioeconomic status, can participate fully in the democratic process.

Moreover, as we navigate this digital transformation, we must remain vigilant against new forms of manipulation and misinformation that can distort public discourse. Transparent algorithms, ethical data practices, and digital education campaigns are essential to maintain the integrity of digital democracy.

In envisioning a future where governance structures reflect the will of an empowered and diverse citizenry, digital democracy stands as a beacon of potential. It is a dynamic tool that, if wielded with care and responsibility, can help to sculpt an inclusive and responsive governance model that not only acknowledges but also thrives on humanity's rich tapestry of diversity.

We will explore how the principles of digital democracy can be applied across various facets of governance. From environmental policy to economic reform, the potential to integrate citizen voices into the heart of governance is a theme that will resonate throughout, painting a picture of a world where every individual has the opportunity to contribute to the harmonious symphony of global society.

*- Ensuring Technological Access and Literacy*

As we inch closer to the horizon of an interconnected future, the symbiosis between technological advancements and democracy becomes increasingly pivotal. In this age of information, technology is not merely a tool but a foundational element that can either enhance or erode the democratic fabric of society. To ensure that it serves as a conduit for democratic enhancement, the twin pillars of technological access and literacy must be fortified.

Access, in its most fundamental sense, is about the democratization of technology. It is about bridging the digital divide that separates the information-rich from the information-poor. A governance model that aspires for inclusivity must prioritize the expansion of digital infrastructure, ensuring that high-speed internet and cutting-edge technologies are not the exclusive preserves of urban metropolises, but are available in the furthest flung rural villages. It is a vision where satellite constellations light up the digital landscapes of the unconnected, and where community-driven initiatives turn local libraries into vibrant hubs of digital learning and participation.

Yet, access alone is a bridge half-built. Technological literacy is the complementary pathway that enables citizens to traverse the digital terrain with confidence and critical acumen. In this envisioned future, educational systems are the incubators of digital wisdom, empowering individuals with not only the skills to use technology but also the discernment to question and shape it. It is a world where coding is as fundamental as reading and writing, and where data privacy rights are taught alongside the principles of democracy.

Let's investigate the dynamic interplay between technological advancements and democracy, advocating for a profound shift in the way we perceive and engage with technology. It is a call to action for policymakers to weave technology into the governance tapestry with deliberate and ethical threads, ensuring that every citizen is equipped with the tools and knowledge to participate in the digital democracy.

In an ideal scenario, technological access and literacy are not seen as end-goals but as the starting points of a virtuous cycle. An informed and connected citizenry is the bedrock of a vibrant democracy, and as they engage with the digital world, they become catalysts for innovation and progress. Governments, in turn, must be agile, ready to evolve and respond to the needs of a technologically-empowered population.

This is not just an exploration of the current landscape but a blueprint for a future where technology is harnessed for the collective good. It is an appeal for a world where every individual is an active participant in the crafting of a democratic, inclusive, and technologically-enlightened society.


1.7 Cultural Studies and Governance

*- Analyzing Cultural Dynamics in Policymaking*

In the intricate dance of governance, culture plays an indispensable role. It is the soul of a society, the undercurrent that shapes identities, values, and norms. To neglect culture in the realm of policymaking is akin to composing a symphony without a melody—it lacks the essence that resonates with the human experience.

The global stage is a mosaic of cultural narratives, each with its unique rhythm and harmony. When governance systems acknowledge this diversity, they tap into a profound source of richness and innovation. Yet, the challenge lies in harmonizing these distinct tunes into a cohesive symphony—a collective aspiration for a better world.

Let's examine how cultural studies can inform and transform governance. It is not merely an academic discipline; it is a compass that guides policymakers through the labyrinth of societal values and practices. By understanding cultural dynamics, leaders can craft policies that resonate with the people's heritage and aspirations, bridging the gap between governance and the governed.

Take, for instance, the delicate task of educational reform. When policymakers steep themselves in the cultural context of the community, they discern the pedagogical traditions that have shaped generations. They learn to value storytelling as a means of knowledge transmission in one culture, or communal learning in another. Such insights lead to educational policies that are not only effective but also culturally empowering.

Similarly, environmental governance benefits from a cultural lens. By recognizing indigenous practices of land stewardship, policymakers can design conservation strategies that are both sustainable and respectful of ancestral wisdom. This not only safeguards biodiversity but also affirms the cultural identity of indigenous communities, weaving their practices into the fabric of modern environmental policy.

In the realm of economic governance, cultural studies shed light on varying perceptions of wealth, work, and well-being. A policy that supports communal ownership may thrive in a society that values collective over individual success. Conversely, a culture that prizes innovation and entrepreneurial spirit may respond better to policies that encourage startup ecosystems and private enterprise.

To analyze cultural dynamics in policymaking is to engage in a dialogue with the heart of society. It demands humility, empathy, and a willingness to listen. It requires the policymaker to become an anthropologist, a sociologist, and a historian, all in one. But the rewards are manifold—a governance that is vibrant, inclusive, and deeply connected to the people it serves.

As we chart our course through the ever-shifting seas of global governance, let us hold fast to the compass of cultural studies. It will guide us to ports of understanding and collaboration, where policies are not just decrees from on high, but invitations to a collective journey toward harmonious worlds.


*- Preserving Cultural Identities Within Governance*

The patchwork quilt of human civilization is a mosaic of cultures, each thread woven from the fibers of language, art, tradition, and belief. The challenge of preserving these rich cultural identities within the framework of governance is akin to conducting an orchestra of diverse instruments, each with its unique timbre and pitch, into a symphony that resonates with harmony rather than discord.

To construct a governance system that not only respects but also celebrates this diversity requires an understanding of cultural heritage as a living entity. It is not merely the preservation of ancient monuments, the retelling of ancestral stories or the continuation of age-old customs. It is about creating spaces within the political discourse for these identities to evolve and to influence policy-making.

Consider, for instance, how indigenous knowledge systems can offer invaluable insights into sustainable land management, or how traditional conflict-resolution practices might inform modern legal frameworks. In recognizing the value of these cultural contributions, governments can foster a sense of inclusion and pride among communities that might otherwise feel marginalized or overlooked.

Moreover, cultural studies advocate for a participatory approach to governance, where citizens are not passive subjects but active contributors to the decision-making processes. This could manifest in community-led initiatives, which are given official support and integration into larger policy structures. Such an approach ensures that the governmental narrative is not monolithic but a polyphonic dialogue that reflects the multitude of voices within society.

Yet, this is not without its challenges. Balancing the preservation of cultural heritage with the exigencies of modernization requires careful negotiation. There is a delicate interplay between the universal and the particular, between the need for a cohesive social framework and the imperative to allow for cultural autonomy. The essence lies in creating policies that are flexible and sensitive to local contexts, that acknowledge the inherent worth of cultural diversity as a cornerstone of human progress.

In this pursuit, the role of education is paramount. By embedding multicultural perspectives within the educational curriculum, governance can cultivate citizens who are both proud of their own heritage and respectful of others. It is about nurturing a collective identity that is rooted in the understanding that while we may sing different melodies, we are all part of the same human chorus.

The vision of unity in diversity is not utopian; it is a pragmatic aspiration grounded in the recognition that governance is not merely the management of resources or the enforcement of laws. It is the art of weaving the many threads of humanity into a tapestry that is as enduring as it is exquisite, ensuring that no color is faded and no pattern is lost in the grand design of our shared existence.

*- Overcoming Societal Segregation*

In the mosaic of humanity, each piece embodies its own beauty, form, and color; yet, when assembled together, these pieces reveal a grand design that surpasses the sum of its parts. The pursuit of governance for unity does not entail blending these unique elements into uniformity but rather positioning them in such a way that their individual strengths contribute to the integrity and vibrancy of the whole.

Societal segregation, whether it be along lines of ethnicity, class, religion, or ideology, poses a formidable barrier to this pursuit. It fractures communities, engenders mistrust, and perpetuates inequality. Governance aimed at unity, therefore, must focus on building bridges across these divides, fostering a sense of shared identity, and cultivating an environment where differences are not just tolerated but celebrated.

One of the most powerful tools at the disposal of inclusive governance is the implementation of policies that are not merely blind to differences but are keenly aware of them and strategically crafted to accommodate and leverage diversity. This involves a profound understanding of the social fabric—a recognition of historical contexts, an appreciation of cultural nuances, and a commitment to equitable representation.

Education systems serve as the bedrock for such understanding. Through curricula that highlight the interconnectedness of human experiences and the value of cultural exchange, young minds can be nurtured to appreciate the pluralism that defines our world. From the stories read in classrooms to the histories recounted, education should serve as a canvas where every student can see themselves and others, not as adversaries, but as fellow architects of the future.

Public spaces and institutions also play a vital role in bridging societal segregation. By designing inclusive public forums, libraries, parks, and community centers that encourage interaction and dialogue among various groups, governance can facilitate the organic growth of social cohesion. These spaces should serve as common grounds where individuals from different walks of life can come together in pursuit of shared interests and goals.

At the heart of these efforts must lie a commitment to participatory governance, where decision-making processes are accessible and responsive to all segments of society. This entails not only formal mechanisms for participation but also the fostering of a civic culture that empowers every citizen to believe in the potential of their voice to effect change.

In overcoming societal segregation, governance for unity requires a vigilant and ongoing effort to dismantle the barriers of prejudice and discrimination. It calls for policies and practices that are rooted in empathy, equity, and justice—a governance that tirelessly works to ensure that no one is marginalized or left behind.

Bridging the divide is not a task for the faint-hearted. It is a journey of a thousand miles that begins with the single step of acknowledging our common humanity. In the subsequent chapters, we will explore the specific strategies and frameworks through which governance can rise to this challenge, knitting together the fabric of a society that is not only diverse but truly unified.

*- Examples of Successful Integrative Policies*

In the bustling corridors of power and the quiet corners of community gatherings, there is a yearning for a governance that mirrors the mosaic of humanity. A governance that not only recognizes diversity but thrives on it, transforming potential fractures into unifying strengths. In this pursuit, the world has witnessed remarkable examples of integrative policies that bridge divides and foster unity.

Consider the case of Rwanda in the aftermath of the genocide. The country embarked on a courageous journey towards national healing and unity. At the heart of Rwanda's transformation was the Gacaca court system – a blend of traditional communal justice and modern legal frameworks. By empowering local communities to participate In the reconciliation process, Rwanda nurtured a sense of collective ownership and accountability. The Gacaca courts served not only as a means to justice but also as a platform for dialogue and understanding, helping to weave a torn society back together.

On a different continent, the Nordic model showcases another approach to inclusive governance. Characterized by a strong welfare state, comprehensive social security, and an emphasis on consensus-building, the Nordic countries have consistently ranked high in measures of social cohesion and equality. Their education systems, free and accessible to all, serve as a great equalizer and a foundation for informed citizenship. By investing in people and prioritizing social welfare, these nations have crafted a governance model that promotes unity without sacrificing individual freedoms.

In the realm of environmental governance, the tiny nation of Bhutan stands out with its innovative Gross National Happiness (GNH) index. Rather than merely measuring economic success through Gross Domestic Product (GDP), Bhutan incorporates factors such as sustainable development, environmental conservation, cultural preservation, and good governance. This holistic approach transcends the traditional metrics of progress, uniting economic, cultural, and environmental policies under a shared vision of collective well-being.

And finally, there is the bold experiment of digital democracy in Estonia. By leveraging technology, Estonia has created an e-governance system that allows for unprecedented levels of transparency and citizen participation. Online voting, e-residency, and digital public services not only streamline governance but also ensure that every voice can be heard, every vote counted. In doing so, Estonia has broken down barriers to participation, fostering a sense of unity and trust between the government and its people.

These examples, each unique in its cultural and historical context, serve as beacons of what is possible when governance structures embrace inclusivity and integration. They illustrate that when policies are crafted with the intention to unify, they can transcend divisions and cultivate a harmonious world where diversity is not a liability but our most cherished asset.


## 1.9 The Quest for Common Purpose

*- Identifying Shared Goals Across Cultures*

In a world where the confluence of cultures often results in a vibrant mosaic, the quest for common purpose stands as a testament to our collective human spirit. It is a journey that transcends geographical boundaries, socio-economic divides, and ideological differences, and it begins with the simplest of recognitions—that despite our divergent paths, we all gaze upon the same stars and walk the same Earth.

The harmonious world we envision is rooted in shared aspirations. These aspirations may vary in expression but converge in essence. They are the universal desires for peace, prosperity, and the betterment of our children's future. To uncover these shared goals, we must embark on a quest that requires us to listen intently, to understand deeply, and to empathize fully.

We start by acknowledging the rich tapestry of human experience, where every thread is a narrative, every color a unique perspective. From the bustling marketplaces of Cairo to the serene fjords of Norway, from the technological hubs of Silicon Valley to the agricultural heartlands of India, we find recurring themes—security for one's family, education for the young, health and wellbeing for all, and justice that upholds the dignity of the individual.

Our approach to governance must, therefore, be a delicate dance—a choreography that aligns these varied rhythms into a symphony of collective action. It is about finding the harmony in diversity, the patterns that emerge when we view our differences not as divisions but as complementary strengths.

Identifying shared goals across cultures is not about imposing a monolithic set of values but about discovering the common ground on which all cultures can stand with respect and recognition. It is a dialogue that does not seek to erase the uniqueness of each voice but instead aims to create a chorus that resonates with the shared hopes of humanity.

In practice, this means crafting policies that reflect universal human rights while also honoring local customs and traditions. It involves creating platforms where voices from different cultures can converge, discuss, and deliberate on the issues that affect us all. It requires flexibility, creativity, and a resolute commitment to the idea that what unites us is far greater than what divides us.

As we move forward, we explore practical strategies and real-world examples of how inclusive governance has been achieved, where diverse societies have found their common purpose and where governance has become an expression of our shared human experience. The journey ahead is one of discovery, one that holds the promise of a harmonious world—a world where unity in diversity is not merely an aspiration but a reality.


*- Mechanisms for Collaborative Governance*

The concept of unity in diversity is not a mere philosophical ideal—it is the pragmatic skeleton key that can unlock the doors to a truly inclusive and effective governance. It calls for a symphony of voices, a confluence of disparate streams of thought and culture into a river that flows toward a common sea of shared goals and aspirations. Here we dissect the anatomy of collaborative governance, where the sum is indeed greater than its parts.

At the heart of collaborative governance lies the recognition of interdependence among diverse stakeholders. To forge a common purpose, governance must be envisioned as a platform for dialogue, where every voice, however faint, is amplified to contribute to the harmony of collective decision-making. This is not a fantasy but a tangible possibility made feasible through the meticulous crafting of mechanisms that prioritize participation, transparency, and mutual respect.

One such mechanism is the establishment of cross-cultural councils—think-tanks composed of representatives from various societal segments. These councils act as crucibles for policy-making, where the heat of debate tempers the steel of strong policies. Here, the youth can speak to the wisdom of the elders, the technocrats can tune into the concerns of traditionalists, and the marginalized can stand on equal footing with the powerful. These councils, when adequately empowered, can become the engines of innovative governance, driving forward policies that resonate with the vibrancy of a diverse populace.

Another pivotal mechanism is the integration of technology in the decision-making process. Digital platforms can serve as virtual agoras, where citizens engage in policy discussions and cast their opinions through e-voting systems. This digital democracy ensures that the quest for common purpose is not confined to physical council halls but extends its reach into the very pockets of the citizenry through their smartphones. It ensures that governance is not a distant concept, but an everyday practice, as accessible as the latest newsfeed on one's screen.

Moreover, collaborative governance requires the scaffolding of education that instills the values of empathy, critical thinking, and civic engagement. Education systems must transcend the mere impartation of knowledge to become nurseries of active citizenship where the seeds of a collaborative mindset are sown and nurtured. This educational approach ensures that the quest for common purpose is ingrained in the very DNA of future generations, making collaborative governance a self-perpetuating reality.

In the quest for common purpose, the role of leadership cannot be understated. Leaders in a collaborative governance model are not autocrats or figureheads but facilitators and mediators. They are the conductors of the orchestra, ensuring that each instrument contributes to the symphony and that the melody of unity is neither discordant nor monotonous but rich with the textures of diversity.

We have outlined the mechanisms that can lead to collaborative governance, but we will delve deeper into how these mechanisms can be operationalized across various domains. As we turn the page, we embark on a journey through the landscapes of digital democracy, environmental stewardship, economic equality, cultural preservation, and more—all through the lens of collaborative governance. The quest for common purpose is not only a call to action but an invitation to reimagine the art of governance itself.

# 2. The Digital Polis

*Bytes of freedom ring,*
*Tech bridges voices afar,*
*Democracy sings.*

## 2.1 Exploring Digital Citizenship

*- The evolving concept of digital rights and responsibilities*

In the crisp morning air of the digital age, we find ourselves on the cusp of a revolution, not unlike the dawn of democracy in ancient Athens. The concept of citizenship itself is undergoing a profound transformation, morphing with the pixels and data streams to form what we now term 'Digital Citizenship'. It is within this virtual polis, the online communities and networks that crisscross our planet, that our rights and responsibilities as citizens are being rewritten.

In the gleaming expanse of the digital realm, citizenship extends beyond the traditional geographic and political boundaries to include a new set of criteria, behaviors, and ethical considerations. Here, the keystrokes of an individual can ripple across the globe with the same impact as the spoken word once did in the public squares of old. But what does this mean for our understanding of rights and responsibilities?

Digital rights speak to the heart of human autonomy and freedom in the online world. They encompass the right to privacy, where personal data should be protected as fiercely as property was in the physical world. The freedom of expression finds new wings online, enabling voices to soar over digital landscapes, but it also raises questions about the boundaries of speech and the consequences of cyberbullying, misinformation, and hate speech.

Responsibilities, on the other hand, are the invisible threads that hold the fabric of digital society together. With the power of widespread connectivity comes the duty to use it wisely. Digital literacy becomes a cornerstone of modern responsibility, ensuring that citizens can not only navigate the complex online world but also discern truth from falsehood, and contribute positively to the collective knowledge base.

As we explore the contours of this new citizenship, we must ask ourselves how we can foster a digital society that is inclusive and equitable. How can technology be harnessed to enhance democratic participation, not just for the tech-savvy but for all layers of society? How can we ensure that the digital divide does not become a new axis of inequality, segregating those with access and know-how from those without?

To address these questions, governments and institutions are beginning to craft policies that aim to secure digital rights and outline clear responsibilities. From the European Union's General Data Protection Regulation (GDPR), which gives individuals control over their personal data, to initiatives that promote digital education and access to technology in underserved communities, the seeds of inclusive digital governance are being sown.

Here, we shall delve deeper into the intricate dance of rights and responsibilities within digital citizenship. We shall explore cases where digital governance has succeeded and where it has faltered, drawing lessons from each. The goal is to paint a vision of a digital democracy that is not only robust and transparent but also compassionate and just, ensuring that every netizen is an empowered member of the global digital polis.

*- Pathways to digital literacy for an inclusive political process*

In the gleaming agora of our modern society, where digital interactions weave the fabric of our civic life, the concept of digital citizenship becomes as vital as the air we breathe in sustaining the health of our democracy. Just as the ancient Greeks congregated in the public square to debate and shape the destiny of their city-states, today's citizens gather in virtual spaces to discuss, decide, and direct the course of our digital polis.

Let's journey through the labyrinth of the internet, seeking to democratize knowledge and empower all members of society. For digital citizenship is not merely about having access to the internet; it is about wielding that access with skill, responsibility, and a sense of community.

To cultivate an inclusive political process, we must first recognize that digital literacy is the cornerstone of participation. It is not enough for a citizen to merely log in; they must also be able to navigate the vast sea of information, discern fact from fiction, and contribute their voice with confidence and clarity. As such, governments and educational institutions bear a sacred duty to provide citizens with the tools and training necessary to become adept digital navigators.

Let's explore various pathways to digital literacy. We begin by examining educational curricula that integrate technology from the earliest years of schooling, thus weaving digital fluency into the very fabric of a child's learning experience. We highlight the importance of continuous adult education and the role of public libraries and community centers as sanctuaries of knowledge where citizens of all ages can sharpen their digital skills.

Moreover, we delve into the transformative power of e-governance platforms that not only increase government transparency but also invite citizens to take an active role in policy-making. Through digital petitions, public consultations, and interactive policy labs, individuals from diverse backgrounds can contribute to the legislative process, ensuring that the tapestry of laws reflects the rich and varied threads of our society.

But the path to digital literacy does not come without its challenges. The digital divide—stemming from economic disparity, geographical isolation, and generational gaps—threatens to exclude segments of the population from the digital polis. We must, therefore, be vigilant in our efforts to bridge this divide, ensuring that access to technology and the internet is recognized as a fundamental right, akin to access to education and healthcare.

Here, we will encounter stories of triumph and tales of caution, all serving to illustrate that an inclusive political process in the age of technology is not only possible but essential. For when every citizen is equipped with digital literacy, the chorus of democracy sings in harmony, and the governance of our digital polis thrives in the collective wisdom of its people.


## 2.2 E-Democracy Platforms

*- Assessing current e-voting systems and their security*

In the heart of the digital polis lies the e-democracy platform, a virtual agora where citizens not only speak but also vote, shaping the destiny of their societies. The allure of such systems is undeniable: they promise convenience, increased participation, and a real-time pulse on the public's will. However, as we wade deeper into the waters of technological governance, we must pause to assess the security and reliability of current e-voting systems.

At first glance, e-voting seems like a natural progression of democratic evolution. In Estonia, where e-voting has been a reality for years, the system has been lauded for its robustness and user-friendliness. Yet, beneath the surface, concerns linger like shadows at dusk. Cybersecurity experts caution that internet-based systems are inherently vulnerable to attacks that could compromise the integrity of the vote. From phishing scams targeting individual voters to large-scale denial-of-service attacks, the threats are as vast as the digital landscape itself.

The sanctity of the ballot is the cornerstone of democracy, and so the security provisions around e-voting systems must be impregnable. This requires an intricate ballet of encryption methods, such as blockchain technology, which can create an immutable record of votes cast. However, technology is only as strong as its implementation. A single misstep in software updates or key management can open the gate to tampering and diminish public trust in the democratic process.

Moreover, beyond malicious interference, the reliability of the system in accurately capturing voter intent is paramount. User interface design plays a crucial role here; even a well-secured system can fall prey to the perils of poor design, leading to unintentional votes or voter confusion. The lessons from the infamous 'butterfly ballot' of the 2000 U.S. presidential election are still fresh in the collective memory, reminding us that the bridge between voter and vote is sacred and must be tread with the utmost care.

To navigate these turbulent waters, independent audits and penetration tests are vital. They provide the checks and balances that can reassure the public that their electronic vote is as sound as one cast on paper. Transparency in these processes is also key; the black box of technology must be made visible and understandable to the citizenry so that trust in the system can be established and maintained.

In the final analysis, the quest for the perfect e-voting system may be akin to chasing the horizon - always just out of reach. Yet, the pursuit is noble and necessary. For the digital polis to thrive, the security and reliability of e-democracy platforms must remain at the forefront of our minds, evolving with each technological advancement and steadfast in the face of challenges. Only then can we hope to craft an inclusive governance that harnesses the full potential of a diverse humanity, united in the harmonious worlds we strive to create.


*- Case studies of effective digital public forums*

As we delve into the realm of e-democracy, it is instructive to examine successful case studies that have harnessed technology to create vibrant digital public forums. These platforms not only enhance democratic participation but also foster a sense of community among users. They provide a blueprint for what effective digital governance can look like when executed with the right mix of innovation, inclusivity, and security.

One of the most compelling examples of an e-democracy platform is Estonia's e-Governance system. Known for being one of the most digitally advanced countries, Estonia has effectively created a digital society where 99% of public services are online 24/7. Every citizen has a digital identity, which enables them to vote, sign documents, and access their medical records through secure online portals. The Estonian government's commitment to transparency and efficiency is evident in the e-Governance system's ability to save over 800 years of working time annually, a testament to the power of digital democracy.

Another pioneering case is Taiwan's vTaiwan platform, which combines online and offline methods to engage citizens in the legislative process. vTaiwan uses digital tools to crowdsource opinions and ideas on various legislative issues. This platform has been instrumental in shaping policies ranging from online alcohol sales regulations to the management of Uber's entry into the Taiwanese market. The success of vTaiwan lies in its open-source approach and its facilitation of consensus between stakeholders through a process called 'Pol.is', which visualizes public opinion to help policymakers understand the crowd's perspective.

Further afield, Iceland's Better Reykjavík is an online platform where citizens can propose and discuss ideas for the city's development. This collaborative platform has seen over 70% of its proposals implemented, demonstrating the impactful convergence of civic engagement and municipal governance. It has enabled a more direct form of democracy, where residents have a real stake in urban planning decisions.

The key takeaway from these case studies is that effective e-democracy platforms are designed with the end-user in mind. They prioritize ease of access, ensuring that every citizen can participate regardless of their technical expertise. Additionally, they employ robust security measures to protect user data and maintain trust in the system. Finally, they are built on the principle of inclusivity, ensuring that the digital divide does not exclude any segment of the population from the democratic process.

These platforms are more than just tools for governance; they are the digital agoras of the modern era, spaces where citizens gather not just to vote but to deliberate, discuss, and co-create the policies that shape their lives. In the quest for inclusive governance for a diverse humanity, e-democracy platforms like these are lighthouses, guiding the way toward more engaged, transparent, and harmonious worlds.


2.3 Bridging the Digital Divide

- *Strategies for technology access in underserved communities*

In a world where the digital polis is no longer a futuristic concept but an evolving reality, the question of inclusivity becomes paramount. As we reimagine the agora of the 21st century, we must forge pathways that connect every citizen—regardless of economic status, geography, or cultural background—to the global conversation. In this section, we explore strategies that aim to bridge the digital divide and ensure technology access in underserved communities.

First and foremost is the need to recognize that access to technology is a fundamental right in the digital age. It is the gateway to education, economic opportunity, and full participation in democratic processes. To this end, one of the most effective strategies is the implementation of community-driven technology hubs. These hubs, often located in public spaces such as libraries or community centers, provide not only access to high-speed internet and computing equipment but also training programs that empower individuals with the digital literacy skills necessary to navigate and contribute to the digital polis.

Another strategy involves public-private partnerships that leverage the resources and expertise of tech companies with the outreach capabilities of government and non-profit organizations. These collaborations can result in the rollout of affordable broadband services, the donation of devices to low-income families, and the development of localized apps and platforms that cater to the specific needs of a community.

Mobile technology is a potent tool in this quest for connectivity. With the proliferation of smartphones, even remote areas can tap into the digital stream. Innovations in mobile education and health services can dramatically transform the lives of those in underserved regions, providing a lifeline to essential information and resources.

Yet, access alone is not the panacea. A truly inclusive digital polis requires that we address the content and language barriers that can perpetuate exclusion. Cultivating a digital ecosystem rich in diverse languages and culturally relevant content ensures that the digital polis is a welcoming space for all. This calls for initiatives that encourage local content creation and the translation of existing digital resources into multiple languages.

Additionally, governance structures must be responsive to the dynamics of the digital divide. Policies that incentivize the deployment of infrastructure in neglected areas, subsidies for low-income users, and the protection of net neutrality all play a crucial role in cultivating an equitable digital landscape.

By embracing these strategies, we lay the foundation for a digital polis that is not an exclusive enclave of the privileged, but a vibrant, inclusive forum where every voice can be heard and every citizen can partake in the shaping of our collective future. The digital divide is a chasm that can—and must—be bridged, for it is in the fertile soil of connectivity that the seeds of a harmonious world are sown.


*- Policies for equitable digital infrastructure development*

In the quest to create a more inclusive governance, one of the fundamental challenges we face is the digital divide. This schism between those who have access to the internet and digital technologies and those who do not is not merely a gap—it is a chasm that separates citizens not just by geography but also by opportunity.

To bridge this divide, our policies must be visionary in their scope and compassionate in their intent. They must recognize that digital access is as essential as any other utility in the modern world. Therefore, the first step is to declare internet access a fundamental right, much like access to clean water or education. This declaration is the cornerstone upon which we build a new edifice of digital democracy.

Once this right is enshrined, we must embark on the ambitious task of constructing the necessary infrastructure. This involves significant investment in high-speed broadband to reach the most remote areas. It requires laying down fiber-optic cables, erecting cell towers, and deploying satellite systems to achieve comprehensive coverage. Governments can incentivize private companies to extend their services to underserved areas through tax breaks, grants, and public-private partnerships.

However, infrastructure alone is not enough. Affordability is a critical component of digital inclusion. Subsidized connectivity programs, along with providing low-cost or free hardware, can ensure that economic status does not dictate digital access. We must also consider innovative solutions like community Wi-Fi hubs, which can serve as local access points in impoverished areas.

Education is another key pillar in bridging the divide. Digital literacy programs must be integrated into school curricula from a young age. For adults, community centers and libraries can offer training courses to enhance digital skills. This approach serves dual purposes: it prepares individuals for a workforce increasingly reliant on digital proficiency, and it empowers them to participate fully in the digital polis.

In parallel, we must safeguard against the monopolization of digital infrastructure. Antitrust regulations should be implemented to prevent the accumulation of too much power in the hands of a few providers, ensuring that the digital landscape remains competitive and diverse.

Finally, we should not overlook the importance of content. Localized, multilingual content that is relevant to the needs and interests of various communities will drive digital engagement. When individuals find value in the content, they are more likely to seek out digital access, thus perpetuating a virtuous cycle of inclusion.

We have outlined not just the skeleton but the very sinews that must be strengthened to support a digital democracy. It is a democracy where every citizen—irrespective of their location, economic standing, or social background—has the tools to engage, influence, and benefit from the governance that shapes their lives. By embracing these policies, we pave the way for a world where digital infrastructure serves as the bedrock for an equitable and harmonious society.

## 2.4 Social Media and Political Mobilization

*- Analyzing the role of social networks in grassroots movements*

In the digital agora of our times, social media platforms have evolved from mere virtual spaces for socializing into powerful engines for political mobilization and grassroots movements. The phenomenon of social networks as conduits for change is neither incidental nor trivial; it is the manifestation of a new kind of polis, one that transcends geographical boundaries and empowers the individual voice.

The role of social media in political mobilization can be dissected into three primary functions: amplification, organization, and galvanization. Firstly, social media amplifies messages to audiences that were once unreachable by traditional means. A single tweet, post, or video can ripple out to millions, circumventing the gatekeepers of information and allowing for a more democratized spread of ideas. This amplification turns the ordinary citizen into a potential influencer, with the power to shape public discourse and attract attention to causes that may have otherwise remained in obscurity.

Secondly, the organizational capabilities of social networks are unprecedented. With the advent of event pages, groups, and hashtags, rallying individuals around a common cause has never been more efficient. The ease with which one can organize protests, fundraisers, and awareness campaigns is a testament to the transformative power of digital tools. These platforms enable swift coordination and collaboration, fostering a sense of community and shared purpose among disparate individuals who may never physically meet.

Social media has the capacity to galvanize people into action. The emotional resonance of shared stories and the communal reinforcement of beliefs can inspire individuals to move from passive observers to active participants. The Arab Spring, the #MeToo movement, and the global climate strikes are salient examples of how social media can ignite the spark of activism. These platforms have become the modern-day megaphone, broadcasting calls to action that resonate deeply with personal values and societal aspirations.

Yet, while the potential of social media as a tool for political mobilization is immense, it is not without its challenges. The same features that empower can also be manipulated, spreading misinformation and inflaming polarization. The echo chambers created by algorithms can distort reality and hinder constructive dialogue. As we strive to harness the positive aspects of social networks for political engagement, we must remain vigilant against their darker tendencies to fracture and mislead.

We will delve into case studies that highlight the dual-edged nature of social media in grassroots movements. We will explore how digital platforms have been leveraged to achieve remarkable feats of collective action, while also examining the pitfalls that threaten the integrity of democratic discourse. Through these analyses, we will uncover strategies to cultivate a digital polis that is both vibrant and responsible, one that champions the ethos of participation while safeguarding against the erosion of truth.

*- Challenges of misinformation and its impact on democratic discourse*

In the digital agora, where voices from every corner of the globe can mingle and amplify, the power of social media as a tool for political mobilization is undeniable. It has the capacity to unite disparate individuals around common causes, enabling swift organization and action that would have been inconceivable in the pre-internet era. However, this same connective tissue that brings people together can also become a conduit for the spread of misinformation, posing significant challenges to democratic discourse.

The term "misinformation" refers to false or inaccurate information that is spread, regardless of whether there is intent to deceive. In the context of social media, misinformation can go viral at astonishing speeds, outpacing the spread of accurate information and entrenching incorrect beliefs in the public consciousness. The impact of this on democracy is profound: when citizens are misinformed, their ability to make rational, informed decisions about their governance is compromised. The integrity of elections, the foundation of representative democracy, is consequently put at risk.

Let's examine the heart of these challenges. Social media algorithms, designed to engage users by showing them content that aligns with their interests and beliefs, inadvertently create echo chambers. These echo chambers reinforce preexisting views and can isolate individuals from information that challenges their perspectives, making them susceptible to accepting and spreading misinformation.

Moreover, the role of bad actors who intentionally disseminate false information to manipulate public opinion cannot be overlooked. Whether it's a foreign power seeking to destabilize a rival nation or a political group attempting to sway voter sentiment, the strategic use of misinformation campaigns can undermine the very processes that democratic governance relies upon.

Free speech in the age of social media is highly complex. While democratic societies value the freedom of expression, the unchecked spread of harmful misinformation raises the question of where to draw the line between protecting free speech and protecting the democratic process.

Despite these challenges, there is a glimmer of hope. Through digital literacy education, the development of fact-checking tools, and the responsible stewardship of social media platforms, it is possible to mitigate the impact of misinformation. Let's cultivate a more discerning audience, capable of critically evaluating the information they encounter online.

As we navigate the tumultuous waters of the digital age, it becomes clear that our ability to harness the potential of social media for positive political mobilization depends on our willingness to confront the specter of misinformation head-on. In doing so, we can protect the sanctity of democratic discourse and ensure that the digital polis serves as a true platform for the voices of an informed citizenry.


## 2.5 Transparency and Open Government

*- Tools for data transparency and citizen oversight*

In the digital age, the polis—the body of citizens—must be reimagined. Digital tools have the power to transform the relationship between governments and citizens, fostering a new kind of transparency that's foundational to democracy. This transparency is not merely about the flow of information, but about creating channels for active citizen oversight and participation.

Consider the power of open data initiatives. By making government data freely available and easily accessible online, citizens can scrutinize budget allocations, track legislative progress, and monitor public service outcomes. These data repositories become the bedrock for a host of applications and platforms that empower citizens to be the vigilant sentinels of democracy.

Take, for example, the imaginary "PolisWatch" platform. This application aggregates government data from multiple sources and presents it in a user-friendly dashboard. Citizens can set alerts for specific areas of interest—perhaps education funding or infrastructure projects—receiving notifications whenever relevant data is updated or a related decision is on the government's agenda.

But it goes beyond mere observation. Interactive features allow users to annotate datasets, flag discrepancies, and crowdsource fact-checking. This collective vigilance ensures that discrepancies and inefficiencies are not just identified but highlighted for public scrutiny. It democratizes the watchdog function that was once the preserve of investigative journalists and regulatory bodies.

In this transparent environment, the onus is also on government officials to be proactive in their disclosures. Regular 'open forums'—live-streamed sessions where policymakers present their initiatives and field questions from the public—become a norm rather than an exception. This direct line of communication between the elected and the electorate reduces the distance that so often leads to distrust and disengagement.

Furthermore, blockchain technology offers a secure and immutable record of governmental transactions, contracts, and decisions. This incorruptible ledger ensures that once something is recorded, it cannot be altered retroactively, providing a historical trail of governance that is verifiable and indisputable.

Transparency and open government are not panaceas, but they are powerful tools that, when coupled with engaged and informed citizenship, can lead to more responsive and responsible governance. In the harmonious worlds we envision, technology is the handmaid of democracy, and data transparency is the wellspring of trust—a trust that is earned, renewed, and deepened with every byte of shared information and every interaction between the governing and the governed.

In this digital polis, the ancient agora is reborn, not as a physical space, but as a digital commons—a realm where every citizen is an active participant in the grand dialogue of governance, and where the watchful eyes of the polis ensure that the levers of power are operated in full view and with the consent of the people.

In the realm of digital democracy, the concept of an open government stands as a beacon of modern governance, where transparency is not just a buzzword but the cornerstone of trust between citizens and their elected officials. As we navigate the intricacies of a connected society, success stories of open governance initiatives serve as lighthouses guiding us toward a more accountable and participatory future.

One such tale of transformation begins in the Baltic region, in the small but technologically advanced nation of Estonia. With the launch of the e-Estonia initiative, the country pioneered an unprecedented level of governmental transparency. By digitizing public services and making governmental data readily available online, Estonia created an ecosystem where citizens could not only view legislative processes in real time but also access their personal data held by the state. This radical openness has fostered a high degree of civic engagement and trust in public institutions, setting a global standard for transparent governance.

Another heartening narrative unfolds in the vibrant democracy of South Korea, where the government introduced the Open Data Portal. This online platform serves as a repository of public data, released for creative and commercial use by citizens and entrepreneurs alike. The initiative spurred innovation, with startups using this data to create apps and services that address social issues and improve daily life. By recognizing the collective intellect of its populace, South Korea demonstrated how open data can catalyze societal progress.

Across the Atlantic, we find the city of Chicago, which, under the banner of the Open Data Ordinance, committed to releasing all non-sensitive city data to the public. The city's data portal quickly became a treasure trove for civic hackers and researchers, who developed tools ranging from crime pattern analysis to real-time public transportation tracking systems. Chicago's commitment to openness not only enhanced city services but also invigorated civic tech communities, proving that open governance can spark local innovation.

These stories, while unique in setting and scope, share a common thread—a belief in the power of transparency to empower citizens and strengthen the fabric of democracy. Open governance initiatives, such as those in Estonia, South Korea, and Chicago, show us that when governments peel back the curtains and invite citizens to partake in the decision-making process, they lay the groundwork for a truly inclusive and harmonious society.

As we contemplate the future of democracy in the digital age, these success stories serve as a testament to what is possible when governments embrace transparency. They remind us that open governance is not a utopian ideal but a practical approach to fostering engagement, nurturing trust, and creating a symphony of voices where every citizen has the opportunity to be heard and contribute to the governance of their society.


2.6 Digital Identity and Privacy

*- Balancing the need for identity verification with privacy concerns*

In the digital agora, the twin pillars of identity and privacy stand as the gatekeepers of participatory democracy. The harmonious world we envision is one where every voice can resonate through the halls of governance, yet without sacrificing the sacred sanctuary of personal privacy. This delicate equilibrium is the subject of our current discourse.

Imagine, if you will, a society where digital identity serves as both shield and key: a shield to protect an individual's most intimate data from the prying eyes of malevolent forces, and a key to unlock the full potential of democratic engagement. Here, we delve into the intricacies of forging a system that honors this dual mandate.

The cornerstone of such a system lies in the concept of self-sovereign identity—a model where individuals have full control over their personal information. This paradigm shift moves us away from centralized repositories of data, vulnerable to breaches and misuse, and towards a decentralized architecture of trust, built upon the bedrock of blockchain technology. In this vision, one's identity credentials are encrypted, with access granted only through explicit consent, ensuring that privacy is not merely an afterthought but a foundational principle.

However, the path to achieving this is riddled with challenges. How do we ensure that the digital identities are robust enough to prevent fraudulent activities and yet not so intrusive as to become instruments of surveillance? To navigate this labyrinth, governance must be at the forefront of designing digital identity systems that are transparent in their operations and intentions. It is imperative to establish clear regulations that delineate the boundary between legitimate verification and overreach.

The harmonious world requires a new social contract—a covenant between the state, the individual, and the digital realm. Within this agreement, there must be an understanding that identity verification serves the public good, enabling fair and secure participation in the democratic process, while also upholding the right to privacy as an inviolable human right. Education plays a crucial role in realizing this balance, for an informed citizenry is the best defense against the erosion of privacy.

In this digital polis, privacy-enhancing technologies become the artisans of governance, weaving intricate patterns of security that allow the individual to engage in the public sphere with confidence and assurance. Features such as zero-knowledge proofs present promising avenues, where one can prove eligibility to vote or access services without revealing any more information than necessary.

As we charter the course for inclusive governance in a diverse humanity, the principles that guide us in reconciling digital identity with privacy will be the lighthouse guiding our journey. Let us commit to systems that respect the individual, safeguard freedoms, and enable the collective will to manifest through the bits and bytes of our connected existence. It is within this digital polis that the future of democracy will flourish, rooted in trust and flowering into a vibrant tapestry of engaged and empowered citizens.

*- The implications of biometrics and AI in governance*

In the bustling agora of our modern Digital Polis, where the keystrokes of citizens echo louder than the orations of ancient statesmen, a new form of identity has emerged. This identity, woven from the very fabric of our digital interactions, poses profound questions for the governance of a pluralistic society. It is here, in the intricate dance of biometrics and artificial intelligence (AI), that we must find our balance between the promise of security and the sanctity of privacy.

Imagine a world where every citizen is as unique in the eyes of governance as the whorls upon their fingertips—a world where one's identity is the key to every lock, from bank accounts to ballot boxes. Biometrics has made this a reality, turning the human body into a password that cannot be forgotten, stolen, or misplaced. But in this convenience, we find ourselves on the precipice of a double-edged sword. With each iris scan and fingerprint, we leave indelible marks on the canvas of our digital world, marks that can be traced, mapped, and potentially misused.

The role of AI in this landscape of identity is that of an omniscient gardener, tending to the vast gardens of data with algorithmic precision. It is AI that sifts through the noise, identifying patterns and anomalies that speak to who we are, what we desire, and where we may falter. It promises a governance that is predictive, preemptive, and profoundly personal. Yet, this promise comes laced with peril. For in its quest to know us better than we know ourselves, AI may inadvertently strip away the very anonymity that fosters freedom of thought and action.

To navigate this new frontier, governance must act as a steward, safeguarding the rights of citizens while embracing the efficiencies of technology. It must craft policies that are as agile as the systems they seek to regulate, embedding within them the principles of consent, transparency, and accountability. Consent, to ensure that citizens understand and willingly participate in the systems that recognize them. Transparency, to shine a light on the algorithms that govern their lives, making them subjects of scrutiny and not suspicion. And accountability, to provide recourse in the face of error or abuse, preserving trust in the institutions that serve them.

As we venture further into this digital domain, we must also remember that identity is not merely a matter of bits and bytes. It is the cornerstone of dignity and self-determination. Thus, the task at hand is not to forsake privacy in the pursuit of progress, but to weave them together into a tapestry that honors both the individual and the collective. In this harmonious world, governance will not be a looming specter over the digital agora, but a partner in crafting a society where technology empowers, protects, and unites.


<u>2.7 Online Deliberation and Decision Making</u>

*- Innovations in crowd-sourced policymaking*

In the quest to forge a harmonious world, the digital arena stands as a modern-day agora, a place where citizens not only gather to exchange ideas but also actively participate in the collective process of policymaking. This digital polis has given rise to revolutionary platforms for online deliberation, where the wisdom of the crowd is harnessed to inform, debate, and ultimately shape the decisions that govern our lives.

Crowd-sourced policymaking is not merely a technological novelty; it is a reimagination of democratic engagement. It embodies the principle that the many can be wiser than the few and that diversity in thought and experience leads to more robust and inclusive policies. Through digital tools, citizens from all walks of life are invited to contribute to the policymaking process, their voices amplified and their perspectives valued.

One such innovation is the policy wiki—a dynamic, collaborative online space where participants can co-create legislation, edit proposals, and discuss ramifications in real-time. Here, drafts evolve with each contribution, reflecting a spectrum of insights until a consensus emerges. The policy wiki does not replace the role of elected officials, but rather serves as a conduit for collective intelligence, offering legislators a richer tapestry of public opinion and expertise to draw upon.

Another pioneering approach is the use of virtual town halls, which transcend geographic barriers, allowing for inclusive and wide-reaching engagement. These online forums can be synchronous, hosting live debates and polls, or asynchronous, permitting reflection and response at one's own pace. The result is a participatory environment in which individuals can deliberate on issues with the same passion and civility that once animated the physical spaces of ancient democracies.

Online deliberation also benefits from the power of data analytics and machine learning. Algorithms can distill large volumes of contributions into coherent patterns, identifying common themes and emerging consensus, or flagging areas of contention that require further debate. These technologies, while neutral tools, must be wielded with caution to ensure that they facilitate rather than dictate the democratic dialogue.

Of course, the realm of online deliberation is not without its challenges. Ensuring cybersecurity, protecting privacy, and preventing the manipulation of discussions are paramount concerns that must be addressed to maintain the integrity of digital democracy. Additionally, the digital divide poses a significant hurdle, as not all citizens have equal access to the technology required to participate in these online platforms. Bridging this gap is essential to avoid the marginalization of certain groups and to uphold the democratic principle of equal voice.

As we advance into the future, crowd-sourced policymaking serves as a testament to the human capacity for innovation in governance. It is a beacon of hope that democracy can be both rejuvenated and made more resilient by the very technologies that have transformed our world. The digital polis, with its online deliberation and decision-making platforms, stands ready to welcome citizens into the heart of governance, forging policies that resonate with the collective voice and wisdom of a diverse humanity.


*- Overcoming polarization through online deliberative processes*

The digital age has encapsulated the world in a web of instant communication, creating unprecedented platforms for the exchange of ideas. But can this web hold under the weight of a world divided? Can it be a cradle for democracy's rebirth? The chapter now turns to online deliberation and decision-making, a beacon of hope for a society seeking to bridge the chasm of polarization.

Imagine a digital agora, a space where citizens gather not beneath the shadow of marble columns, but within the glow of their screens. Here, in this contemporary forum, the art of deliberation is being redefined. Online deliberative processes have the potential to transcend geographical boundaries and social divisions, allowing a diverse tapestry of voices to weave together in the pursuit of collective solutions.

In these virtual chambers, citizens are not just passive recipients of decrees from distant leaders; they are active participants, creators of the very policies that shape their lives. This is the essence of digital democracy—where every click, every post, every shared story is a testament to the power of the people.

To overcome polarization, however, we must first address the architecture of these online spaces. They must be designed to foster constructive dialogue and respectful debate. Algorithms must be tuned not to amplify sensationalism and conflict but to elevate reasoned discourse and consensus-building. Moderation is key, not to censor, but to maintain a focus on productive conversation and to deter the spread of misinformation that can inflame divisions.

Let us then outline the contours of an effective online deliberative process:

1. Inclusivity: Every individual must have equal access and opportunity to contribute, ensuring that marginalized voices are not only heard but are integral to the conversation.
2. Anonymity and Safety: Participants may choose anonymity to express opinions without fear of retribution, creating a safe environment that encourages honest and open discussion.
3. Structured Interaction: Dialogues are structured to allow for a phased progression of topics, from broad discussion to specific, action-oriented conclusions.
4. Facilitation: Trained facilitators guide conversations to prevent digression and ensure that all points of view receive consideration.
5. Decision Mechanisms: Clear methods are established for how decisions are made, whether through consensus, majority vote, or other democratic practices.

The power of online deliberation lies in its potential to transform the cacophony of clashing viewpoints into a symphony of collaborative action. Through these processes, consensus can emerge from chaos, and diverse perspectives can blend into a vision that reflects the collective will.

In this digital polis, the voices of humanity do not cancel each other out in a relentless battle of wills; they come together in a mosaic of thought, a testament to the strength that lies in our differences. As we continue to navigate the complexities of our world, the principles of online deliberation and decision-making stand as a guidepost for creating a more harmonious and inclusive democracy.


<u>2.8 Cybersecurity and Electoral Integrity</u>

*- Safeguarding elections in the cyber age*

As the digital age deepens its roots into the fertile soil of our social construct, the very essence of democracy—free and fair elections—faces unprecedented challenges. In this section, we turn our focus to the critical intersection of cybersecurity and electoral integrity, essential for preserving the sanctity of the democratic process in an era where information is both currency and weapon.

The advent of digital technology has provided a plethora of tools to enhance voter access and engagement, but it has also opened Pandora's box of vulnerabilities. The shift towards electronic voting systems, online voter registration, and virtual campaigning has exposed electoral processes to cyber threats including hacking, misinformation campaigns, and data breaches. It is no longer enough to safeguard the physical ballot box; we must now protect an intangible digital polis from threats that are borderless and often anonymous.

In recognizing these challenges, our approach must be twofold: proactive defense and resilient response. Proactive defense involves the implementation of robust cybersecurity measures. This includes the encryption of sensitive data, regular security audits and updates, and the employment of blockchain technology to create immutable and transparent voting records. Furthermore, the separation of the internet from critical voting infrastructure serves as an additional safeguard, providing a digital moat against would-be attackers.

However, cybersecurity is not solely a technological endeavor; it is also a human one. Thus, education and awareness are paramount. Electoral officials, political parties, and voters must be literate in the potential cyber threats and the means to counteract them. Regular training sessions, public awareness campaigns, and the inclusion of cybersecurity topics in educational curricula build a knowledgeable electorate that is less susceptible to manipulation.

Resilient response acknowledges that, despite our best efforts, breaches may occur. In such cases, having a swift and effective incident response protocol is essential. This includes real-time threat detection, rapid containment, and recovery strategies to ensure the integrity of the electoral process.

Transparency with the public during these incidents is crucial to maintaining trust in the system.

Furthermore, international cooperation plays a pivotal role in combating cyber threats to elections. Just as these threats know no borders, our defense and response must also be collaborative. Sharing intelligence, best practices, and technologies across nations enhances the global community's ability to protect the democratic process.

The dream of a harmonious world rests upon the foundation of trust in democratic systems. Cybersecurity and electoral integrity are not simply items on a checklist of governance; they are the bulwarks that stand against the forces seeking to undermine the collective will of the people. As we continue to navigate the shifting landscapes of technology and democracy, let us commit to the vigilant defense of our digital polis, ensuring that every vote is a voice heard and every election a testament to our unwavering dedication to democratic ideals.


*- International cooperation to combat election interference*

In the digital age, the sanctity of electoral processes has become vulnerable to a new breed of threats that transcend physical borders and traditional defense mechanisms. With this revelation, we turn a critical eye toward the urgent imperative of cybersecurity in safeguarding democracy.

The global community has witnessed the insidious nature of election interference through cyber means: data breaches that compromise personal information, disinformation campaigns that skew public perception, and direct attacks on election infrastructure that threaten to undermine the very foundations of democratic governance. These are not just theoretical concerns but tangible incursions that have left Indelible scars on tho fabric of several societies.

International cooperation emerges not merely as an option but a necessity when confronting such transnational challenges. Consider a symphony orchestra, with each musician contributing to a harmonious whole. In much the same way, every nation has a unique role in the ensemble of global cybersecurity, where the dissonance of one player can unsettle the entire performance.

Here we propose a multipartite framework for international collaboration. First, the development and adoption of global cybersecurity standards is paramount. These standards would serve as the sheet music from which all nations play, ensuring a baseline of security measures that protect against the most common cyber threats.

Second, the book advocates for real-time intelligence sharing between countries. The swift exchange of information regarding potential cyber threats functions much like the quick communication needed among ensemble members to address sudden changes in tempo or dynamics. This collaborative vigilance enables the early identification of threats and a coordinated response that is more effective than isolated efforts.

Third, we envision a robust international legal framework to prosecute cybercrimes, especially those that target democratic institutions. This framework would define the acts that constitute election interference and establish the consequences for violating these international norms, much as a code of conduct sets the expectations for behavior within an orchestra.

Lastly, we emphasize the importance of joint cyber-defense exercises, akin to rehearsals that prepare the orchestra for a flawless performance. These drills would simulate attacks on electoral systems, allowing nations to practice their defensive strategies and improve coordination.

With these measures in place, global governance can harmonize efforts to ensure that the digital polis—the virtual city square where democratic discourse thrives—remains a bastion of free expression, debate, and the will of the people. As we navigate the complexities of this interconnected world, the orchestration of international cooperation in cybersecurity becomes a pivotal movement in the symphony of inclusive governance, resonating with the promise of a diverse humanity united in its quest for a harmonious global society.


## 2.9 Blockchain for Trust and Verifiability

*- Utilizing blockchain for transparent governance processes*

In the heart of this new digital polis lies a revolutionary concept that may redefine the very essence of trust in governance: blockchain technology. As a digital ledger that is immutable and decentralized, blockchain has the potential to create a new architecture for democratic processes that is both transparent and resistant to fraud.

Imagine a world where every legislative action, every government decision, and every public expenditure is recorded on a blockchain. In such a world, citizens can verify the authenticity of governmental actions with a few clicks, and the perennial specter of corruption is banished to the annals of history. This is not merely a utopian dream but a tangible possibility within our grasp.

The use of blockchain stands as a bulwark against the manipulation of records, ensuring that once a piece of data is entered into the chain, it cannot be altered without a clear, traceable record of what was changed, when, and by whom. This characteristic of blockchain technology is particularly potent in the realm of elections. By recording votes on a blockchain, we create an electoral system that is virtually immune to tampering. Each vote becomes a block in the chain, providing a level of verifiability that traditional paper ballots or even electronic voting systems have struggled to match.

Let's explore the practical applications of blockchain in governance. It starts with the premise that the key to inclusive governance is trust – trust that every voice is heard, every vote counts, and that the systems we rely on to organize our society are as incorruptible as we aspire our leaders to be.

Blockchain-enabled governance also holds promise in the realm of public finance. By making budgets and transactions visible on a blockchain, citizens can see where their tax dollars are going, effectively turning the opaque walls of bureaucracy into windows. This transparency fosters accountability, as officials know their actions are not just recorded, but also easily scrutinized by the public they serve.

Furthermore, such a system can streamline governmental processes, reduce administrative costs, and eliminate many of the inefficiencies associated with bureaucracy. Smart contracts, self-executing agreements with the terms directly written into code, could automate many routine tasks, freeing up resources for more substantial and meaningful work.

Yet, the path to a blockchain-based governance system is not without challenges. The technical complexity of blockchain and the digital divide may exclude those without access to technology or the knowledge to use it effectively. The section concludes by examining these obstacles, stressing the need for education and infrastructure to ensure that the blockchain revolution in governance is as inclusive as it promises to be.

Blockchain is more than a technological innovation; it is the bedrock upon which a new era of trust and verifiability in governance can be built. We do not merely present this as a theoretical exploration but as an actionable blueprint for a future where governance is truly by the people, for the people, and accessible to all.

*- Case studies in blockchain-enabled voting systems*

In the search for a more inclusive and transparent democracy, technology has emerged as a beacon of hope. Blockchain technology, with its inherent characteristics of decentralization, immutability, and transparency, promises a future where governance can be both participatory and secure. Let's delve into the pioneering case studies of blockchain-enabled voting systems, showcasing how they pave the way for trust and verifiability in the digital age.

The first case study takes us to the small but technologically ambitious country of Estonia. Estonia's e-Residency program has become a global benchmark for digital governance, and the country has extended its digital frontier by experimenting with blockchain in its voting systems. Known as i-Voting, Estonia's system allows citizens to cast their votes from any internet-connected device. Blockchain technology ensures that once a vote is recorded, it cannot be altered or deleted, thus safeguarding the integrity of the electoral process. This bold initiative has dramatically increased participation, especially amongst the younger demographic and those living abroad, demonstrating the potential for blockchain to bridge distances and bring a dispersed citizenry into the fold of active governance.

Moving across the globe, the city of Tsukuba in Japan presents another fascinating implementation. Here, blockchain was used in a different context: to vote on social contribution projects. Residents were given the opportunity to participate in decision-making regarding the development of science and technology in the city. The success of this pilot not only highlighted the efficacy of blockchain in reducing fraud and errors, but also its potential to engage citizens in a direct and meaningful way, fostering a sense of community and shared responsibility.

However, these case studies are not without their challenges. Critics point out that while blockchain can ensure the verifiability of the voting process, it is not a panacea for all democratic ailments. Issues related to digital literacy, accessibility, and the digital divide must be addressed to prevent the creation of a new class of disenfranchised citizens. Moreover, the security of these systems, while robust, is not infallible. The threat of sophisticated cyberattacks necessitates continuous vigilance and advancement in security protocols.

Despite these hurdles, the promise of blockchain-based voting systems remains alluring. They offer a glimpse into a future where governance is not only conducted with the consent of the governed but done so in a manner that is open to scrutiny and beyond reproach. As these case studies continue to evolve and multiply, they collectively chart a path toward a digital polis founded upon the bedrock of trust and verifiability, where the ethos of democracy flourishes in the fertile soil of technology.

<u>2.10 The Future of Representative Democracy</u>

*- Rethinking representation in the age of direct digital participation*

In the luminous glow of our screens, democracy is undergoing a renaissance. The Digital Polis, a term reminiscent of ancient Greek city-states, is now being reimagined in the age of technology. Here, the marketplace of ideas is not confined to a physical agora but spans the infinite cyberspace, engaging citizens from every corner of the globe. This digital transformation beckons us to reconsider the very nature of representative democracy and the role of direct digital participation.

For centuries, representative democracy has been the cornerstone of governance in many societies, a system designed to elect individuals who would act on behalf of their constituents. This grand experiment in social organization has been largely successful. However, the rise of the Internet and digital platforms presents an unprecedented opportunity to enhance this system, to morph it into something more interactive and immediate.

As we forge ahead into this brave new world, the question emerges: How can we harness the power of digital technology to create a more participatory form of representative democracy?

The answer lies in the delicate interweaving of tradition and innovation. Representative democracy need not be replaced but rather augmented by the tools of our time. We can envision a system where elected officials are not the sole custodians of decision-making but act as conduits for the amplified voice of the populace. Digital platforms can facilitate a constant dialogue between representatives and the represented, creating a feedback loop that informs policy decisions in real-time.

Consider the potential of digital town halls, where constituents interact directly with their representatives, not just during campaign seasons but as a regular fixture of governance. Picture legislative agendas influenced by online petitions and forums, where the number of likes and shares carries real weight in the legislative process. Imagine a world where the pulse of public opinion is not measured by the occasional survey but by a continuous stream of data.

This is not to say that we should leap blindly into direct digital democracy. The risks of misinformation, the digital divide, and the erosion of deliberative processes are genuine concerns that must be addressed. Our challenge is to create digital platforms that are accessible, secure, and designed to promote informed discussion rather than reactionary populism.

In this new paradigm, representatives will become curators of public sentiment, tasked with the responsibility of translating the digital will into actionable policy. They will still play a pivotal role in shaping and guiding the legislative process but will do so with a mandate that is more directly informed by those they serve.

The future of representative democracy in the digital age is not a zero-sum game where the rise of one system precipitates the fall of another. It is a symbiotic evolution, a chance to breathe new life into our institutions and empower citizens as active participants in governance. It is, in essence, a return to the very ideals of democracy, reimagined for the world we live in today—a world where the harmonious integration of technology and civic duty creates not just a more efficient government but a more vibrant and inclusive polis.



As the digital age accelerates, artificial intelligence (AI) emerges as a double-edged sword in the heart of democratic governance. It holds the potential to revolutionize decision-making processes, yet simultaneously poses profound challenges to the principles of representative democracy. This section delves into the intricate dance between human judgment and algorithmic precision, envisioning a future where AI augments rather than undermines the will of the people.

The promise of AI in governance is tantalizing – vast amounts of data can be processed to inform policy decisions with an unprecedented level of detail and predictive power. The capacity to analyze complex patterns in human behavior, economic trends, and social movements could lead to more responsive and efficient governance. However, the reliance on AI raises critical questions about transparency, accountability, and the very nature of political representation.

If not approached with caution and foresight, AI could inadvertently erode the human element that is the cornerstone of democracy. The nuanced understanding that elected representatives bring to the table – empathy, moral judgment, and the ability to negotiate – might be overshadowed by the cold calculus of algorithms. The risk is that decision-making becomes a mere optimization problem, detached from the ethical and cultural dimensions that define our societal fabric.

To prepare for this future, it is imperative to establish frameworks that ensure AI is used to enhance rather than replace human decision-makers. This involves creating systems that are interpretable, where the rationale behind AI-generated recommendations is transparent and can be scrutinized by human officials and the public alike. It is about ensuring that AI serves the public interest, governed by principles that prioritize human rights, social justice, and democratic values.

Moreover, there must be an emphasis on AI literacy within the political sphere. Elected officials and civil servants should be equipped with the knowledge to understand the potential and limitations of AI, enabling them to make informed decisions about its implementation. By fostering a collaborative relationship between human expertise and AI capabilities, the potential for a more dynamic and representative democracy unfolds.

A critical component of integrating AI into governance is the establishment of ethical oversight committees. These bodies, composed of technologists, ethicists, and representatives from diverse communities, would evaluate AI systems for bias, fairness, and alignment with societal norms. They would play a pivotal role in ensuring that AI does not perpetuate existing inequalities but instead operates as a tool for greater inclusivity and equity.

The future of representative democracy in the era of AI is not predetermined. It is a tapestry we must weave with intention and care, threading the needle between technological innovation and the enduring values of democratic society. By embracing the challenges AI presents, we can craft a governance model that is not only more efficient and informed but also deeply human – a model for a harmonious world that respects and empowers its diverse citizenry.

# 3. Green Governments



### 3.1 The Genesis of Green Policy

*- Tracing the Roots of Environmental Governance*

In the verdant cradle of human civilization, our forebears lived in an intimate dance with nature, their lives woven into the rhythm of the seasons and the bounty of the earth. It was from this symbiotic relationship that the earliest notions of environmental governance emerged, though they were not named as such. The ancient practices of crop rotation, sacred groves, and the communal stewardship of water resources are but echoes of this primal understanding that the land was not merely a resource to be exploited, but a living entity to be honored and sustained.

Yet, as the wheels of progress churned, this deep-seated respect for the natural world was often overshadowed by the relentless pursuit of industrialization and economic expansion. It was not until the palpable consequences of such unbridled exploitation began to manifest in the form of smog-choked cities, ravaged landscapes, and poisoned waters that the necessity of environmental governance was thrust into the stark light of collective awareness.

The genesis of green policy in modern governance can be traced to the awakening of the 20th century, a period of burgeoning environmental consciousness. Pivotal moments like the publication of Rachel Carson's seminal work "Silent Spring" in 1962 laid bare the insidious impact of unchecked industrial practices on the environment, catalyzing a global environmental movement. This movement gave rise to the first Earth Day in 1970, a clarion call to the guardians of governance that the health of the planet could no longer be ignored.

In the following years, environmental governance began to take shape through a series of landmark conferences, treaties, and national policies. The United Nations Conference on the Human Environment, held in Stockholm in 1972, marked the first major international gathering focused on reconciling human activity with environmental preservation, leading to the creation of the United Nations Environment Programme (UNEP). This was an acknowledgment that green policy was not merely a national concern, but a global imperative.

Subsequent decades brought forth a proliferation of environmental legislation and initiatives. Governments, once the enforcers of industry and expansion, began to fashion themselves as protectors of the planet. Green policies were woven into the very fabric of governance, from the local to the international level. Initiatives such as the Brundtland Commission's report "Our Common Future" in 1987 introduced the concept of sustainable development, marrying the need for economic growth with environmental stewardship and social equity.

The transformation was not without its challenges. Vested interests, economic pressures, and political inertia often slowed the pace of reform. Yet, the green tendrils of policy continued to spread, driven by the tireless efforts of activists, forward-thinking policymakers, and a populace increasingly attuned to the fragility of the world around them.

Today, as we stand at the crossroads of environmental crisis and opportunity, the genesis of green policy serves as both a lesson and a beacon. It reminds us that environmental governance is not a static entity, but a living, evolving construct that must be nurtured and adapted to the ever-changing needs of both humanity and the planet. It is a journey that began with the first human societies, one that continues to unfold with each policy drafted, each tree planted, each step taken towards a sustainable future.


*- Milestones in Global Sustainability Agreements*

In the grand tapestry of human endeavor, the thread of sustainability weaves a pattern of hope and urgency. The genesis of green policy is not a modern epiphany but a continuum of awakening, a series of milestones that reflect humanity's growing consciousness of its place within the natural world. It is a journey marked by pivotal moments when the globe's leaders came together to acknowledge their shared responsibility for the planet's health and the well-being of future generations.

The story begins in earnest with the Stockholm Conference of 1972, the first significant global gathering focused on reconciling human advancement with environmental protection. It was a seminal event that laid the foundation for international environmental governance, sparking a global conversation about the need for concerted action. The resulting declaration and action plan may seem modest by today's standards, but they were the first drops of rain in what would become a transformative downpour of green policy.

Fast forward to 1987, when the Brundtland Report, "Our Common Future," introduced the term "sustainable development" to the world stage, defining it as development that meets the needs of the present without compromising the ability of future generations to meet their own needs. This document, crafted by the World Commission on Environment and Development, provided a philosophical cornerstone for green governance, emphasizing the interdependence of economic progress, social equity, and environmental stewardship.

The 1992 Earth Summit in Rio de Janeiro represented another critical waypoint, giving birth to the Rio Declaration and Agenda 21, a comprehensive blueprint for sustainable development. It also saw the establishment of the United Nations Framework Convention on Climate Change (UNFCCC), the bedrock treaty underlying subsequent climate agreements. The summit was a moment of collective realization that the environment was not merely a backdrop to human activity but a vital player in the story of civilization.

One cannot discuss the evolution of green policy without pausing at the doorstep of the Kyoto Protocol in 1997, the first agreement to set binding emission reduction targets for developed countries. Though its impact was hampered by significant political and economic hurdles, the protocol was a clear signal that the winds of change were picking up speed.

The Paris Agreement of 2015 stands as the current zenith of international climate efforts, a beacon of collaborative ambition. It encapsulates the spirit of unity and resolve, with nations pledging to limit global warming and transition towards low-carbon economies. It is a testament to the power of cumulative action, built upon the milestones that came before it.

These milestones are not merely historical footnotes but stepping stones leading us to a future where green policy is not an afterthought but the guiding principle of governance. They are the legacy of those who dared to imagine a harmonious world where human progress and planetary health are not adversaries but allies in a dance of delicate balance. As we continue to build upon these foundations, the story of green policy evolves with each new commitment, each innovative practice, and each act of courage in the face of daunting challenges. It is a narrative of hope, of a humanity united in the pursuit of a sustainable and equitable existence for all who call Earth home.

3.2 Legislative Frameworks for Eco-Governance

- *Crafting Effective Environmental Laws*

In the verdant chamber of the heart lies the seed of eco-governance, where laws are not merely inscribed in books but are living extensions of our collective reverence for nature. In the crafting of these legislative frameworks, we must approach with the delicate touch of an artist and the astute mind of a scientist, for the laws we create will shape the very canvas of our natural world.

The world's legislatures stand as the guardians of tomorrow's earth, and their charge is to craft laws that will ensure the integrity of our environment. The drafting of such laws is an intricate dance between the needs of the present and the preservation of the future. Herein lies the art of legislative craftsmanship in eco-governance: the creation of laws that are robust, flexible, and above all, just.

The artistry in legislation begins with a clear vision. It requires an understanding that environmental laws are not merely prohibitive but are constructive frameworks that guide the sustainable use and stewardship of natural resources. Effective laws must incentivize innovation in green technologies and practices, fostering a culture of environmental responsibility across all sectors of society.

To achieve this, lawmakers must engage in a collaborative process with scientists, economists, and the public. This synergy allows for the creation of laws that are informed by the latest scientific research, economic impact assessments, and the lived experiences of those most affected by environmental issues. It is a process that requires humility, for no single discipline holds all the answers, and it is through this interdisciplinary dialogue that the most resilient and adaptive laws are born.

Moreover, eco-governance necessitates a spirit of international cooperation. Environmental laws must transcend borders, as rivers flow and air currents drift beyond the lines drawn on maps. Agreements such as the Paris Climate Accord exemplify the global commitment required to address climate change, and similar cooperative efforts must be made in the drafting of national legislation.

Transparency and accountability are the twin pillars upon which trust in these laws is built. The public must be assured that environmental laws are enforced equitably, without favor or corruption, and that violators are held to account. This transparency extends to the process of lawmaking itself, where public participation is paramount. Citizens should have a voice in the decisions that will shape their environment, and this participatory approach lends legitimacy and strength to the laws enacted.

In enacting these legislative frameworks, we must also be mindful of the intrinsic value of the natural world. Laws should protect not only the resources that have economic value but also the ecosystems and species that enrich our planet in immeasurable ways. It is a recognition of the right of the environment to exist and flourish, independent of its utility to humanity.

As we look to the horizon, the task before us is clear. We must continue to refine our legislative tools, to polish and adapt them, in the service of a world where governance and nature exist in harmonious balance. The green governments of the future will be those that have mastered the art of crafting laws that honor the earth and safeguard it for generations to come.


*- International Regulation and Compliance Mechanisms*

In the grand mosaic of eco-governance, legislative frameworks are the grout that binds the colorful pieces of policy and practice into a coherent whole. It is through the intricate lattice of laws and regulations that nations can harmonize their efforts to protect our shared environment, transcending borders and differences to uphold a collective responsibility.

International regulation on environmental conservation and sustainability is not a novel concept. Treaties like the Paris Agreement on climate change and the Convention on Biological Diversity are testaments to the world's capacity for collective action. However, the true artistry lies not in the creation of these agreements but in their implementation and the compliance mechanisms that ensure their effectiveness.

To paint a picture of successful eco-governance, one must appreciate the subtleties of international regulation. It requires a careful balance between the sovereign right of nations to govern their realms and the necessity for global standards that prevent environmental degradation. This is where compliance mechanisms come into play, serving as the tools to maintain this delicate equilibrium.

These mechanisms often take the form of regular reporting requirements, where states disclose their environmental policies and progress to international bodies. This transparency fosters a culture of accountability and encourages a race to the top, where nations strive not only to meet but to exceed the agreed-upon standards.

Another tool in the arsenal of eco-governance is the use of sanctions or incentives. Economic sanctions can deter states from flouting international norms, while incentives, such as financial aid or technology transfer, can assist developing nations in their journey towards sustainability. The Green Climate Fund, for instance, is an innovative financial mechanism designed to support emerging economies in their climate change mitigation and adaptation efforts.

Moreover, international environmental law is increasingly recognizing the role of non-state actors. Corporations, NGOs, and even individuals are being empowered to participate in the eco-governance process. The Equator Principles, a voluntary set of guidelines adopted by financial institutions, illustrate how the private sector can help enforce sustainable development by ensuring that projects they finance are environmentally and socially responsible.

Yet, these frameworks and mechanisms are not without their challenges. Enforcement remains a complex issue, as it often relies on the political will of member states. Additionally, the dynamic nature of environmental challenges necessitates adaptive legislation that can evolve in tandem with scientific understanding and technological innovation.

As we forge ahead, the quest for an effective legislative framework for eco-governance continues. It is a journey that demands collaboration, creativity, and commitment from all corners of the globe. For it is only through concerted, inclusive action that we can hope to sculpt a future where governance and green policies are harmoniously intertwined, safeguarding the planet for generations to come.

## 3.3 Economic Instruments for Environmental Protection

*- Taxation and Fiscal Policies for Sustainability*

Imagine a world where the very structure of our economic system aligns with the rhythms of the Earth, where fiscal policies are not simply about growth but about nurturing the planet. In this section, we take a magnifying glass to the role of economic instruments, specifically taxation and fiscal policies, as vital tools for environmental protection and the promotion of sustainability.

Taxation, often viewed merely as a means of revenue generation, can be artfully repurposed to foster sustainable practices. Environmental taxes, such as carbon taxes, seek to internalize the external costs of environmental damage, effectively making it more expensive to pollute. By setting a price on carbon emissions, governments send a clear market signal that encourages companies and individuals to shift towards cleaner technologies and practices. The beauty of such a tax lies not just in its deterrent effect but also in its ability to raise funds that can be reinvested into renewable energy projects, conservation efforts, and green infrastructure.

While the mere mention of taxes can cause a stir of unrest, it is essential to paint the picture of a tax system that is not punitive but protective. It is a canvas where the polluter pays principle is not a penalty but a pathway to a greener future. These fiscal policies must be designed to be equitable, with careful consideration to prevent undue burdens on those least able to bear them. Rebates, exemptions, or a progressive structure can ensure that the transition to a sustainable economy is just and inclusive.

Fiscal policies extend beyond taxation. Government spending is a powerful brushstroke in the portrait of a sustainable society. By prioritizing investments in sustainable agriculture, clean energy, and public transportation, governments can lead by example, demonstrating the viability and benefits of such practices. Subsidies for sustainable initiatives, often overshadowed by those for fossil fuels, need a reversal of fortune. By redirecting subsidies to support renewable energy and energy efficiency, governments can foster industries that will power a sustainable future.

Public procurement policies also have a significant role to play. When governments choose to purchase eco-friendly products and services, they not only reduce their own environmental footprint but also stimulate market demand for green goods, encouraging more producers to consider the environmental impact of their offerings.

In this mosaic of fiscal measures, it is crucial that the policies are transparent, consistent, and predictable. Such clarity allows businesses and consumers to plan and invest with confidence in sustainability-oriented markets. With the right economic instruments, governments can turn the tide, crafting an economy that is a friend, not a foe, to our environment.

In sum, taxation and fiscal policies for sustainability represent the intricate dance between economy and ecology. They are the levers of change in our quest for a harmonious world, where the pursuit of prosperity does not come at the expense of the planet. It is a delicate balance, a symphony of policies harmonized to achieve the greatest composition of all—a sustainable and thriving Earth.


*- Incentives and Subsidies to Encourage Green Practices*

In the verdant embrace of a world where the economy and the environment are not at odds but in a harmonious dance, lies the promise of green governance. Here we delve into the heart of this promise, exploring the myriad ways in which governance can pave the way for a sustainable future. Let's unfold the tapestry of potential fiscal levers and incentives that can be wielded to foster a culture of conservation and sustainable practices.

Imagine a world where the invisible hand of the market is gently guided by the visible hand of enlightened governance, directing economic activities towards green practices. In such a world, subsidies are not mere financial handouts but strategic investments in the future of our planet. They become catalysts for change, encouraging businesses and individuals alike to adopt environmentally friendly technologies and sustainable practices.

One might consider the case of renewable energy sources, such as solar or wind power. Traditional energy production has long been subsidized, inadvertently promoting the use of fossil fuels. However, shifting such subsidies to renewable energy can reduce our carbon footprint and hasten the transition to a cleaner future. By reducing the cost of installation for solar panels or wind turbines, governments can make green energy more accessible and attractive to the masses.

Furthermore, taxation can be reimagined as a tool for environmental stewardship. By imposing taxes on carbon emissions or plastic production, governments create a financial disincentive for polluting activities. Conversely, offering tax credits to those who engage in practices that benefit the environment, such as maintaining green spaces or restoring natural habitats, rewards and proliferates positive action.

Incentives also come in the form of grants for research and development in sustainable technologies. By funding the quest for innovative solutions to environmental challenges, governments can spur scientific advancement and economic growth in tandem. These grants signal to the market that sustainability is not just a moral choice but an economically viable and profitable one.

Moreover, the concept of 'pay-for-performance' incentives can be applied to conservation efforts. In this model, businesses or communities that achieve verifiable environmental outcomes, such as reduced pollution levels or increased biodiversity, receive financial rewards. This not only incentivizes progress but ensures that funds are allocated effectively, with tangible results for the environment.

In all of these economic instruments, the underlying principle is clear: aligning financial gain with environmental gain. It is a strategy that speaks the language of both the economist and the ecologist, bridging the gap between prosperity and preservation. Through incentives and subsidies, green governance can encourage a culture of sustainability that permeates every level of society, from the individual to the corporate, from the local to the global.

As we continue our journey, let us keep in mind that the seeds of sustainable governance we plant today are the forests of tomorrow. They are the legacy we leave for future generations—a world not just surviving but thriving in a delicate balance with nature.


<u>3.4 Urban Planning and Sustainable Development</u>

*- Designing Cities for the Future*

Cities are the pulsing hearts of civilization, the vibrant hubs where culture, commerce, and community converge. Yet, as we gaze into the future, we see an urban tapestry frayed by the pressures of population growth, resource depletion, and the stark realities of climate change. The quest for sustainable urban development is not merely an option; it is an imperative. To weave the future of our cities with the threads of sustainability and resilience, we must reimagine the very fabric of urban planning.

The dawn of this renaissance in urban planning emerges from a confluence of innovation and ancient wisdom. It requires us to look beyond the concrete jungles and envision green, living cities—metropolises that breathe with the rhythm of nature and pulsate with the heartbeat of a community united in diversity. In this future, the city is not a blight upon the landscape but a harmonious extension of it.

Imagine streets lined with verdant canopies, where the air is purified by the very trees that shade our daily commutes. Envision buildings not merely constructed but grown from materials that sequester carbon, standing as living monuments to our commitment to the planet. Picture public spaces that are not just places of transit but destinations in themselves—parks and plazas that invite contemplation and community.

In these cities of tomorrow, renewable energy sources power our homes, workplaces, and transport systems. Rooftop gardens and vertical farms rise towards the sky, providing local, organic produce that reduces the need for long-haul transportation, simultaneously revitalizing urban economies and reducing our carbon footprint. Water management systems, inspired by ancient aqueducts and modern technology, ensure that every drop is treasured and that our cities become models of efficiency and stewardship.

The role of governance in this urban metamorphosis cannot be overstated. It is the government that must lay the foundation upon which these sustainable cities will grow. Policies must be designed that incentivize green building practices, promote the use of public transportation, and ensure that urban development does not come at the expense of the natural environment. It is a governance that understands the intrinsic link between the health of the environment and the well-being of its citizens.

Urban planning and sustainable development must also be inclusive, recognizing that every citizen has a stake in the city's future. Public participation in the planning process ensures that the diverse needs of the community are met and that the voices of often marginalized groups are heard. It is the collective wisdom of the populace, harnessed through digital democracy and participatory governance, that will drive the innovation necessary to confront the challenges we face.

In crafting cities for the future, we must be architects of hope, building not just for survival but for a thriving existence that honors the diversity of humanity and the planet we share. These green governments will stand as beacons of progress, guiding us towards a world where urban landscapes are as lush and vibrant as the forests from which we once emerged.

*- Green Spaces and Urban Biodiversity*

In the heart of the city, where the hum of traffic merges with the rhythm of human bustle, there lies an oasis of tranquility—a park, with lush green canopies and the soft murmur of a brook. Such are the green spaces that dot the urban landscape, vital lungs in a body of concrete and steel. These are not mere aesthetic charms or recreational retreats; they are the cornerstones of sustainable urban planning, essential to the well-being of both the environment and the populace.

As we delve into the fabric of urban ecosystems, we find that green spaces are far more than patches of vegetation. They are dynamic habitats, fostering urban biodiversity and offering a refuge for native flora and fauna. In the seamless weave of a city's planning, these spaces must be integrated thoughtfully, connecting neighborhoods with verdant corridors that allow species to flourish and migrate.

Indeed, the crafting of such spaces requires an artful balance. Urban planners and ecologists must join hands, envisioning a metropolis where skyscrapers and parks coexist, where the built environment does not encroach upon the natural but rather enhances it. Sustainable development in this realm is not only about conserving energy or reducing emissions—it is about creating a symbiotic relationship between urban life and the ecosystem.

To achieve this, cities must transform. Vacant lots can blossom into community gardens; rooftops, into sky-high meadows; and walls, into vertical forests. These initiatives not only beautify and cool the city but also serve as vital habitats and green corridors. The rewilding of urban areas with native species revitalizes ecosystems, encouraging bees to pollinate, birds to sing, and life to cycle in its myriad forms.

Moreover, green spaces are not islands unto themselves; they are interwoven with the social fabric, promoting community engagement and offering a communal heart. They are where children learn the rhythms of nature, where adults find respite from the grind, and where the elderly stroll through the memories of seasons past. In these spaces, the governance of a city finds one of its most profound expressions of care for its citizens.

The governance that champions such urban planning must be visionary, recognizing that sustainable development is not a constraint but a canvas for innovation. It must embrace the concept that green spaces are not just amenities but necessities, as integral to urban infrastructure as roads and utilities. By prioritizing urban biodiversity and sustainable development, governments pave the way for communities that are not only resilient but harmonious—where the natural and the man-made dance in delicate balance, and where humanity thrives amidst the green sanctuaries of the world it has built.

Thus, we sketch the outlines of a future where governance is not only green in rhetoric but verdant in reality—a world where each city breathes life into the vision of a harmonious world.


<u>3.5 Energy Policies for a Cleaner World</u>

*- Transitioning to Renewable Energy Sources*

The shift toward renewable energy sources is not just an environmental imperative but a testament to the ingenuity and adaptability of humankind. In this era of transformation, governments around the world are tasked with the grand challenge of reengineering their countries' energy infrastructures. This is a pivotal movement, where the quest for sustainability aligns with the aspirations of diverse communities seeking a healthier planet.

At the heart of this transition lies the recognition that fossil fuels, which have powered our societies for centuries, come with an unsustainable cost— environmental degradation, health risks, and the exacerbation of climate change. The age of coal and oil is giving way to the sun, wind, and water; an epoch marked by clean skies and revitalized ecosystems is upon us.

The journey towards renewable energy is both a moral and a practical one. It requires visionary leadership and a collective commitment to reimagine our relationship with the Earth's resources. Solar panels, wind turbines, and hydroelectric dams are not merely technological marvels but symbols of a renewed covenant with nature.

Governments pioneering sustainable policies are laying the groundwork for a robust green economy. They are investing in research and development to make renewable technologies more efficient and affordable. Incentives for solar and wind installations, carbon credits, and green bonds are tools in the policy-maker's kit, each contributing to an intricate mosaic of solutions.

Education plays a critical role in this transformation. Public awareness campaigns and curricula that emphasize the importance of sustainable energy create a culture of conservation and responsibility. Moreover, the green energy sector promises a wealth of job opportunities, requiring a workforce skilled in new technologies and sustainability practices.

Yet the transition to renewable energy is not without its challenges. The infrastructure for harnessing and distributing clean energy requires significant investment. The intermittency of some renewable sources demands innovative solutions for energy storage and grid management. And as with any shift in the economic order, there are interests vested in the status quo that resist change.

Despite these obstacles, the momentum is undeniable. Cities are becoming smarter, integrating renewable sources directly into their power grids. Islands once dependent on imported oil are harnessing the wind and waves that surround them. Nations are setting ambitious targets for carbon neutrality, recognizing that the health of the planet and the well-being of its inhabitants are inextricably linked.

Here, we see a blueprint for energy policies that are not only cleaner but also more equitable. The democratization of energy—where power is generated and owned by communities—emerges as a theme that resonates deeply with the vision for inclusive governance. As we embrace renewable energy, we are not just powering our homes and businesses; we are fueling a movement toward a more harmonious world.


*- Reducing Dependency on Fossil Fuels*

In the verdant landscape of sustainable governance, energy policy stands as a crucial pillar, supporting the overarching architecture of a cleaner, greener world. We must meticulously unfold the layers of environmental stewardship necessary for the health of our planet. Here we shine a light on the path that leads away from the carbon-heavy footsteps of our past.

The transition to renewable energy sources is not merely an environmental imperative but a moral one, challenging the very sinews of governance to adapt and innovate. As I delve into the intricacies of energy policy, we must appreciate that the shift from fossil fuels to renewable energy is akin to a caterpillar's metamorphosis into a butterfly—a complete transformation of form and function, requiring both patience and persistence.

The historical reliance on coal, oil, and natural gas has woven itself into the fabric of modern economies. Today, we stand at the crossroads of change. However, the geopolitical and socio-economic impediments have hindered the adoption of cleaner energy sources. Let's analyze the inertia that plagues our energy policies.

Governments must invest in research and development of renewable technologies, such as solar, wind, and hydroelectric power. These investments not only reduce carbon emissions but also create new industries and job opportunities. Incentives for both producers and consumers form another cornerstone of this framework. By restructuring tax codes, offering subsidies for clean energy initiatives, and implementing carbon pricing, governments can make renewable energy the most economical and rational choice. Additionally, the gradual phasing out of fossil fuel subsidies is a controversial yet necessary step to level the playing field for renewables.

A critical element is the role of international cooperation. No single nation can shoulder the burden of climate change alone. Global alliances must share technology, resources, and best practices, weaving a tapestry of collective action against the specter of environmental degradation.

This is a clarion call to action. We must envision a future where energy does not pollute, degrade, or divide, but rather sustains, unites, and invigorates. There is a world where governance is not a barrier to innovation but a conduit for it, channeling the human spirit's inexhaustible energy towards the most noble of goals—a harmonious existence with the Earth that nurtures us all.


<u>3.6 Waste Management and Recycling Initiatives</u>

*- Strategies for Reducing Waste Production*

In the shadow of towering landfills and amidst the swirling currents of oceanic garbage patches, the urgent need for robust waste management and recycling initiatives becomes glaringly apparent. Our quest for a harmonious world is inextricably linked to our ability to reduce waste production at its source and to reimagine our throwaway culture as a cycle of renewal and reuse.

The first strategy in pioneering sustainable policies for waste management is to promote the concept of a circular economy. This economic system emphasizes the continual use of resources, minimizing waste by designing products and processes that allow for repair, refurbishment, and recycling. Governments can play a pivotal role by incentivizing businesses that adopt circular economy principles. Subsidies, tax breaks, and grants geared toward companies that prioritize sustainable design, packaging reduction, and material innovation can drive a significant shift toward waste reduction.

A cornerstone of this transformation is the implementation of extended producer responsibility (EPR) programs. EPR policies require manufacturers to bear the cost of disposal for the products they create, thus encouraging them to design products with longer lifespans and that are easier to disassemble and recycle. When producers are held accountable for the entire lifecycle of their products, a dramatic reduction in waste generation follows.

Education campaigns also serve as a vital tool in reducing waste. By informing citizens about the environmental impact of their consumption choices and the benefits of reducing, reusing, and recycling, governments can foster a culture of environmental stewardship. Schools can integrate waste management principles into their curricula, instilling in the younger generation the values of sustainability and conservation.

Furthermore, the adoption of zero-waste policies in local governments can act as a beacon of possibility. These policies aim to eliminate all waste sent to landfills and incinerators through comprehensive recycling, composting, and smart design. Cities that commit to zero-waste goals become laboratories for innovation, developing best practices that can be replicated and scaled up.

Infrastructure investment is also key. By building state-of-the-art recycling centers, composting facilities, and waste-to-energy plants, governments can ensure that waste is seen not as an insurmountable problem but as a resource that can be harnessed. These facilities not only process waste more efficiently but also generate jobs and stimulate the local economy.

Governments must facilitate the transition to sustainable waste management by fostering collaboration between stakeholders. Public-private partnerships, community-led initiatives, and international cooperation can all contribute to the development of waste management solutions that are both locally relevant and globally informed.

Through an amalgamation of these strategies, governance can transform waste management from a daunting challenge into an opportunity for sustainable growth. As we craft our inclusive governance for a diverse humanity, let us remember that our relationship with the Earth's resources sets the tone for our collective future. It is only by managing our waste with foresight and ingenuity that we can hope to foster a truly harmonious world.


*- Innovation in Recycling and Upcycling*

In the verdant heart of governance, there lies a commitment to the earth: a promise to maintain the delicate balance of nature while nurturing the growth of human civilization. This commitment is perhaps most tangibly expressed in the policies surrounding waste management and recycling. It is here, in the alchemy of recycling and upcycling, that governments can both show respect for our planet and inspire their citizens to participate in a circular economy.

The innovation in recycling and upcycling is not merely a technical challenge but a cultural shift. It requires reimagining what we consider "waste" and seeing it instead as a resource—a potential raw material for new creations. The most forward-thinking governments have begun to weave this principle into the fabric of their policies, encouraging industries and individuals alike to transcend the traditional linear economy of "take, make, dispose."

One exemplary case is that of a small coastal city that transformed its waste management system into a beacon of sustainability. Here, the government launched an initiative that not only facilitated recycling but fostered an upcycling culture. Local artisans were given access to materials recovered from the waste stream, such as glass, plastics, and metals, which they transformed into high-quality products. From discarded bottles emerged intricate mosaic tiles that graced the city's public spaces, while reclaimed plastics were reborn as components of stylish furniture that adorned local cafes and parks.

This initiative did more than reduce waste—it created jobs, supported local craftspeople, and infused the economy with unique goods that carried a narrative of transformation and responsibility. The city's innovative approach to upcycling became a source of pride and a tourist attraction, with visitors marvelling at the ingenuity of repurposing what would have otherwise been trash.

Governments in harmonious worlds recognize that education is crucial in encouraging recycling and upcycling. They invest in public awareness campaigns that elevate the status of recycled products and inform citizens about the environmental and economic benefits of waste reduction. Schools incorporate sustainability and waste management into their curricula, fostering a new generation of environmentally conscious citizens.

On a larger scale, green governments incentivize businesses to adopt cradle-to-cradle design principles, ensuring products are created with their eventual recycling or upcycling in mind. By providing tax breaks, subsidies, or other forms of support, they encourage companies to develop innovative recycling technologies and to design products that can be easily disassembled and repurposed at the end of their life cycle.

In this harmonious world, the act of recycling transcends utility and becomes an art form, a testament to human ingenuity in the face of environmental challenges. Upcycling, as a governmental policy, becomes a bridge connecting the preservation of natural resources with the enrichment of cultural heritage. It is here, in the mindful transformation of what was once discarded, that the true potential of sustainable governance is realized.


<u>3.7 Water Conservation and Management</u>

*- Policies for Protecting Water Resources*

In the symphony of sustainable governance, water is the most delicate and vital of melodies, a resource that courses through the lifeblood of civilizations and ecosystems alike. The crafting of policies for water conservation and management is a testament to humanity's capacity to harmonize with nature's rhythms, ensuring that the purity and abundance of water endures for generations.

As we delve into the intricacies of this precious resource, we see that the key to safeguarding water lies in the embrace of a holistic approach. This approach intertwines the wisdom of traditional practices with the innovative solutions of the modern world, creating a governance model that is as fluid and adaptable as water itself.

Consider the ancient rainwater harvesting systems, a dance with the clouds that has quenched the thirst of communities for millennia. Governments can draw inspiration from these systems, implementing policies that incentivize the revival and modernization of such practices. By integrating rainwater harvesting into urban planning, we mitigate the strain on municipal water supplies and reduce the impact of stormwater runoff, a concerto of ecological and practical benefits.

Further, the protection of water resources necessitates a vigilant stance against pollution. Legislation must be stringent, yet flexible, capable of confronting the myriad threats that emerge in an era of rapid industrialization. Policies that enforce strict waste management protocols and penalize contaminant discharge not only preserve water quality but also signal a government's unwavering commitment to the health of its people and the land.

Agriculture, the great consumer of water, presents its own set of challenges and opportunities. Here, governance must take on the role of a maestro, orchestrating the adoption of water-efficient irrigation techniques, such as drip irrigation and soil moisture monitoring technologies. Subsidies and educational programs can be instruments of change, encouraging farmers to adopt practices that reduce water usage and safeguard this vital resource.

In urban landscapes, where concrete often usurps the permeability of natural soil, innovative infrastructure becomes indispensable. Green roofs, permeable pavements, and urban wetlands not only capture and reuse water but also act as verdant oases amidst the city's hustle, a visual and functional homage to the value of water in our lives.

Governance must also play the role of a global steward, fostering international cooperation in the management of transboundary water resources. Treaties and agreements can ensure equitable distribution, prevent conflicts, and facilitate knowledge exchange on best practices for water conservation.

The policies that protect our water resources are not merely legal documents; they are declarations of our collective resolve to be custodians of the planet's most life-sustaining element. It is through these policies that governments can compose a future where every drop of water is valued, conserved, and shared, and where every community, irrespective of latitude or longitude, has access to the clean, abundant water that is their birthright.

By embracing innovation and tradition, by legislating with both firmness and foresight, and by engaging every citizen in the quest for water sustainability, we can achieve a world where our governance not only echoes but amplifies the natural harmony of water, an essential refrain in the melody of harmonious worlds.


*- Sustainable Water Use and Reuse Practices*

Water is the essence of life, a precious resource that flows through the veins of our ecosystems and societies. In this section, we explore the innovative governance policies that underpin sustainable water use and reuse practices, essential for the survival and prosperity of our planet.

The concept of sustainable water management is not new, but its implementation remains a challenge in many regions of the world. The harmonious world we envision is one where water is respected as a communal treasure, not merely an economic commodity. To achieve this, governments must pioneer policies that incentivize conservation, enhance efficiency, and encourage the development of new technologies for water reuse.

One of the most promising approaches is the adoption of decentralized water management systems. These systems empower local communities to take charge of their water resources, tailoring solutions to their specific needs and environmental conditions. By harnessing the power of rainwater harvesting, greywater systems, and constructed wetlands, communities can reduce their reliance on centralized water treatment facilities, which often consume vast amounts of energy and resources.

In the realm of agriculture, which accounts for a staggering 70% of global freshwater withdrawals, the shift towards precision irrigation practices represents a transformative change. Smart irrigation systems that deploy sensors and satellite imagery can optimize water use, ensuring that crops receive the exact amount of water they need to thrive, no more, no less. This not only conserves water but also minimizes runoff and reduces soil erosion.

Urban landscapes, too, can become havens of water efficiency through green infrastructure. Green roofs, permeable pavements, and urban gardens not only beautify our cities but also act as natural sponges, capturing rainwater and reducing stormwater runoff. These initiatives, when supported by policy and public Investment, can transform urban centers into models of water sustainability.

The governance of water must also extend to its reuse. Advances in water treatment technologies have made it possible to safely recycle wastewater for non-potable uses, such as agriculture, industry, and even replenishing aquifers. By integrating these systems into urban planning, governments can create closed-loop water cycles that significantly reduce the demand for freshwater.

In this harmonious world, education plays a pivotal role. A well-informed citizenry is the bedrock of sustainable governance. By integrating water conservation education into school curricula and public campaigns, governments can foster a culture of water stewardship that transcends generations.

Sustainable water use and reuse practices are not just environmental imperatives but also opportunities for innovative governance. By embracing these practices, governments worldwide can secure the health of their nations and the planet, ensuring that water, our most vital resource, is preserved and cherished for all humanity. The journey to harmonious worlds begins with each drop of water saved, each policy enacted, and each community empowered to make a difference.


<u>3.8 Agriculture and Food Security</u>

*- Promoting Sustainable Farming Techniques*

Within the verdant embrace of Earth's arable lands lies a profound truth: the sustainability of our societies is rooted in the soil. It is within this matrix that the harmonious world we envision must take root, particularly through the prism of agriculture and food security. As we explore the pioneering sustainable policies that green governments are implementing, we uncover a fertile ground for innovation and resilience.

Sustainable farming techniques are the seedlings of a robust food system, one that nourishes both people and the planet. Governments that have embraced these practices are leading by example, demonstrating that it is indeed possible to satisfy our present needs without compromising the ability of future generations to meet their own.

The shift toward sustainable agriculture is not merely a change in techniques; it is a transformation in mindset. It requires us to rethink the relationship between the land and the food it yields. This section delves into the array of methods that policy and practice can cultivate to ensure a bountiful and balanced harvest.

Crop rotation, a venerable practice as old as agriculture itself, has seen a resurgence. By alternating the crops on a given plot of land, farmers can naturally replenish soil nutrients, break pest and disease cycles, and reduce the need for chemical fertilizers and pesticides. Green governments are incentivizing this practice through subsidies and educational programs, recognizing that the health of the soil is inextricably linked to the health of the population.

Another significant stride in sustainable farming is the adoption of agroforestry. By integrating trees and shrubs into agricultural landscapes, farmers can create microclimates that protect crops from harsh weather, improve water retention, and foster biodiversity. Governments promoting agroforestry are not only investing in the present but also planting the seeds for a more resilient agricultural system—one that can withstand the climatic tempests on the horizon.

Urban agriculture is yet another green frontier. As cities expand and the distance between farm and fork grows, innovative governance has sparked a revolution in local food production. Rooftop gardens, vertical farms, and community plots are springing up, supported by policies that make urban spaces available for cultivation. These initiatives not only reduce the carbon footprint of food transportation but also reconnect urban dwellers with the agrarian rhythms that sustain life.

We must discuss the role of technology in sustainable agriculture. Precision farming, powered by sensors and data analytics, allows for the meticulous application of water and nutrients, minimizing waste and maximizing yield. Governments are fostering the development and dissemination of these technologies, ensuring that farmers—regardless of their scale—have access to the tools necessary for sustainable stewardship of the land.

As we cultivate these practices and policies, we nourish the roots of a harmonious world. Green governments are leading the way, proving that sustainability in agriculture is not only an environmental imperative but also a catalyst for food security, economic vitality, and societal well-being. The harvest of such governance is plentiful, promising a future where humanity grows in sync with the Earth that sustains us.


*- Addressing the Challenges of Climate Change on Food Production*

In the golden fields that stretch across the horizon, there is a silent struggle between the bounty of the earth and the changing whims of the climate. Here, the impact of governance on environmental sustainability becomes starkly visible, and the necessity for innovative policies to ensure food security in the face of climate change is undeniable.

Climate change presents a daunting array of challenges for agriculture: altered rainfall patterns, increased frequency of extreme weather events, and the spread of pests and diseases. These phenomena threaten the very foundations of food production, with the potential to disrupt the delicate equilibrium of ecosystems that have sustained human life for millennia.

To address these challenges, green governments worldwide are pioneering sustainable policies that intertwine the threads of ecological wisdom with the fabric of agricultural practice. One such policy is the promotion of climate-resilient crops. Through the development of seed varieties that can withstand erratic weather conditions, governments are helping farmers maintain their yields even as the environment grows more uncertain.

Another innovative approach is the implementation of water-smart agricultural techniques. Techniques such as drip irrigation and rainwater harvesting are becoming instrumental in preserving precious water resources. By optimizing water usage, these methods not only ensure that crops can survive during droughts but also help to mitigate the effects of floods by improving soil absorption and reducing runoff.

In parallel, green governments are fostering the adoption of organic farming practices. By reducing reliance on chemical pesticides and fertilizers, which can exacerbate soil degradation and water contamination, these practices promote biodiversity and build healthier, more resilient agroecosystems. Organic farming also holds the potential to sequester carbon in the soil, contributing to the mitigation of greenhouse gas emissions.

Moreover, forward-thinking policies are encouraging local food production and consumption. By supporting community gardens, urban agriculture, and farm-to-table initiatives, governments are reducing the carbon footprint associated with long-distance food transport. These efforts not only bring fresher produce to consumers but also strengthen local economies and build community resilience.

To catalyze these changes, green governments are investing in agricultural research and extension services that provide farmers with the knowledge and tools they need to adapt to changing conditions. Education campaigns are launched to raise awareness of the benefits of sustainable farming practices, and incentives are offered to those who adopt them.

The challenges are formidable, but the collective will of the world's governance structures—animated by the vision of a harmonious world—can turn the tide. By nurturing the land with policies that protect and enhance its fertility, governments can secure the future of food production, ensuring that the generations to come will continue to reap the harvests of a well-tended earth. The vision of harmonious worlds is not just about governance; it is about sustaining the very lifeblood of humanity—our sustenance.


<u>3.9 Education for Environmental Stewardship</u>

*- Integrating Sustainability into Educational Curricula*

In the verdant classrooms of tomorrow, the seeds of environmental stewardship will be meticulously sown. The vision of a harmonious world is inextricably linked to the way we educate our youth about sustainability. It is not enough to merely inform; we must inspire and empower. As we delve into the role of education in environmental governance, we find that the key lies not only in the content delivered but also in the ethos cultivated.

Imagine a curriculum that breathes life into the principles of sustainability, where each lesson is an invitation to engage with the world as thoughtful custodians. Here, mathematics transcends numbers and equations; it becomes a tool to measure carbon footprints, analyze renewable energy efficiency, and assess the sustainability of supply chains. Science is no longer confined to the laboratory; it spills out into the natural world, teaching students about ecosystems, biodiversity, and the delicate balance that sustains all life.

Language and literature classes serve as the perfect platforms to explore environmental narratives, weaving ecological themes into the tapestry of human expression. Through stories and poems, students learn empathy for the natural world, understanding the profound interconnectedness of all beings. History becomes a lens through which to view the evolution of human-environment relations, learning from past mistakes and successes to shape a more sustainable present and future.

But this integration extends beyond academic subjects. Real-world application is paramount. School gardens become living laboratories for biology and ecology, while recycling and composting initiatives serve as practical exercises in resource management. Energy audits conducted by students transform abstract concepts into tangible actions, bridging the gap between theory and practice.

Central to this educational paradigm is the development of critical thinking. It encourages students to question the status quo, to envisage alternative futures where society harmonizes with nature rather than dominating it. This critical approach fosters a generation of innovators and problem-solvers, ready to tackle the environmental challenges that lie ahead.

Service learning and community projects enable students to step out of the classroom and into the heart of their communities, applying their knowledge to real-world environmental issues. These experiences solidify the connection between learning and living, reinforcing the notion that every individual has a role to play in the stewardship of our planet.

And as students grow into informed citizens, they carry with them the values of sustainability into all spheres of life. The ripple effect is profound – sustainable practices become embedded in culture, economy, and governance, leading to a societal transformation that starts in the classroom but echoes throughout the world.

The harmonious world we yearn for begins with education – an education that does not end with graduation but evolves into a lifelong commitment to environmental guardianship. By integrating sustainability into educational curricula, we cultivate a generation equipped not only with knowledge but with the passion and purpose to create a future where green governance is not an exception, but the rule.

*- Public Awareness Campaigns and Community Engagement*

In the verdant crucible of environmental governance, the seeds of sustainable living must be sown early and nurtured with care. It is through education that these seeds find fertile ground, growing into the robust trees of environmental stewardship that stand tall against the winds of ecological ignorance and indifference. Here we examine the quintessence of public awareness campaigns and community engagement as the twin pillars supporting the edifice of environmental education.

The narrative of Earth's fragility has long been confined to the margins of academic discourse, whispered in the cloisters of environmental science departments, or echoed in the fervent rallies of activists. Yet, the urgency of our times demands a chorus, not a whisper. Public awareness campaigns are the megaphones that amplify this message, transforming the narrative from a sotto voce to a resonant call to action that reverberates through the consciousness of the populace.

These campaigns wield the power of storytelling, creating compelling narratives that resonate with the collective spirit. They transcend the mere dissemination of facts and figures, instead weaving a tapestry of emotional and intellectual engagement that inspires individuals to see themselves as part of a larger, interconnected ecosystem. Innovative mediums—ranging from immersive virtual reality experiences to interactive social media movements—bring the plight of the planet into the personal realm, making the abstract tangibly urgent.

Moreover, the synergy between public awareness and community engagement engenders a sense of ownership and responsibility. Local initiatives, such as tree-planting drives and community gardens, serve as practical workshops for the principles espoused in environmental campaigns. These grassroots efforts cultivate a hands-on understanding of sustainability and empower citizens to be active participants in the stewardship of their environment.

There are a mosaic of case studies, illustrating successful campaigns that have sparked significant behavioral changes. One such example is the 'Green Ribbon' initiative, which encouraged citizens to symbolically and literally 'tie' themselves to the commitment of reducing their carbon footprint. The campaign was a confluence of education and action, with each ribbon representing both a pledge and a plan to plant a new tree in the community.

Furthermore, schools are positioned as the crucibles of change, integrating environmental education into curricula and fostering a generation of eco-literate citizens. Children who are taught the value of biodiversity, the intricacies of ecosystems, and the importance of conservation grow into adults who naturally incorporate these values into their decision-making processes.

Public awareness campaigns and community engagement are not peripheral activities but central components of a holistic approach to environmental governance. They are the lifeblood of sustainable policy, ensuring that the heartbeat of environmental consciousness echoes through the chambers of society. By embracing these initiatives, governments can pioneer a future where green is not merely a color, but the very ethos of a harmonious world.

<u>3.10 Monitoring, Reporting, and Accountability in Environmental Governance</u>

*- Tools for Tracking Policy Impact*

The canvas of environmental governance is vast, and its colors blend the hues of policy with the intricate shades of ecological impact. At the heart of this mosaic lies a critical process that ensures the vibrancy and authenticity of the entire artwork: monitoring, reporting, and accountability. The tools employed in this process are not mere instruments but brushes that paint the portrait of policy impact, revealing the true picture of sustainability efforts.

To begin, monitoring serves as the watchful eyes of governance, constantly surveying the landscape of implementation. It is through meticulous monitoring that policymakers can discern whether the seeds of their initiatives are flourishing or withering. For instance, the deployment of satellite imagery and remote sensing technologies has revolutionized the way governments track deforestation, encroachment on protected areas, and the health of coral reefs. These digital sentinels silently observe the Earth, providing real-time data that can trigger swift corrective action.

Reporting, on the other hand, is the voice that narrates the story of environmental policy. It is an exercise in transparency, a recitation of facts and figures that illustrates the journey from intent to impact. The Global Reporting Initiative (GRI) has set standards that encourage organizations to disclose their environmental performance, offering a template for governments to emulate. By adhering to such frameworks, administrations can produce reports that not only reflect their accomplishments but also identify areas in need of improvement.

Accountability is the backbone of effective governance. It is the promise that actions align with words, and it stands tall when policies are questioned or challenged. Environmental accountability entails the establishment of regulatory bodies, such as environmental ombudsmen and watchdog agencies, that possess the authority to enforce regulations and impose penalties for non-compliance. These guardians of green governance act as arbiters, ensuring that environmental policies do not become hollow declarations lost in the wind.

Innovative tools like the Environmental Performance Index (EPI) offer a comprehensive metric to evaluate and compare the environmental performance of countries, fueling a healthy competition towards sustainability. Citizen science initiatives empower individuals to contribute data on local environmental conditions, thereby weaving a grassroots network of monitoring that complements official efforts.

The effectiveness of monitoring, reporting, and accountability tools hinges on their integration into a holistic governance framework. This requires the synchronization of technology, legislation, and human resources to ensure that the mechanisms for tracking policy impact are robust and responsive.

In crafting inclusive governance for a diverse humanity, these tools are not optional; they are essential threads in the tapestry of sustainable policy-making. They enable governments to adjust their strategies, celebrate their successes, and above all, remain steadfast in their commitment to the environment. The harmonious world we envision is one where every policy stroke is guided by these principles, creating a masterpiece of governance that endures for generations.

*- Ensuring Transparency and Public Participation in Environmental Decision-Making*

The pursuit of sustainability is not merely a policy initiative; it is a covenant with future generations. This sacred bond requires steadfast monitoring, meticulous reporting, and unwavering accountability. Here, we explore how environmental governance can be crafted to ensure that these principles are not only upheld but celebrated as cornerstones of a thriving, green government.

The heartbeat of transparent environmental governance lies in the constant, rhythmic pulse of data. Monitoring systems must be sophisticated, yet accessible, capturing the myriad interactions between human activity and the natural world. State-of-the-art sensors and satellites can track everything from deforestation rates to urban air quality, providing a stream of real-time data. But technology is only part of the equation. There must be a harmonious blend of scientific expertise and local knowledge, where indigenous wisdom and citizen observations contribute to an overarching understanding of environmental health.

Reporting this data is equally crucial. Environmental data repositories should be as engaging as they are enlightening, presenting information in formats that resonate with both policymakers and the public. Interactive maps, compelling infographics, and narrative storytelling can transform raw numbers into powerful testimonies of our planet's condition. These reports must be frequent and forward-looking, not just assessing current states but projecting future scenarios. They should inform policy decisions, but also spark public discourse, encouraging communities to discuss the state of their environment and the efficacy of current policies.

Accountability in environmental governance is the lynchpin that ensures policies transcend rhetoric and manifest into tangible outcomes. Governments must be held answerable for their environmental commitments through a framework of legal and societal checks and balances. Independent environmental watchdogs, equipped with legal authority and public support, can oversee government actions, ensuring that environmental goals are pursued with diligence. When governments know they are being watched, and that there are consequences for negligence or misconduct, their incentive to adhere to sustainable practices is significantly reinforced.

Public participation is the lifeblood of a democratic approach to environmental governance. Citizens should not only have access to environmental information but also the opportunity to contribute to decision-making processes. Public forums, citizen juries, and online platforms can facilitate robust discussions where community members can voice concerns, propose solutions, and collaborate with officials. By involving the public in environmental governance, governments can harness a wealth of diverse perspectives and foster a sense of shared responsibility for the health of the planet.

Monitoring, reporting, and accountability are not mere bureaucratic necessities but are the pillars upon which green governments can build a legacy of sustainability. It is through these processes that the abstract concepts of transparency and public participation become tangible actions, weaving the thread of responsibility through the tapestry of governance. As we endeavor to create harmonious worlds, let us remember that the fabric of a sustainable future is only as strong as the commitment to these principles.

# 4. Economic Inclusivity



## 4.1 Redefining Wealth

*- The philosophical underpinnings of wealth*

As we venture into the realm of economic inclusivity, it is imperative to pause and ponder upon the philosophical underpinnings of wealth. The concept of wealth has traditionally been associated with the accumulation of material assets and financial prosperity. It has been the yardstick by which societies have measured success and the objective towards which individuals have tirelessly strived. Yet, this narrow definition belies the richness and complexity of what it means to be truly wealthy.

Wealth, in its most enlightened form, transcends the mere aggregation of possessions. It embodies the availability and accessibility of opportunities, the inclusivity of one's community, and the health of the environment that sustains us all. A society that is wealthy in this holistic sense is one where every individual has the means to fulfill their potential, where no one is left behind in abject poverty while others bask in opulence, and where the natural world is not sacrificed on the altar of economic growth.

To redefine wealth, we must first acknowledge that our current economic systems often perpetuate disparities rather than alleviate them. The pursuit of wealth has too frequently led to the exploitation of resources, both human and environmental, creating deep chasms of inequality that threaten the very fabric of our societies. The philosophy that should guide our reconceptualization of wealth is one that harmonizes individual ambition with collective well-being, one that regards the prosperity of the community as inseparable from the success of the individual.

In this new paradigm, wealth is not hoarded but shared, not flaunted but utilized for the common good. It is a recognition that the most valuable assets are not always quantifiable — the trust within a community, the wisdom passed down through generations, the diversity of cultures that enrich our understanding of the world, and the resilience of ecosystems that nurture life on our planet.

The redefinition of wealth demands a bold reimagining of our governance structures. It calls for innovative economic models that prioritize equitable resource distribution, ensuring that every member of society has access to the essentials: clean water, nutritious food, healthcare, education, and the means to participate fully in the civic life of their communities. The governance that emerges from this philosophy is one that measures prosperity not by the stockpiles of the few but by the upliftment of many, where the success of a policy is gauged by the breadth and depth of its impact.

As we forge ahead in this book, we will explore the practical steps necessary to transition from a world fixated on financial wealth to one that cherishes and cultivates wealth in its most expansive, inclusive, and sustainable form. It is a journey that promises to redefine not just our economies but the very essence of what it means to live in a harmonious world.

*- Current global wealth distribution and its impacts*

In the shadow of towering skyscrapers and amidst the bustle of market squares around the world, there lies a silent witness to the great paradox of our times— the coexistence of extraordinary wealth and abject poverty. As we delve into the heart of this dichotomy, we unravel the tapestry of global wealth distribution and its profound impacts on humanity.

Our world, abundant in resources and technological advancements, is marked by a stark disparity in wealth distribution. A mere handful of individuals command fortunes that surpass the gross domestic product of entire nations, while billions struggle to secure the barest necessities of life. This imbalance is not merely a matter of economic digits; it is a catalyst for social unrest, a barrier to education and health access, and a profound moral quandary.

The concentration of wealth in the hands of the few is not an isolated phenomenon; it is the product of historical processes, economic structures, and power dynamics. The colonial legacies that carved up continents, the industrial revolutions that reshaped societies, and the financial systems that dictate flows of capital—all have played their parts in sculpting the economic landscape we see today.

As we trace the contours of this landscape, we see that wealth is not evenly distributed, neither between nations nor within them. Countries with vast natural resources may find themselves paradoxically impoverished if governance is weak and corruption rampant. Within societies, systemic barriers such as racial and gender discrimination further skew the allocation of wealth, entrenching cycles of poverty that span generations.

The impact of this skewed distribution is manifold. Economies stagger under the weight of inequality, as the consumer base narrows and social mobility stagnates. Social fabrics tear, giving rise to tensions and conflicts. The environment suffers as the drive for profit eclipses the imperative for sustainable practices. Meanwhile, the wealthy, insulated by their affluence, may drift further from the reality of the common populace, their decisions in governance and business reflecting a detachment from the lived experiences of the majority.

But what if we were to redefine wealth? Not as an accumulation of currency and assets, but as a measure of a society's ability to provide for the well-being of all its members? What if our metrics for success included not only gross domestic product but also indices of education, health, and social equity?

In redefining wealth, we challenge the very foundations upon which the current distribution is predicated. We open the door to innovative economic models that prioritize human dignity and environmental stewardship. We envision a new architecture of governance, one where fiscal policies are crafted not solely for the growth of wealth but for its equitable distribution.

In the pages that follow, we shall explore these alternative models, analyzing their potential to create economies where inclusivity is not just an ideal but a cornerstone. We shall embark on a quest to reimagine a world where the wealth of nations is gauged by the prosperity of their people, a world striving toward economic inclusivity—a fundamental step toward the harmonious worlds we seek.


4.2 Equitable Economic Models

- *Exploring the spectrum of economic systems*

In a world where wealth is as diverse as the landscapes we inhabit, the quest for economic systems that distribute resources equitably is akin to the search for the Holy Grail in medieval lore. It is a pursuit fraught with complexity, yet essential for the crafting of harmonious worlds. Let's delve into the spectrum of economic models that endeavor to weave a tapestry of fairness and opportunity across the globe.

The first thread in this tapestry is the concept of a participatory economy, where each individual has a stake and a say in the economic decisions that affect their community. Imagine an economic system where decision-making power is not hoarded by the few but is distributed like seeds in a field, promising a harvest of collective prosperity. In this model, workplaces are democratically controlled, and investment choices are made through communal deliberation, ensuring that the fruits of labor are shared in a manner that reflects the input and needs of all.

Then, we turn our gaze to the principles of a circular economy, a bold reimagining of the traditional linear consumption model—take, make, dispose— into one that is restorative and regenerative by design. Here, resources are kept in use for as long as possible, extracting the maximum value during usage, and then recovered and regenerated at the end of their service life. This model not only champions environmental sustainability but also fosters economic inclusivity by creating jobs and opportunities within the recycling and refurbishing sectors.

Another vibrant hue in this economic mosaic is the cooperative movement. Cooperatives are businesses owned and run by and for their members, whether they are customers, employees, or residents. These entities are not driven by the relentless pursuit of profit but by the goal of fulfilling the needs and aspirations of their members. As such, they prioritize equitable distribution of profits, community development, and social responsibility.

But what of the gig economy, the rapidly growing segment of the labor force that operates on a freelance or short-term contract basis? Here lies a paradox—on one hand, it offers autonomy and flexibility; on the other, it can lead to instability and lack of protection. To harness this model for economic inclusivity, we must reimagine its framework to provide safety nets and benefits, much like those offered in traditional employment, thus ensuring that workers are not left vulnerable.

We explore the potential of universal basic income (UBI) as a means to level the economic playing field. By providing all citizens with a regular, unconditional sum of money, irrespective of employment status, UBI aims to reduce poverty and inequality, and to empower individuals to pursue education, entrepreneurship, or other activities that may contribute to the common good.

Each of these economic systems, with their distinct colors and textures, contributes to the mosaic of equitable resource distribution. As we piece them together, we are not seeking a one-size-fits-all solution, for such a garment would be ill-fitting for the diverse body of humanity. Instead, we are striving for a patchwork quilt of economic models, each tailored to the unique cultural, social, and environmental fabric of a community, creating a global tapestry of economic inclusivity.


*- Criteria for fairness in resource allocation*

In the quest for economic inclusivity, the cornerstone of equitable governance lies in the principles that guide the distribution of resources. Fairness is not a one-size-fits-all concept; it must be a chameleon, adapting to the colors of context, culture, and circumstance. Yet, in the tapestry of human society, certain universal threads can be woven to create a fabric of economic justice that drapes over the shoulders of every nation, providing warmth and security to all its citizens.

The criteria for fairness in resource allocation must begin with the principle of sufficiency. This is a commitment to ensuring that all individuals have access to the basic goods and services necessary for a dignified life. These include, but are not limited to, food, shelter, healthcare, education, and the means to pursue meaningful work. Sufficiency does not demand equal shares for all but rather an equitable floor from which all can stand.

Next, we must embrace the principle of opportunity. Beyond mere sufficiency, fair resource allocation should enable individuals to reach their potential. This requires access to advanced education, professional development, and the economic infrastructure that fosters innovation and entrepreneurship. Opportunity is the seedbed of human creativity; when nurtured by fair economic systems, it can flourish into solutions for society's most pressing challenges.

The principle of transparency undergirds fair allocation. Resources must be distributed in a manner that is open and understandable to all stakeholders. This transparency builds trust and ensures that the processes governing distribution are subject to public scrutiny and accountability. Without clear insight into how decisions are made, the shadow of doubt creeps in, and the legitimacy of the system is eroded.

A fourth criterion is the principle of participation. In a truly inclusive governance system, all affected parties should have a voice in how resources are allocated. This participatory approach democratizes economic decisions, fostering a sense of collective ownership and responsibility. It is not enough for decisions to be made on behalf of the people; they must be made with the people.

We must consider the principle of adaptability. Economic systems must be flexible enough to respond to changing needs and circumstances. The world is in a constant state of flux, and governance structures must be nimble enough to adjust their sails to the winds of change. This includes revising resource allocation in response to environmental challenges, technological advancements, and shifting demographics.

In our envisioned world, fairness in resource allocation is not a static target but a dynamic process that evolves with the ebb and flow of human needs and aspirations. By grounding our economic models in these principles—sufficiency, opportunity, transparency, participation, and adaptability—we forge a path toward a governance that genuinely embodies economic inclusivity. As we traverse this path, we must remain vigilant, ensuring that our strides toward fairness are measured not only by the prosperity they generate but also by the voices they uplift and the lives they dignify.


<u>4.3 Universal Basic Income</u>

*- Rationale behind the Universal Basic Income*

In the tapestry of economic inclusivity, one thread stands out for its bold color and radical promise: Universal Basic Income (UBI). UBI is a model for social security in which all citizens receive a regular, unconditional sum of money from the government, sufficient to ensure a basic standard of living. Let's examine the philosophical and practical underpinnings of UBI, arguing for its potential to weave a new pattern of economic justice into the fabric of society.

At its core, UBI is grounded in the principle of economic human rights. The assertion is that, in a world of plenty, no individual should be without the means to live. UBI is premised on the idea that the wealth of a nation is not solely the product of the current generation's labor but a cumulative legacy of societal advancement. It acknowledges that every member of society contributes to and benefits from the stability and progress of the collective, and thus, everyone should share in the bounty.

UBI is also a response to the nuanced challenges of the modern economy. In an era where automation and artificial intelligence threaten to render traditional employment models obsolete, UBI offers a cushion against the shockwaves of technological disruption. It presents a future where humans are not valued merely for their labor, but for their intrinsic worth, and where creativity and innovation are liberated from the constraints of economic survival.

Moreover, UBI is a tool for simplifying the welfare state. Rather than navigating a labyrinth of conditional assistance programs, each with its own bureaucracy and stigma, citizens would receive a straightforward, stigma-free financial foundation. This not only reduces administrative costs but also empowers individuals to make choices about their own lives, trusting in their capacity to allocate resources wisely.

One cannot discuss UBI without confronting the specter of shared responsibility. Detractors often argue that UBI could diminish the incentive to work. However, studies in various countries have shown that the opposite is true. When the specter of absolute poverty is removed, individuals are more likely to pursue education, take entrepreneurial risks, and engage in community service. UBI fosters an environment where work is not born of sheer necessity, but rather, is a pursuit of passion and contribution to the common good.

In essence, the rationale behind UBI is to emancipate the human spirit from the fetters of economic precariousness. It is a bold reimagining of society's social contract, extending the promise of liberty and justice to encompass economic freedom as well. As we move forward in crafting inclusive governance for a diverse humanity, UBI presents not just an economic model, but a philosophical beacon—a vision of a world where each individual is assured the dignity of choice and the opportunity to thrive in harmonious worlds.

*- Case studies of Universal Basic Income trials*

In the quest for economic inclusivity, few ideas have sparked as much debate and interest as Universal Basic Income (UBI). This radical reimagining of welfare suggests that by providing all citizens with a regular, unconditional sum of money, regardless of employment status, a more equitable and less bureaucratically entangled safety net could be established. We shall embark on a journey into the heart of various UBI trials, examining their outcomes and the lessons they impart.

The Finnish Experiment, conducted from 2017 to 2018, serves as an illuminating starting point. Two thousand unemployed Finns were provided with a monthly stipend of €560, free from the usual tangle of welfare conditions. Initial findings painted a portrait of improved well-being, with participants reporting less stress and greater incentive to seek employment, contradicting critics' fears of diminished work motivation. However, the study did not show a significant increase in employment compared to a control group, suggesting that UBI might not directly influence job markets as some proponents had hoped.

Leap to the west, and you find the Ontario Basic Income Pilot, launched in 2017 but prematurely canceled in 2018. Despite its abrupt end, early reports suggested that recipients experienced better physical and mental health, had more opportunities to invest in their education, and felt empowered to make career changes that could lead to more stable, higher-paying jobs in the long term. The Ontario case thus provides a tantalizing glimpse into the potential long-term societal benefits that a fully implemented UBI could offer.

Crossing to the southern hemisphere, one finds the Namibian UBI experiment in the village of Otjivero. Launched in 2008, residents received 100 Namibian dollars per month for two years, leading to remarkable outcomes. Economic activity flourished, with new businesses emerging and overall transactional activity within the village increasing. School attendance rates soared, while malnutrition and crime rates plummeted. This case study exemplifies UBI's potential to transform economies at the micro-level, suggesting that its effects could be even more profound in struggling communities.

Each of these case studies presents a piece of a complex puzzle. While not a panacea, UBI trials offer compelling evidence that a restructuring of economic safety nets could yield diverse benefits. Improved mental health, increased educational pursuits, entrepreneurial stimulation, and reduced crime rates are among the mosaic of positive outcomes. Yet, the nuanced picture that emerges also shows that UBI is not a straightforward solution to unemployment, and its implementation must be thoughtfully tailored to the specific economic and social fabrics of different societies.

As we contemplate the broader application of UBI, it is essential to consider these trials as guideposts on the path toward a more inclusive economic future. It is a path lined with questions about funding, societal values, and the very nature of work in an evolving world. The trials teach us that UBI's greatest strength lies in its ability to provide a foundation upon which human potential can more freely build, a harmonious note in the symphony of economic inclusivity.


## 4.4 Progressive Taxation

*- The role of taxation in redistributing wealth*

In the tapestry of economic inclusivity, progressive taxation emerges as a vital thread. It is not merely a mechanism for generating government revenue but a powerful tool for wealth redistribution, capable of weaving equity into the fabric of society. The principle behind progressive taxation is elegantly simple: those with greater financial means contribute a larger share of their income to public coffers, thereby helping to level the societal playing field.

The role of taxation in achieving economic balance cannot be overstated. It is the chisel with which we sculpt a fairer world out of the raw marble of capitalism. Through progressive tax policies, we can dampen the sharp edges of inequality, ensuring that everyone, from the most affluent to the most vulnerable, has a stake in society's prosperity.

Let us consider the archetypal tycoon, whose wealth, amassed through a combination of innovation, opportunity, and sometimes sheer happenstance, towers over the average citizen's earnings. Under a progressive taxation system, this tycoon's income is taxed at a rate that rises in proportion to their earnings. The revenue thus obtained is channeled into public goods and services—education, healthcare, infrastructure, and social security—that benefit all, including the tycoon who requires a well-educated workforce, healthy consumers, and stable societal conditions to continue their entrepreneurial ventures.

But progressive taxation is more than an economic instrument; it is a declaration of societal values. It asserts that a citizen's worth is not measured solely by their wealth, but by their contribution to the common good. Through this system, the wealthy are not penalized for their success but are asked to shoulder a greater portion of the financial burden in recognition of the social structure that facilitated their prosperity. It is a modern echo of the ancient ideal of noblesse oblige, where privilege entails responsibility.

Critics may argue that such taxation stifles innovation and ambition, yet evidence suggests that when implemented with care and foresight, it spurs growth by investing in the collective well-being, thereby creating a more robust and resilient economy. It fosters a climate where opportunity is not hoarded but shared, allowing talent and industriousness to flourish regardless of one's starting point in life.

To ensure progressive taxation achieves its aim, transparency and fairness are paramount. Loopholes and shelters that allow for evasion must be sealed, and the tax revenue must be visibly transformed into tangible enhancements in public life. When citizens witness their contributions molding a more equitable society, trust in the system is fortified.

In crafting inclusive governance for humanity's diverse mosaic, progressive taxation stands as an essential pillar—supporting structures that uplift every individual. It encourages us to envision a world not as a collection of disparate economic islands but as a united archipelago, where the tides of wealth lift all boats, big and small, in harmonious ascent.


*- Comparative analysis of global taxation policies*

As we navigate the labyrinthine complexities of crafting inclusive governance, the tool of progressive taxation emerges as a beacon of hope in our quest for economic equity. In essence, progressive taxation is a system where the tax rate increases as the taxable amount rises, ideally ensuring that those with greater financial means contribute more substantially to the public coffers. Here is a comparative analysis of global taxation policies which illuminate the variegated ways in which nations strive to balance fiscal responsibility with social justice.

The Scandinavian model often stands as a paragon of progressive taxation. Countries like Sweden, Norway, and Denmark have implemented tax systems that exhibit a steep progression, where high-income individuals are taxed at rates north of 50%. The result is a robust welfare state that provides universal healthcare, free higher education, and a safety net that catches citizens long before they hit the ground. These countries have managed to weave the threads of taxation into a tapestry of societal support without stifling the entrepreneurial spirit that drives economic growth.

Turning our gaze to the United States, we observe a different tableau. In principle, the U.S. tax code is progressive. However, the reality is often distorted by a myriad of deductions, exemptions, and loopholes that can significantly lower the effective tax rates for the wealthiest individuals and corporations. This muddles the waters of progressivity, leading to public outcry for reform and transparency. The debate rages on whether the tax code should be simplified to ensure the wealthy pay their fair share or whether the current system, with its incentives for investment and innovation, is the engine of American prosperity.

In contrast, flat tax systems, like those in some Eastern European countries, tax all income at the same rate, irrespective of the amount. While this simplifies the tax code and encourages compliance, it does little to redistribute wealth or alleviate the burdens on the lower-income strata of society. Here, the pursuit of simplicity trumps progressivity, challenging the notion that effective governance necessitates an overtly progressive tax system.

What can we glean from this kaleidoscopic array of policies? It is evident that there is no one-size-fits-all solution in the realm of taxation. Each country's historical context, cultural values, economic structure, and societal priorities shape its approach. Yet, amidst this diversity, a common thread binds these systems: the ongoing quest to harmonize revenue generation with societal well-being.

To forge ahead on the path toward economic inclusivity, we must be willing to dissect and learn from these global experiments in taxation. It is a delicate dance between individual wealth and collective welfare, one that requires precision, insight, and above all, a profound commitment to the principle that every individual deserves to partake in the fruits of their society. Progressive taxation, if wielded judiciously, can be a powerful instrument in our symphony of inclusive governance, harmonizing the notes of prosperity and fairness in a melody that resonates across the diverse spectrum of humanity.

*- Establishing a living wage standard*

As we venture further into the labyrinth of economic equality, we encounter a crucial cornerstone of inclusive governance: the establishment of a living wage standard. This is not merely about ensuring that workers can meet their basic needs; it's about recognizing the dignity of labor, fostering societal health, and stimulating economic vitality. It's about crafting a world where every individual has the opportunity to thrive, not just survive.

In the heart of the bustling cityscape, where skyscrapers kiss the heavens and the hum of commerce fills the air, we find Cara, a single mother of two, weaving through the maze of her day. From dawn to dusk, she serves up steaming cups of hope in the form of coffee, all the while her dreams simmering on the back burner. Cara, like millions, is tethered to a minimum wage that fails to acknowledge the true cost of living. The disconnect between her earnings and the price of existence casts a long shadow over her family's future.

The establishment of a living wage standard is a declaration that society values the time and effort of its workforce. It is an admission that the minimum wage, often stagnant and unresponsive to the rising tides of inflation and cost of living, is insufficient. A living wage is not a luxury; it is a calculation based on the actual costs of living in a specific location, including housing, food, healthcare, and other essentials, along with a modicum of discretionary income that allows for participation in the cultural and civic life of the community.

When governance systems embrace the living wage, they sow seeds of sustainability. Workers like Cara suddenly find themselves able to afford decent housing, nutritious food, and quality education for their children. This is not simply altruism; it is sound economic strategy. With the ability to spend more, workers inject vitality back into the economy, supporting local businesses and generating tax revenue. Moreover, the benefits ripple outward, reducing the strain on social services and healthcare systems as the populace leads healthier, more secure lives.

But how do we implement such a standard? It requires a nuanced approach, involving collaboration between government, businesses, and labor representatives. Indexing wages to the cost of living, regular adjustments in line with economic indicators, and tax policies that encourage fair compensation are all pieces of the intricate puzzle. It requires courage from policymakers to reshape the landscape, an acknowledgment from businesses that investing in their workforce is investing in their own success, and a commitment from society to elevate the common good above the siren call of unchecked profit.

Let us envision a world where the Caras are no longer just scraping by, but are empowered to be full participants in the economy and society. Let us strive for a governance that not only hears but heeds the chorus of voices calling for change. In establishing a living wage standard, we step closer to harmonious worlds, where the dignity of each individual is not just recognized but revered, and economic inclusivity is not just a distant dream but a tangible reality.

*- Effects of living wages on economies and societies*

In the quest for economic inclusivity, the concept of a living wage emerges as a beacon of hope, a promise of stability amidst the tumultuous seas of financial inequality. A living wage is defined as a pay rate that allows individuals to afford adequate shelter, food, and other necessities, without government assistance, and is often significantly higher than the minimum wage. Let's explore the transformative potential of living wages on economies and societies and how they can serve as a cornerstone of inclusive governance.

The introduction of living wages into an economy can be likened to the infusion of vitality into a slumbering ecosystem. Workers earning enough to live on are not merely surviving; they are thriving. With the capacity to spend more on goods and services, they invigorate local businesses, which, in turn, can lead to increased job creation. It is a virtuous cycle where prosperity begets prosperity, fostering a sense of communal uplift that extends beyond individual households.

Beyond the economic benefits, living wages have profound social implications. When individuals are no longer preoccupied with the ceaseless struggle to make ends meet, they can engage more fully in the fabric of their communities. Civic participation flourishes, as does investment in education and personal development. The societal tapestry, once frayed by the strain of economic hardship, is rewoven into a stronger, more vibrant mosaic of engaged and empowered citizens.

However, the journey toward the ideal of living wages is not without its challenges. Critics often raise concerns about potential job loss due to increased labor costs, and businesses may resist changes that threaten short-term profits. Yet, the evidence suggests that when implemented thoughtfully, living wages can be integrated into economic systems with minimal disruption. In fact, they often lead to reduced employee turnover, enhanced productivity, and a more loyal and motivated workforce.

For policymakers committed to crafting inclusive governance, living wages offer a powerful tool for reducing poverty and economic disparity. By setting the foundation for a more equitable distribution of resources, living wages can help bridge the divides that have long hindered the creation of harmonious societies. They act as a testament to the belief that a thriving economy is one where no individual is left behind, where each person's labor affords them dignity and a fair share of the collective prosperity.

As we forge ahead into an era where the principles of governance are being reevaluated and reshaped, the inclusion of living wages in our economic framework stands as a testament to our collective commitment to justice, fairness, and the belief that the well-being of all citizens is the bedrock of a harmonious world.


<u>4.6 Gender Equality in Economics</u>

*- Addressing the gender pay gap*

In the journey toward economic inclusivity, the issue of gender equality looms large, casting long shadows on the landscape of fair resource distribution. It is not merely a matter of social justice but of economic necessity. To address the gender pay gap is to unlock a fuller potential of human capital, to harness a more robust and equitable engine of economic growth.

Understanding the gender pay gap requires delving into the complex interplay of societal norms, educational opportunities, workplace practices, and legislative frameworks. It is a gap that is measured not only in terms of salary but also in terms of access to opportunities, career progression, and representation in leadership roles.

As we peel back the layers, we uncover a historical narrative where women's work has been undervalued and undercompensated. It is a narrative punctuated by disparities in education, interrupted career paths due to caregiving responsibilities, and a lack of mentorship and sponsorship in the professional realm. To recalibrate this imbalance, it is essential to implement multi-faceted strategies that operate at both the macro and micro levels of society.

Firstly, policy reform is paramount. Legislation must mandate equal pay for equal work, and employers should be required to conduct regular salary audits to ensure compliance. Transparency in compensation is a powerful tool that can shine a light on unconscious biases and systemic barriers that perpetuate the pay gap.

Secondly, societal attitudes towards gender roles need to evolve. This transformation can be sparked through education that promotes gender equality from the earliest stages, emphasizing the value of diverse skill sets and careers for all genders. Educational curricula should challenge traditional gender stereotypes and encourage young women to pursue studies in fields traditionally dominated by men, such as STEM (Science, Technology, Engineering, and Mathematics).

Thirdly, the corporate sector must champion change by fostering an inclusive culture that actively supports the career advancement of women. This includes offering flexible work arrangements, providing robust parental leave policies for both mothers and fathers, and creating mentorship programs that prepare women for leadership roles.

Moreover, it is critical to address the 'motherhood penalty,' which refers to the career and wage setbacks women often face after having children. Societal and corporate structures must adapt to support working parents, ensuring that career progression is not derailed by the decision to start a family.

In the concluding analysis, the narrative of economic governance must weave gender equality into its very fabric. By addressing the gender pay gap, we are not merely granting women their due; we are investing in a more harmonious and prosperous society. For it is only when every individual has the opportunity to contribute to the economy on an equal footing that we can truly claim to be moving toward a world of economic inclusivity.


*- Women's economic empowerment and its societal benefits*

As the dawn breaks over the horizon of economic inclusivity, one element remains pivotal to the illumination of a just and prosperous society: gender equality. The empowerment of women in the economic sphere is not merely a matter of rights; it is a cornerstone for broader societal benefits that extend beyond the immediate impacts on women's lives.

Historically, women have been relegated to the margins of the economic narrative, their contributions undervalued, their potential untapped. Yet, when women are given equal opportunities to participate in the economy, the entire tapestry of society is enriched. Their economic empowerment fosters a more dynamic labor market, accelerates innovation, and stimulates growth. It is akin to unlocking an ancient reservoir of potential that, once released, nourishes the parched fields of progress.

Studies have consistently shown that when women are economically empowered, the benefits cascade through families and communities like a rejuvenating stream. Women tend to invest more in their children's education and health, seeding the ground for the next generation's success. Their participation in the workforce leads to more diverse decision-making and can even shift societal norms towards greater equality.

Furthermore, women's economic empowerment challenges and reshapes the structural barriers that perpetuate inequality. By fostering policies that support women entrepreneurs, equal pay, and fair representation in leadership roles, governance structures can catalyze a renaissance of inclusivity. For instance, parental leave policies that recognize the roles of both parents not only level the playing field for women but also promote shared responsibility in the home, nurturing a culture of equality.

The societal benefits of women's economic empowerment are as varied as they are profound. They range from reduced poverty and enhanced child welfare to greater resilience in the face of economic downturns. Communities where women are active economic agents tend to be more equitable and peaceful, their governance marked by collaboration rather than competition.

In this light, crafting inclusive governance necessitates a deliberate focus on dismantling the obstacles that impede women's economic participation. It requires legislative frameworks that uphold women's rights, educational systems that prepare girls for a competitive economy, and societal attitudes that celebrate the achievements of women.

To sail toward the horizon of harmonious worlds, the winds of gender equality must fill the sails of our economic vessel. In the following sections, we will delve into the mechanisms of inclusive policies, explore case studies of transformative practices, and chart the course for a future where women's economic empowerment is not an aspiration but a reality. For it is only when the full spectrum of humanity is engaged in the dance of economic creation that the music of societal harmony reaches its most sublime notes.


<u>4.7 Access to Education and Economic Mobility</u>

*- Education as a tool for economic advancement*

Education is often hailed as the great equalizer, a ladder that can lift individuals from the depths of poverty to the heights of prosperity. Yet, the rungs on this ladder are not evenly spaced, and for many, the climb is fraught with insurmountable barriers. In this section, we will explore the intricate relationship between access to education and economic mobility, and how this access – or lack thereof – shapes the distribution of resources within a society.

In societies where education is both esteemed and accessible, a virtuous cycle emerges. Here, education is not merely a service; it is an investment in human capital. Each learned skill, each acquired piece of knowledge, becomes a brick in the foundation of a robust economy. It is in these societies that we witness a burgeoning middle class, reduced income inequality, and increased innovation.

However, access to education is not a given. It is a policy choice, a conscious decision by those in governance to invest in their most valuable resource: their people. To achieve economic inclusivity, educational policies must be crafted with an eye toward equity. This means not just building schools, but also ensuring that those schools are equipped with qualified teachers, modern resources, and curricula that prepare students for the jobs of tomorrow.

Moreover, access to education must be universal, extending beyond the privileged urban centers to reach the rural outposts. It must bridge the gaps between genders, ethnicities, and socioeconomic statuses. Scholarships, grants, and financial aid programs are essential tools in this endeavor, providing a lifeline to those who would otherwise be left adrift in the sea of economic stagnation.

In this light, education transforms into a powerful tool for economic advancement. As individuals climb the educational ladder, their potential for higher earnings increases. With higher earnings, they can invest back into their communities, creating a ripple effect that benefits the economy as a whole. This interplay between education and economic mobility is not just theory; it is observable in the rising tides of nations that have prioritized inclusive education.

Yet, the path is not without its challenges. The rapid pace of technological change means that the education received today may be obsolete tomorrow. Lifelong learning becomes imperative, and here, governance must adapt. It must provide not only foundational education but also avenues for continuous skill development. This includes vocational training, adult education programs, and online learning platforms that cater to the evolving needs of a dynamic workforce.

The pursuit of economic inclusivity through education is a multifaceted endeavor. It demands investment, innovation, and a steadfast commitment to equity. It requires policymakers to envision education not as a line item on a budget but as the beating heart of economic policy. For in the harmonious world we seek to create, every individual must have the opportunity to climb, to reach, and to rise. Only then can we truly unlock the collective potential of our diverse humanity and distribute the resources of our world with justice and foresight.

As twilight fades on the traditional models of resource distribution, where wealth begets wealth and poverty is a self-perpetuating cycle, a new dawn breaks with the promise of education as a cornerstone of economic inclusivity. Yet, this potential remains partially obscured by the shadows of existing disparities. Here, we embark on a scholarly voyage to bridge the educational divide, illuminating pathways that lead to greater economic mobility for all.

Education, often hailed as the great equalizer, has the profound capacity to level the playing field and enrich human capital. However, the promise of education is only as strong as the systems that deliver it. Inequitable access to quality education perpetuates economic stratification, leaving swaths of the population stranded on the lower rungs of the socioeconomic ladder. To dismantle these barriers, we must first understand the intricate tapestry of factors that contribute to the educational divide.

Demographic determinants such as socioeconomic status, race, and geography have historically dictated the quality of education an individual receives. These predetermined factors should not define one's educational journey, yet they continue to cast long shadows over the prospects of many. By addressing these systemic issues, we can begin to redraw the map of opportunity, providing pathways for individuals from all backgrounds to climb upwards.

Investing in early childhood education is a critical first step. This formative stage lays the cognitive and social groundwork upon which future learning is built. By providing universal access to high-quality preschool programs, we can ensure that every child starts on equal footing. Furthermore, integrating technology into classrooms can democratize access to information and resources, opening doors to those who were previously shut out from the corridors of knowledge.

Yet, access alone is not enough. We must also prioritize the relevance and quality of education. Vocational and technical training, tailored to the needs of a changing economy, can create direct avenues to employment and self-sufficiency. Partnerships between educational institutions and industries can bridge the gap between academic knowledge and practical skills, making education a more effective tool for economic advancement.

Moreover, higher education must shed the shackles of exorbitant costs. Scholarships, grants, and income-based repayment plans can make college and university education attainable for those who would otherwise be excluded. By breaking the financial barriers that guard the gates to advanced knowledge, we unlock the potential within each individual to contribute to a more dynamic and inclusive economy.

Here, we traverse the landscape of policy reforms and innovative educational models, seeking out the best practices and shining examples where education has successfully fueled economic mobility. From the Scandinavian countries' approach to free university education to the rise of massive open online courses (MOOCs) that make learning accessible across the globe, we explore the myriad ways in which governance can facilitate an education system that is both equitable and excellent.

In the harmonious world we envisage, education is not a privilege but a right — a powerful instrument of change that can alter the course of an individual's life and, in turn, shape the destiny of entire communities. By bridging the educational divide, we lay the foundation for a society where economic mobility is not just a distant dream but a tangible reality, and where the cycle of opportunity revolves unimpeded, powered by the engine of inclusive education.

<u>4.8 Sustainable Business Practices</u>

*- The triple bottom line: People, Planet, Profit*

In the grand tapestry of economic discourse, the notion of 'sustainability' has woven itself into the very fabric of modern business philosophy. It is a thread that intertwines the destiny of humanity with the health of the planet, and the pursuit of profit. Inclusive governance included the triple bottom line - a principle that proposes businesses should commit to focusing as much on social and environmental concerns as they do on profits.

The traditional view of business success, measured solely by financial gain, has been a driving force behind economic growth. Yet, this growth has often come at a devastating cost to the environment and the social fabric of communities. Here emerges the triple bottom line, a beacon guiding us toward a future where the well-being of people and the planet are not sacrificed for monetary gain but are elevated as pillars of prosperity.

Consider a hypothetical business, 'HarmonyCraft,' a company that produces artisanal goods. Under a triple bottom line approach, HarmonyCraft's ledger extends beyond mere financial transactions. It includes an account of how its operations impact the social realm - the people it employs, the communities it serves, and the societal structures it influences. It calculates its environmental footprint, taking responsibility for the resources it consumes and the waste it generates. Lastly, it measures profitability, for a business must thrive to sustain its mission.

HarmonyCraft's commitment to people involves fair labor practices, equitable pay, and fostering a culture that values diversity and inclusion. It ensures that the very hands that craft its products are cared for, respected, and empowered. By investing in the planet, HarmonyCraft adopts eco-friendly materials, minimizes waste, and reduces its carbon footprint. Its dedication to profit remains, but not as an isolated goal - rather as one that is achieved through ethical, socially responsible, and environmentally conscious means.

Governance structures that champion the triple bottom line encourage businesses like HarmonyCraft to flourish. They implement policies that reward sustainable practices and create economic incentives for companies to prioritize long-term societal and environmental health over short-term gains. By doing so, they lay the groundwork for an economy that is more resilient, just, and harmonious.

In this world we envision, HarmonyCraft is not an outlier but a herald of the norm. Governments, in partnership with businesses and civil society, craft a regulatory environment that balances the scales between people, planet, and profit. They recognize that when these three bottom lines are given equal weight, the dividends are a more equitable society, a healthier environment, and a robust economy that benefits all.

As we turn the page on outdated economic models, we find ourselves at the cusp of a new era. An era where governance and business walk hand in hand toward a horizon of sustainability. The triple bottom line is not just a policy or a practice; it's a pledge to future generations that the worlds we build will be as harmonious as they are prosperous.

*- Encouraging corporate social responsibility*

In a world where the chasm between the haves and have-nots is ever-widening, the role of businesses in bridging this gap cannot be overstated. The traditional paradigm of corporate success, measured solely by profit margins and shareholder returns, is undergoing a transformative reevaluation. There is a burgeoning recognition that businesses, as societal actors, have an ethical obligation to foster economic inclusivity and sustainability. This is where the concept of corporate social responsibility (CSR) takes center stage, emerging as a beacon of hope for a more equitable future.

CSR extends beyond philanthropy; it is a comprehensive approach where businesses integrate social and environmental concerns into their operations and interactions with stakeholders. Sustainable business practices, therefore, become a strategic imperative, not just a charitable add-on. By embracing CSR, companies can contribute to the broader societal goal of inclusive resource distribution, while simultaneously reinforcing their own long-term viability and success.

Consider the case of a multinational corporation that decides to shift part of its supply chain to a developing country. Instead of merely exploiting the cheaper labor costs, the corporation can choose to invest in local communities by paying fair wages, providing vocational training, and ensuring safe working conditions. Such practices not only uplift the local economy but also engender a loyal workforce and a positive brand image. This, in turn, can lead to increased consumer trust and a stronger market presence, creating a virtuous cycle of prosperity and goodwill.

Moreover, sustainable business practices necessitate environmental stewardship. Companies must minimize their ecological footprint by adopting green technologies, reducing waste, and sourcing materials ethically. By doing so, they not only contribute to the preservation of the planet but also align themselves with the growing consumer base that values environmental consciousness. This alignment with public sentiment is not merely a matter of compliance or public relations; it is a strategic pivot towards a future where ecological balance is integral to economic activity.

In this era of digital transparency, where every corporate action is scrutinized under the public lens, businesses cannot afford to neglect CSR. Social media platforms amplify consumer voices, and a company's reputation can be bolstered or battered in real-time. Hence, sustainable business practices are not just the right thing to do; they are a critical component of a company's risk management strategy.

The path to economic inclusivity is paved with corporate accountability and a commitment to sustainable development. As businesses look to the future, they must redefine what success looks like. It is no longer enough to be the best in the world; companies must strive to be the best for the world. Through CSR, organizations can play a pivotal role in crafting a harmonious world where prosperity is not an exclusive privilege but a shared reality.


<u>4.9 Technology and Job Creation</u>

*- The future of work in the digital age*

As the dawn of the digital age unfurls its luminescent wings, the nature of work undergoes a profound metamorphosis, orchestrated by the ceaseless march of technology. The digital age, with its boundless innovation, holds the key to unlocking a future of work that can foster economic inclusivity and bridge the chasms of disparity. Technology plays a significant role in shaping job creation. With digital tools, we can cultivate a workforce that is diverse, skilled, and resilient.

The advent of automation and artificial intelligence has stoked fears of a dystopian future where machines usurp human roles, leaving in their wake a trail of unemployment and societal upheaval. However, this narrative, while cautionary, overlooks the canvas of opportunity that technology paints across the economic landscape. It is through the intricate interplay of human ingenuity and technological advancement that new vistas of employment emerge, teeming with jobs that are yet to be conceived.

Consider the burgeoning fields of green technology and renewable energy. As governance structures worldwide pivot toward sustainability, technology becomes the cornerstone of a revolution that not only mitigates the impact of climate change but also spawns a myriad of occupations. From solar panel technicians and wind farm engineers to sustainability consultants, these roles are the progeny of a symbiotic relationship between technology and environmental stewardship.

Moreover, the digital age cradles the potential to democratize access to meaningful work. The rise of the gig economy, powered by platforms that connect freelancers with global opportunities, exemplifies the dissolution of traditional employment barriers. Technology becomes both the bridge and the destination for those seeking to ply their trade across the digital marketplace, regardless of geographic or socio-economic confines.

Yet, as we charter the waters of this brave new world of work, we must be vigilant stewards of the ship we sail. It is incumbent upon governance to weave a safety net that can cushion the transitions and turbulences of the digital labor market. Educational policies must be attuned to the evolving demands of the workforce, equipping citizens with the digital literacy and adaptive skills necessary to thrive. Furthermore, social security systems must be reimagined to account for the fluidity of modern employment, ensuring that even as jobs fluctuate, the dignity and well-being of workers remain steadfast.

In the digital age, technology is the loom on which the fabric of future work is woven. It is an era where job creation is not merely about quantity but quality— about crafting roles that not only provide sustenance but also meaning and fulfillment. As authors of this unfolding narrative, we must pen a tale where technology is not the harbinger of obsolescence but the artisan of opportunity, sculpting a labor landscape that is as inclusive as it is innovative.

Let us, therefore, embrace the digital age with the resolve to mold it into an epoch marked by economic inclusivity. Through considered governance, strategic foresight, and an unwavering commitment to the common good, we can ensure that technology augments the human experience, creating work that dignifies and unites us in the pursuit of a harmonious world.

*- Preparing the workforce for technological advancements*

In the digital age, the intersection of technology and the labor market presents both unprecedented opportunities and formidable challenges. As technology evolves, so does the need for a workforce that is not only adaptable but also adept at navigating a landscape that is constantly being reshaped by innovation.

Historically, the advent of technology has been a double-edged sword, offering efficiency and new job creation on one hand, while on the other, rendering certain skills obsolete. Today, we stand at a pivotal juncture where technological advancements in artificial intelligence, robotics, and automation are redefining the very essence of work. In this transformative period, it is imperative that governance plays a proactive role in preparing the workforce for the future, ensuring economic inclusivity by fostering environments that encourage skill development and job creation in new tech industries.

To cultivate an economically inclusive society, governments must invest in education and training programs that are attuned to the technological zeitgeist. This includes creating curricula that emphasize STEM (Science, Technology, Engineering, and Mathematics) education, while also valuing the creative and critical thinking skills fostered by the arts and humanities. By doing so, we are not merely preparing individuals for the jobs of today but equipping them with the adaptive skills required for the jobs of tomorrow.

In addition, fostering strong partnerships between the public sector, private enterprises, and educational institutions is crucial. These collaborations can lead to apprenticeship programs that provide hands-on experience and create pathways to employment in emerging tech fields. For instance, a government initiative that pairs tech startups with community colleges could offer students real-world experience in software development, while simultaneously providing startups with a pool of talented and trained candidates.

Public policy must also address the needs of those whose jobs are displaced by technology. This includes providing social safety nets and retraining programs that assist individuals in transitioning to new employment opportunities. A responsive governance model would include "transition credits" to fund education or vocational training for displaced workers, ensuring that no one is left behind in the shift toward a technology-driven economy.

Moreover, governments can encourage the growth of the tech sector by offering incentives for innovation and investment in research and development. These incentives not only stimulate job creation but also contribute to a nation's competitive edge in the global economy. By championing technological advancement and its integration into the fabric of society, governance can pave the way for a thriving, inclusive economy where every citizen has the opportunity to contribute and benefit.

As we venture further into the 21st century, the harmonious worlds we seek are contingent upon our ability to meld the realms of technology and workforce development. In this section, we explore the multifaceted strategies and policies that can foster a robust, technologically empowered workforce, ensuring that economic inclusivity is not just an ideal, but a tangible reality for all.

<u>4.10 Global Trade and Local Economies</u>

*- The effects of globalization on local industries*

In the tapestry of today's global economy, local industries weave intricate patterns of livelihoods, cultural identity, and social fabric. As the threads of international trade pull tighter, they often strain the seams of these local entities, challenging their survival and testing their resilience.

Globalization, for all its promise of economic integration and shared prosperity, carries with it a paradox. While it creates vast markets and opportunities for multinational corporations, it also subjects local economies to fierce competition from abroad. This competition can lead to a homogenization of products and services, as well as a devaluation of local practices and knowledge that have been honed over generations.

In a small town nestled in the verdant hills of a developing country, an artisan community once thrived on the production of handmade textiles. Each pattern was a story, a lineage of tradition that connected the present with the past. But as the gears of global trade turned, cheaper, mass-produced fabrics flooded the market, making it nearly impossible for these artisans to compete. The looms grew silent, and the stories began to fade.

This scenario is not unique. Across the globe, local industries, from agriculture to crafts, face similar existential threats. The question then arises: how can governance structures foster economic inclusivity in the face of such challenges?

Policymakers must recognize the intrinsic value of local industries beyond their immediate economic contribution. They are custodians of cultural heritage, incubators of innovation, and pillars of community cohesion. To support these industries, governments can implement protective measures such as tariffs and subsidies judiciously, ensuring they do not incite retaliatory trade wars but instead provide a buffer for local industries to adapt and find their niche in the global market.

Governance can promote the branding of local products by emphasizing their unique qualities and origins, a concept known as 'geographical indication.' By doing so, they not only protect the intellectual property of local artisans but also enhance the marketability of their products on the international stage.

Investment in education and training programs tailored to local industries can enhance the skills and knowledge of workers, enabling them to innovate and increase the competitiveness of their products. Coupled with access to new technologies, these investments can revitalize traditional industries, allowing them to flourish in a modern context.

International trade agreements must be crafted with a sensitive understanding of their impact on local economies. Governance that prioritizes inclusive dialogue and considers the voices of those likely to be affected can lead to more equitable trade practices that do not disadvantage smaller local players.

As we navigate the complex web of globalization, the governance of trade must not only consider the efficiency of markets but also the equity of outcomes. By doing so, we can ensure that local industries are not merely surviving in the shadow of globalization but thriving in the light of a harmonious world economy.

*- Strategies for supporting local economies within the global market*

As the tendrils of global trade stretch further across borders, intertwining economies with a delicate complexity, we must turn our attention to the local communities that form the backbone of global prosperity. Here, we explore the nuanced strategies that can support and empower local economies, ensuring they are not just participants but beneficiaries in the grand ballet of international commerce.

The stage upon which this intricate dance occurs is vast and often seems skewed towards the larger players, with multinational corporations often dictating the rhythm. Yet, there is an art to ensuring that local economies not only survive but thrive within this global market. The key lies in choreographing policies that elevate and protect local interests while encouraging sustainable growth and innovation.

One such strategy involves fostering local industries through protective tariffs and subsidies, creating a protective cocoon that allows them to metamorphose into entities robust enough to compete on the global stage. This approach, however, requires a deft touch, as overprotection can lead to dependency and stifle the very innovation needed for global competition. Instead, a balanced approach that supports local industries while simultaneously encouraging them to elevate their standards and outputs is essential.

Moreover, we must celebrate the diversity of local products and services by promoting them on the global stage. Initiatives like geographical indications and trademarks can help preserve the unique cultural heritage embedded in local goods, allowing them to command premium prices and recognition worldwide. By doing so, we not only bolster local economies but enrich the global market with a tapestry of cultural depth and variety.

Technology also plays a pivotal role in harmonizing global trade with local economies. E-commerce platforms can open up new avenues for local artisans and small-scale producers, directly connecting them with a global customer base. By reducing the barriers to entry and providing the tools for digital marketing and logistics, we empower local economies to take their place in the global orchestra without being overshadowed by the louder instruments of multinational conglomerates.

Investing in education and skill development within local communities ensures that the workforce is adaptable and equipped for the evolving demands of the global market. A populace that is well-educated and versatile becomes the fertile ground from which innovation sprouts, drawing investors and businesses to local shores.

In the harmonious world we envision, local economies are not mere satellites in the orbit of global trade, but vibrant, self-sustaining planets in their own right. Through thoughtful policies and the embrace of technology, we can create a symphony of economic activity where each local note is as vital as the global melody, and together, they compose an anthem of inclusivity and prosperity.

# 5. Guardians of Heritage



## 5.1 The Fabric of Tradition

*- Weaving history into contemporary life*

In the gentle embrace of tradition, the past is not merely remembered—it is lived and breathed into the very essence of the present, shaping identities and informing futures. This delicate interplay between the old and the new forms the crux of our cultural continuity, and it is within this fabric that societies find their unique patterns, colors, and textures. To weave history into contemporary life is both an art and a responsibility, a task requiring the finesse of a skilled artisan and the wisdom of a sage.

The Fabric of Tradition is not a relic to be sequestered away in the dusty corners of memory but rather a vibrant tapestry, perpetually expanding with each generation's contributions. It offers a shared narrative, a common language of symbols, rituals, and values that bond a community together. The challenge for inclusive governance lies in embracing this narrative while fostering growth and innovation, ensuring that the tapestry remains relevant and reflective of the entire society.

At the heart of this balance is education. In schools, children must learn not only the history of their ancestors but also the context in which these traditions arose. By understanding the origins and evolutions of their cultural heritage, they can appreciate its significance and contribute to its ongoing narrative. Education systems that incorporate local history, folklore, and traditional arts into their curricula not only enrich students' learning experiences but also anchor them to their cultural roots.

Modernization, while often seen as a force that erodes traditional ways of life, can also be harnessed to preserve and promote them. Technology provides unprecedented opportunities to document and disseminate cultural practices. From virtual reality experiences that transport users to historical events to online platforms that allow artisans to sell traditional crafts globally, innovation can bridge the gap between the ancient and the contemporary.

Governance that values heritage must also recognize the importance of physical spaces in the continuity of tradition. The preservation of historical sites and the encouragement of community gatherings at these locales are vital. Such spaces serve as tangible links to the past, where stories are embedded in stone and soil.

Incorporating tradition into modern governance also means recognizing and respecting the diversity of cultural expressions within a society. Policies must be crafted to protect minority cultures and their unique traditions from being overshadowed or assimilated by dominant narratives. This requires a commitment to multiculturalism and a willingness to provide platforms for all voices to be heard and celebrated.

In weaving history into the fabric of contemporary life, we must endeavor to create a governance that is as much about guarding the treasures of the past as it is about ensuring their relevance for the future. It is a governance that listens to the whispers of ancestry and allows them to sing in harmony with the chorus of modernity, crafting a symphony that resonates with the richness of human experience.


*- Guarding intangible cultural heritage*

In the tapestry of human civilization, the threads of tradition weave patterns of identity, belonging, and continuity. As societies stride into the future, the challenge of preserving these delicate strands becomes increasingly complex, particularly in the face of relentless modernization. Let's explore this delicate dance between progress and preservation.

Here, we delve into the heart of what it means to protect the non-material aspects of our collective past. Intangible cultural heritage encompasses the practices, representations, expressions, knowledge, and skills that communities recognize as part of their cultural heritage. This includes oral traditions, performing arts, social practices, rituals, festive events, knowledge and practices concerning nature, and the universe or the knowledge and skills necessary to produce traditional crafts.

As the world becomes increasingly globalized, the guardians of intangible cultural heritage face a formidable challenge: How can they safeguard these practices against the homogenizing forces of modernity without stifling the organic growth and evolution inherent to culture?

Consider the example of language, the most potent vessel of intangible heritage. A language is not merely a means of communication; it is the repository of a community's collective memory, a carrier of its history, literature, and worldview. Yet, languages are disappearing at an alarming rate, taking with them the unique perspectives they embody. In response to this, innovative governance must create spaces where endangered languages can be taught, learned, and spoken freely, incorporating technology to document and disseminate these linguistic treasures.

Similarly, traditional crafts, which often struggle to find a place in the modern economy, can be revitalized through policies that promote their value — not only as tourist curiosities but as living expressions of cultural identity. Subsidies, grants, and educational programs can empower artisans to continue their craft while adapting to contemporary markets, ensuring that these skills are not lost to time but rather evolve with it.

Rituals and social practices, too, must be approached with sensitivity. While some may be at odds with contemporary values, outright prohibition rarely serves the purpose of preservation. Instead, governance that encourages dialogue and education, aiming to find a harmonious balance between respect for tradition and adherence to modern principles of human rights and equality, is key.

Here, we discover how inclusive governance can be artfully designed to protect the intangible heritage that knits the social fabric together, while also making room for the innovation and change that drive societies forward. It is a call to become the custodians of our collective memory, not through rigid resistance to change, but through dynamic engagement with the living, breathing cultures we seek to preserve.

As we navigate this intricate landscape, we must remember that the goal is not to freeze culture in time but to ensure that it continues to flourish, enriching the present and informing the future. In this pursuit, governance becomes an act of balance, a delicate art where every decision can either contribute to the vibrant pattern of tradition or unravel the threads that hold our shared humanity together.


5.2 Architectural Conservation

- *Preserving historic skylines*

The silhouette of a city is like a visual symphony, each building a note that contributes to the grand composition of its skyline. Within these skylines lie tales of our ancestors, architectural marvels that have withstood the ravages of time and serve as tangible links to our shared past. Yet, as we march toward an era marked by glass and steel, there is a pressing need to harmonize the crescendo of modernity with the delicate legato of tradition.

Let's raise the baton to conduct a discussion on the preservation of historic skylines—an endeavor that is far more than an aesthetic choice; it is a commitment to the cultural continuity of our urban landscapes. Architectural conservation is the art of preserving these structures not merely as relics, but as living entities that contribute to the identity and spirit of a place.

In the shadow of gleaming skyscrapers, the ancient facades often tell stories of bygone eras—each cornice, column, and cobblestone a testament to the craftsmanship and vision of their time. They remind us that progress need not come at the expense of our heritage. Indeed, the most vibrant cities are those that manage to weave the old with the new, creating a tapestry that honors history while embracing the future.

But how does one ensure that these historic skylines are not only preserved but celebrated amidst the relentless push for urban development? It requires a governance that values the past as much as it anticipates the future—a governance that enacts policies to protect significant buildings and districts from the wrecking ball of progress. This can include establishing heritage sites, enforcing strict zoning laws, and providing incentives for restoration projects.

Moreover, it is imperative to engage the community in these conservation efforts, for a building's soul is animated by the lives that have passed through its doors. When citizens take pride in their historic landmarks, they become the most ardent guardians of their preservation. Participatory governance can foster a sense of collective stewardship over these architectural treasures, ensuring they are not only maintained but integrated into the fabric of contemporary urban life.

Here, we delve into case studies that illustrate successful conservation initiatives, from the cobblestone streets of Old San Juan to the Art Deco wonders of Miami Beach. These stories highlight the ingenuity and dedication required to protect our historic skylines against the pressures of modernization. They serve as blueprints for crafting inclusive governance that recognizes the intrinsic value of our architectural heritage, ensuring that the skylines we bequeath to future generations are as rich in culture and history as they are in ambition and innovation.

We posit that true progress is not the erasure of the past but its incorporation into a future where every building tells a story, and every skyline sings a song of diversity and unity. The conservation of historic skylines is not a quixotic nod to nostalgia; it is an essential chapter in the narrative of inclusive governance and the crafting of a diverse humanity.



*- Adaptive reuse of heritage buildings*

In the heart of every city lies the pulse of its past, the architectural embodiments of times gone by. These structures, ranging from grandiose temples to humble cottages, not only tell the stories of the societies that built them but also form an intrinsic part of a community's cultural identity. As societies evolve, the challenge of preserving these historical edifices while repurposing them for modern use becomes a vital task for inclusive governance.

Adaptive reuse of heritage buildings is an artful dance between conservation and innovation. It requires a delicate touch, one that respects the original architecture and its historical significance while infusing it with new life to serve contemporary needs. This approach to governance embodies a reverence for the past with a vision for the future, ensuring that the legacies of our ancestors find a place in our modern world.

Imagine an 18th-century warehouse that once stored the spoils of maritime trade. Its sturdy walls and timber beams have withstood the test of time, but its purpose has long been relegated to the pages of history. Through adaptive reuse, this relic can transform into a vibrant community center, a hub for local artisans, or a museum dedicated to the city's seafaring heritage. In each case, the building's historical character is not only maintained but also celebrated as part of the urban landscape.

Adaptive reuse is not without its challenges. It requires a governance framework that is flexible and creative, one that can navigate the complexities of modern building codes, the intricacies of historical preservation standards, and the often competing interests of stakeholders. It demands a collaborative approach, where architects, historians, urban planners, and the community engage in a dialogue to envision a shared future for these structures.

Inclusive governance in the realm of architectural conservation is about more than just maintaining walls and windows; it's about preserving the soul of a community. It's about understanding that heritage buildings are the physical manifestations of our collective memory and as such, they are irreplaceable treasures that connect us to our roots.

By embracing adaptive reuse, governance bodies send a clear message: heritage structures are not obstacles to progress but rather keystones in the arch of a society's ongoing narrative. They stand as testaments to the fact that change and continuity are not mutually exclusive but can coexist in harmony, each enriching the other.

The adaptive reuse of heritage buildings is a testament to a governance system's commitment to cultural sustainability. It is a practice that recognizes the importance of the past in shaping the future, ensuring that our built heritage continues to contribute to the vibrancy and diversity of our communities. It is through such practices that we can aspire to craft a world where the tapestry of human experience is not only acknowledged but interwoven into the fabric of our daily lives, creating a truly harmonious existence.

## 5.3 Language Revitalization

*- Strategies for saving endangered languages*

In the luminous tapestry of human expression, language is the thread that weaves together the narratives of our past, present, and future. Each idiom carries the essence of a culture, the intellect of a society, and the soul of a people. Yet, as the world marches inexorably towards a homogenized future, the breathtaking diversity of our linguistic heritage is at risk.

Language revitalization is a resolute act of cultural defiance and preservation, a means of saving not just words, but worlds within those words. It is a commitment to resuscitate the lifeblood of a community, ensuring that its unique voice continues to echo through the ages. To this end, a confluence of strategies emerges, each a beacon of hope for endangered tongues.

First and foremost is the creation of immersive language environments where native speakers and learners are encouraged to engage in everyday communication. These linguistic islands become sanctuaries of practice, safeguarding the veracity and usage of the language. Educational programs, from preschools to universities, must integrate these languages into their curriculum, treating them not as relics of study but as vibrant vehicles of instruction.

Technology, our double-edged sword, offers a gleaming edge for language preservation. Digital platforms can host repositories of language resources, from dictionaries to oral histories, making them accessible to a global audience. Social media, often a purveyor of dominant languages, can be harnessed to create virtual communities where minority language speakers can connect, share, and grow.

Governmental support, however, is the cornerstone of any substantial revitalization effort. Policies that recognize and protect linguistic diversity are crucial. These can range from official recognition of minority languages and financial support for cultural initiatives to the inclusion of these languages in administrative and judicial settings.

Moreover, collaborations with linguists, anthropologists, and native speakers can produce comprehensive language documentation. Such scholarly work ensures that even if a language ceases to be spoken, its knowledge is not lost to the sands of time. These records become the lexicons for future generations who may seek to revive their ancestral tongue.

We must recognize the intangible value of each language as part of the collective human heritage. Public awareness campaigns can illuminate the existential threat to linguistic diversity, fostering a sense of global responsibility towards its preservation.

In my envisioned harmonious world, the guardians of heritage stand vigilant, ensuring that the symphony of human language—each note precious and unique—resounds with the richness it has always possessed. Language revitalization is more than an act of conservation; it is an affirmation of identity and an investment in the cultural wealth of our shared future.


*- The role of technology in language preservation*

In the heart of the digital era, technology emerges as both a vessel and a beacon for the preservation of linguistic diversity. The dwindling numbers of native speakers of certain tongues have painted a somber picture, one that foretells the extinction of cultural identities embedded in the syntax and semantics of these languages. Yet, there is hope amidst this digital revolution— a hope that we may harness the very tools of modernity to safeguard the relics of our past.

Language revitalization programs have traditionally relied on community involvement and educational initiatives, but these are now being augmented with an arsenal of technological innovations. Mobile applications, online dictionaries, and digital archives are creating accessible platforms for language learners across the globe. Social media, too, serves as a contemporary agora where speakers of minority languages can connect, converse, and cultivate their linguistic heritage in a global conversation.

One notable example is the initiative to revive the Cherokee language, once on the verge of silence. Through a collaboration between tribal linguists and tech companies, smartphones now possess the capability to text and type in Cherokee syllabary, allowing the language to flow through modern channels of communication. This endeavor illustrates the potential of technology not just to preserve but to breathe life into a language, enabling it to evolve and adapt to the currents of the present world.

Moreover, artificial intelligence (AI) and machine learning are playing increasingly pivotal roles. AI-driven language learning platforms tailor educational content to individual learners, using algorithms to enhance the acquisition process. Speech recognition and synthesis technologies are also being refined to accommodate the phonetic and tonal complexities of less-documented languages, thereby providing an auditory dimension to written words.

However, this intersection of technology and tradition is not without its challenges. The democratization of access remains a paramount concern, as not all communities possess the necessary resources to leverage such tools. Furthermore, there is a delicate balance to be struck between the allure of new technologies and the maintenance of traditional methods of language transmission, such as oral storytelling and face-to-face tutelage.

As we navigate this confluence of the ancient and the cutting-edge, we must strive for inclusivity and sustainability. Technology should be viewed not as a replacement but as a complement to the human element, an extension that enriches and amplifies the voices of those who carry the torch of their ancestors' words. It is through this synergy—this harmonious melding of the old and the new—that languages once at the brink can find new vigor, and with them, the cultures they express can continue to thrive in a modern world that acknowledges the value of every voice within the grand chorus of humanity.

## 5.4 Living Traditions in Modern Society

*- Folklore and customs in the digital age*

In an age where the digital world often overshadows the physical, we are presented with an unprecedented opportunity to preserve and promote our folklore and customs. The digital age, rather than being a force that dilutes our cultural heritage, can act as a guardian, a medium through which living traditions breathe anew and find resonance with younger generations.

The key lies in the artful fusion of technology with tradition. This fusion allows us to craft a bridge between the past and the future. Take, for instance, the storytelling traditions of indigenous communities. Once confined to the communal firesides and village squares, these rich narratives can now be shared across the globe through podcasts and virtual reality experiences. They can be augmented with digital illustrations and interactive elements that bring the tales to life for a global audience, ensuring that these stories do not fade into obscurity but thrive in a new, more connected world.

Within this digital framework, customs and folklore become living entities, not static relics to be observed behind the glass of museum displays. Instead, they are integrated into the daily lives of people everywhere. Social media campaigns can celebrate traditional festivals, using hashtags to encourage the sharing of photos, recipes, and stories that highlight the vibrancy of these customs. This not only preserves the tradition but also fosters a sense of unity and understanding across cultures.

Moreover, e-commerce platforms can serve as modern marketplaces for traditional crafts, allowing local artisans to reach a global customer base. This not only provides economic benefits but also ensures that the skills and techniques passed down through generations continue to be practiced and valued.

However, to maintain the authenticity of these traditions in the digital realm, governance plays a pivotal role. Policies must be put in place to protect intellectual property rights and prevent cultural appropriation. Governments can work alongside tech companies to create digital archives that are respectful of the source communities, offering platforms for these communities to tell their stories in their own voices. The Ainu of Japan have leveraged digital media to share their language and culture, and the annual celebration of Dia de los Muertos has found new expression through online platforms.

As we navigate the complexities of governing a diverse humanity, we must recognize that living traditions can coexist harmoniously with modern technology. By embracing the digital age as an ally, we ensure that our collective heritage remains a vibrant and integral part of our modern society, fostering a governance that truly resonates with the spirit of its people.


- *Cultural festivals as a bridge between eras*

In the pulsating heart of modern society, where the glass of skyscrapers reflects the dreams of a digital age, cultural festivals emerge as vibrant arteries, pumping lifeblood into the urban sprawl. These festivals are not mere echoes of the past; they are the rhythmic drumbeats of tradition, reverberating through the streets, inviting all to dance to the tune of heritage.

As we navigate the intricate dance of modernity and tradition, it is essential to recognize that cultural festivals serve as powerful conduits for living traditions.

They are not static relics to be observed from a distance but dynamic celebrations that invite participation, adaptation, and renewal. In the kaleidoscope of these gatherings, ancient stories are retold, traditional garments are draped over contemporary fashion, and age-old recipes are savored alongside fusion cuisine.

Consider the Lantern Festival in East Asia, a spectacle of light that dates back millennia, now intertwined with innovative technologies that enhance the visual feast. Or the Day of the Dead in Mexico, where marigold petals and sugar skulls find new expression in art installations and multimedia performances. These festivals do not resist the currents of change; they ride them, allowing the essence of the past to flow into the veins of the present.

In the context of governance, festivals are more than entertainment; they are an essential policy tool. By investing in these celebrations, governments can foster an environment that respects and revitalizes cultural identities. It is through the medium of festivals that citizens can engage with their heritage while contributing to a collective narrative that honors diversity and encourages social cohesion.

Moreover, cultural festivals offer a unique opportunity for intergenerational dialogue. They open spaces where the wisdom of elders meets the innovation of youth, creating a fusion of ideas that ensures traditions are not only preserved but also allowed to evolve. In this exchange, the role of governance is to provide the platforms and support necessary for these interactions to flourish.

To bridge the gap between eras, modern governance must adopt a dual approach: protecting the sanctity of cultural heritage while promoting its contemporary relevance. This can be achieved through policies that encourage community-driven festival programming, support local artisans and performers, and integrate educational components that highlight the significance of cultural practices.

Cultural festivals stand as testaments to the enduring human spirit, a spirit that refuses to be confined by time. As guardians of heritage, it is our collective responsibility to ensure that these living traditions are not only celebrated but also woven seamlessly into the fabric of modern society. Through the shared joy of festivals, we can construct a bridge between eras, one that is strong enough to carry the weight of history and flexible enough to reach the horizons of tomorrow.


5.5 Traditional Knowledge and Intellectual Property

In the labyrinthine alleys of cultural governance, the protection of indigenous knowledge stands as a beacon, illuminating the path to a future where tradition and modernity do not just coexist but coalesce. Traditional knowledge, an amalgamation of cultural expressions, wisdom, and practices, has been passed down through generations, shaping the identity and resilience of communities across the globe. These knowledge systems encompass a wide array of cultural facets, including medicinal practices, agricultural expertise, ecological wisdom, and artistic expressions.

Yet, in our contemporary era, where the global market's maw is ever-expanding, the guardianship of such heritage faces unprecedented threats. Intellectual property rights, primarily designed for the commodification of innovation, often fall short in safeguarding the collective custodianship that indigenous communities exercise over their knowledge. The conundrum herein lies in the anachronistic application of Western legal frameworks to a realm that operates on an entirely different cultural and philosophical axis.

To navigate this complex terrain, we must first acknowledge that traditional knowledge is not merely a 'thing' to be protected but a living, breathing process that sustains communities. It is both intangible and tangible, vested not in the individual but in the community as a whole. Therefore, the challenge is to craft governance mechanisms that respect these unique attributes while providing robust protection against exploitation and misappropriation.

One innovative approach is the development of sui generis systems, tailored to the specific nature of traditional knowledge. These systems can recognize and enforce communal rights, providing legal standing to indigenous communities to control the use of their knowledge. By integrating customary laws and practices into formal legal structures, such systems ensure that the holders of traditional knowledge are the primary beneficiaries of its utilization.

Furthermore, the creation of registries and databases that document traditional knowledge, with the consent and active participation of indigenous communities, can serve as a tool for both preserving and protecting this knowledge. These repositories can act as evidence of prior art, thwarting attempts at unauthorized patenting, and can also facilitate the sharing of benefits when traditional knowledge leads to commercial applications.

At the international level, the discourse must evolve beyond the mere recognition of the value of traditional knowledge to the implementation of conventions and treaties that mandate its protection. This includes the expansion of the scope of the Convention on Biological Diversity and the

Nagoya Protocol to encompass not just genetic resources but the cultural wisdom that informs their use.

As we tread into this new chapter of governance, we must do so with the understanding that the protection of traditional knowledge is not a concession but a crucial component of a harmonious world. It is an affirmation of the dignity and rights of indigenous peoples and a testament to the profound insight that diversity—in knowledge, in culture, in governance—enriches humanity as a whole. It is this tapestry of diverse wisdom that will guide us as we forge a future that honors our past while embracing the promise of innovation.


*- Ethical considerations in commercializing tradition*

In the labyrinthine corridors of global commerce, where the voracious appetite for novelty often clashes with the sanctity of tradition, lies a delicate balance that governance must navigate. Here, we confront the ethical considerations inherent in commercializing tradition. This intricate dance between progress and preservation compels us to question: How can we honor the guardians of heritage in a world that is constantly seeking to reinvent itself?

Consider the intricate patterns of indigenous textiles, the healing wisdom contained in ancient herbal remedies, or the unique flavors of traditional cuisines. These are not just commodities; they are the lifeblood of cultural identity, passed down through generations like a sacred trust. As such, their entry into the marketplace should not be a surrender to exploitation, but rather a controlled sharing that benefits the original custodians of this knowledge.

The ethical framework for commercializing traditional knowledge must be rooted in consent, respect, and equitable benefit-sharing. Governments, acting as mediators and enforcers, have the responsibility to ensure that local communities have a voice in the decision-making process. This includes actively participating in negotiations and receiving a fair portion of the profits derived from their traditional knowledge. Intellectual property laws must be adapted to recognize the collective ownership inherent in many traditional practices, which often clash with the Western notion of individual intellectual property rights.

Moreover, the narrative surrounding traditional products in the global market must be shaped with care. It is not merely a matter of branding but of storytelling; the cultural context of these products must accompany them to their new audiences. This safeguard helps prevent cultural appropriation—a phenomenon all too common in these transactions—and fosters a deeper appreciation for the origins and significance of these cultural expressions.

Education plays a pivotal role in ethical commercialization. Consumers must be informed about the origins of the products they purchase and understand the impact of their consumer choices on preserving cultural heritage. Similarly, the guardians of tradition require knowledge of their rights and the means to assert them, ensuring they are not left at the mercy of more powerful commercial entities.

Let's explore case studies that illustrate successful partnerships between traditional knowledge holders and commercial enterprises. These partnerships not only brought traditional products to a wider audience but did so in a way that reinforced the cultural significance of these products and provided tangible benefits to their originators.

We will also probe the challenges that arise when traditions are not just shared but are severed from their roots, repackaged in ways that dilute their essence and deprive the original guardians of their due recognition and compensation.

In our journey toward harmonious worlds, the respect for and protection of traditional knowledge and intellectual property is not merely an ethical imperative but a cornerstone of inclusive governance. It is a testament to our collective commitment to honoring the past while embracing the future, ensuring that the tapestry of human heritage remains vibrant for generations to come.


## 5.6 Education and Cultural Heritage

*- Curriculum design for cultural continuity*

In a world where the relentless march of progress often threatens to trample the delicate gardens of cultural heritage, education stands as a bulwark against the erosion of ancestral identity. Indeed, the very heartbeat of tradition finds its rhythm in the stories, rituals, and knowledge passed down through generations. To ensure that these treasures are not lost to the sands of time, education systems must be meticulously designed to weave cultural threads into the tapestry of curriculum, fostering cultural continuity while embracing modernity's advances.

The curriculum is the vessel through which the wisdom of ages can travel into the future. It is in the alchemy of curriculum design that we must blend the old with the new, crafting learning experiences that honor the past while equipping students for the future. Cultural heritage must not be relegated to the annals of history, to be studied as a relic of bygone eras; instead, it should be presented as a living, breathing aspect of students' identities, informing their worldview and enriching their contemporary lives.

In this endeavor, educators serve as the custodians of continuity. They curate lessons that highlight the contributions of their culture to the world's tapestry, celebrating achievements in art, science, governance, and philosophy. They bring to light the narratives of their people, ensuring that students see themselves reflected in the curriculum, fostering a sense of pride and belonging. This commitment to representation is paramount, for it is through seeing one's heritage honored in education that a deep connection to one's roots is nurtured.

Moreover, in designing curricula that honor cultural heritage, we cultivate respect and understanding among diverse student populations. It is through this exposure to the myriad ways of knowing and being that we prepare young minds for the multicultural world they will inherit. Lessons are enriched with the languages, literature, and lore of various cultures, enabling students to traverse the globe within classroom walls. It is a journey of discovery that instills empathy and encourages a reverence for the great mosaic of human expression.

Yet, the challenge lies in balancing the preservation of tradition with the necessity for innovation. The curriculum must not become a museum, static and unchanging. It must be dynamic, evolving with the times, and integrating technological advancements that can further the cause of cultural education. Digital archives, virtual reality experiences, and interactive platforms can bring ancient wisdom to life, allowing students to explore worlds once confined to dusty tomes or the fragile memories of elders.

To achieve this equilibrium, curriculum designers engage with community leaders, cultural practitioners, and historians, ensuring that the knowledge imparted is both authentic and relevant. They harness the power of storytelling, leveraging narratives that have captivated human imagination for centuries, and presenting them in ways that resonate with the digital age.

Education can act as a conduit for cultural heritage. Curricula should not only be cognizant of the past but also visionary, looking ahead to a future where cultural continuity is not merely preserved but celebrated as the cornerstone of a vibrant and harmonious world.


*- Experiential learning and heritage*

In the crucible of modern education, the glowing embers of cultural heritage are often neglected, at risk of being swept away by the winds of technological advancement and global homogenization. Yet, it is precisely within the hallowed halls of learning that the preservation of cultural legacies can be most effectively ensured. Education is not merely the transmission of facts and figures, but the delicate art of cultivating a deep, visceral connection to the past.

Experiential learning, the pedagogical approach that emphasizes engagement through direct experience, emerges as a powerful guardian of heritage. It invites students to step beyond the confines of the traditional classroom and immerse themselves in the living, breathing reality of their cultural inheritance. This is where the abstract becomes tangible, and the historical becomes personal.

Consider, for example, a history lesson on the indigenous peoples of a given region. Instead of confining the discussion to textbook narratives, students could be taken on a journey to visit the ruins of ancient dwellings, participate in traditional crafts, or engage in the oral storytelling traditions of local tribes. Such encounters foster an empathetic understanding, a sense of stewardship over these cultural treasures that cannot be replicated through passive learning.

By integrating cultural heritage sites into educational curricula, schools become conduits for intergenerational exchange. Students learn not only about the practices of their ancestors but also come to appreciate the wisdom embedded within these traditions. They develop a sense of identity and continuity, recognizing their role in a story that began long before them and will continue long after.

Furthermore, experiential learning in the context of cultural heritage does not simply preserve the past; it reinvigorates it. When students are tasked with designing a modern use for an ancient technique or reinterpreting a traditional art form in a contemporary context, they become active participants in the evolution of their culture. They learn that tradition is not static but a living dialogue between the past and present.

The challenge, then, is to weave these experiential threads into the fabric of education systems. Policymakers and educators must collaborate to identify and protect sites of cultural significance, develop programs that facilitate hands-on learning, and allocate resources that allow heritage to be a cornerstone of the educational experience.

In this way, education becomes more than a mere guardian of heritage; it becomes its champion, ensuring that the rich tapestry of human history informs the present and inspires the future. It is through this melding of learning and legacy that a truly harmonious world can be cultivated, one where modernity and tradition dance in elegant balance, each step informed by the knowledge of a thousand yesteryears.


5.7 Traditional Arts in the Global Marketplace

In the vibrant tapestry of human culture, traditional arts hold a treasured place, encapsulating the essence of a community's heritage, history, and identity. Yet, as the world gallops towards an ever-connected, modern future, these cultural keystones risk being swept into obscurity. Let's delve into the delicate dance of balancing modernity with tradition, particularly within the global marketplace. We not only celebrate these art forms but must also examine practical strategies for their promotion and preservation in the face of globalization.

Imagine a world where the intricate Ikat patterns of Indonesia, the rich tapestry of Native American beadwork, and the delicate brushstrokes of Chinese calligraphy are as commonplace and revered in global commerce as the latest fashion trends from Milan or New York. This is a vision not of cultural appropriation, but of appreciation and integration, where traditional arts are given a platform to thrive and evolve, rather than merely survive.

To this end, inclusive governance must play a pivotal role. Governments, in partnership with cultural organizations and local communities, can implement policies that facilitate the entry of traditional arts into the global marketplace. Such policies might include grants for artisans, subsidies for craft cooperatives, and tax incentives for businesses that incorporate traditional arts into their products in a respectful and ethical manner.

Moreover, technology can serve as a bridge between the local and the global. Online marketplaces, social media, and virtual reality experiences can introduce traditional arts to a worldwide audience, creating a new wave of appreciation and demand. These platforms can tell the stories behind the crafts, connecting consumers with the artisans' heritage and the cultural significance of their work.

However, it is crucial that these initiatives are not exploitative. Artisans should be the primary beneficiaries of their labor, with fair trade practices ensuring that their work is compensated justly. Intellectual property rights must also be safeguarded to prevent cultural theft and to ensure that communities maintain control over their artistic expressions.

Education plays a role as well; through awareness campaigns and inclusion in school curricula, the value of traditional arts can be instilled in the next generation. This not only nurtures a domestic market but also raises ambassadors who can champion these crafts in international arenas.

We posit here that by fostering an ecosystem where traditional arts are valued assets within the global marketplace, we not only enrich the cultural fabric of our societies but also empower the guardians of heritage to weave their legacies into the future. This is a clarion call for policymakers, entrepreneurs, and consumers alike to embrace the myriad of traditional arts as part of our shared human narrative, ensuring they continue to flourish in our collective consciousness.

*- Fair trade and cultural products*

In the labyrinth of globalization, traditional arts emerge as a beacon of identity and heritage. They whisper tales of ancient wisdom, of hands that weaved, carved, and painted through the ages. Yet, these cultural products often face the harsh winds of the global marketplace, where their intrinsic value risks being lost amidst mass-produced commodities. It is within this context that fair trade principles have become a vital lifeline, ensuring that the artisans behind these cultural treasures are justly rewarded and their crafts preserved for posterity.

Fair trade, at its core, is about equitable exchange. It is a movement that advocates for better wages, working conditions, and sustainability for producers. When applied to traditional arts, fair trade becomes the bridge that connects the local artisan to the global consumer, fostering a relationship of respect and mutual benefit. The principle extends beyond economics; it is a cultural dialogue that affirms the worth of ancestral legacies.

Imagine a handwoven basket from a remote village finding its place in a chic boutique halfway across the world. The basket carries more than functionality; it is a narrative of community, of a lineage of weavers who have passed down their skills through generations. Fair trade ensures that when this basket is sold, the artisans receive a fair share of the profit, enabling them to continue their craft and sustain their families.

But this relationship is not one-sided. Consumers, increasingly aware of the stories behind their purchases, seek authenticity. They are drawn to the human connection that traditional arts provide, to the sense of owning a piece of cultural heritage. This growing market for ethically sourced cultural products opens up new opportunities but also poses challenges.

The guardians of heritage must navigate this global marketplace with care, ensuring that the commoditization of cultural products does not dilute their significance. The authenticity of traditional arts must be maintained, and clear labeling and education can help consumers discern genuine articles from those that merely mimic tradition. Moreover, governing bodies and trade organizations can support artisans by providing platforms to showcase their work, away from the shadow of mass production.

In a world where the exotic becomes accessible, where a click can bring a piece of distant culture to our doorstep, we must ask ourselves: Are we merely consumers, or are we custodians of this intangible heritage? By embracing fair trade principles, we choose the latter. We acknowledge the value of cultural products, not merely in monetary terms, but as repositories of human creativity and diversity. We ensure that as these traditional arts traverse borders, they are not stripped of their soul, but rather, they enrich the global tapestry with their vivid hues of history and humanity.

Thus, in the harmonious worlds we strive to build, traditional arts flourish, supported by systems that recognize their worth and the dignity of those who create them. We foster a marketplace that is not only fair but also a forum for cultural exchange, where every transaction is an act of solidarity with the guardians of heritage.

<u>5.8 Modern Governance of Ancient Practices</u>

- *Policy frameworks for heritage preservation*

In the labyrinth of modern governance, the preservation of ancient practices poses a unique challenge. It is the delicate dance between the seductive pull of modernization and the steadfast grip of tradition. As we navigate this dance floor, the question arises: How can policy frameworks be constructed to honor the past while accommodating the present and future?

To address this, we must first recognize that ancient practices are not relics to be displayed in a museum, but living traditions that continue to breathe life into communities. They are the threads that weave the social fabric, the narratives that define identities, and the customs that enrich humanity's collective heritage. With this understanding, modern governance can begin to outline policies that not only protect but also revitalize these cultural treasures.

The key lies in participatory policymaking, where stakeholders—ranging from community elders to the youth—are engaged in the decision-making process. It is a governance that listens before it legislates, ensuring that the voices of those who are the custodians of these traditions are heard and respected. By creating platforms for dialogue, governments can develop policies that reflect the collective wisdom of the community and the practicalities of contemporary life.

For example, the incorporation of traditional agricultural methods into sustainable development initiatives can offer an alternative to industrial farming, preserving biodiversity while providing economic opportunities. Similarly, educational curricula can be enriched by integrating local history and arts, fostering a sense of pride and continuity among younger generations.

Moreover, technology, often seen as a harbinger of cultural erosion, can become an ally in heritage preservation. Digital archives can document and disseminate ancient knowledge, virtual reality can recreate historical sites for global audiences, and social media can build networks of cultural practitioners, amplifying their reach and influence.

Yet, alongside these initiatives, there must be legal safeguards. Intellectual property rights tailored for cultural heritage can protect against the commodification and misappropriation of traditional knowledge and expressions. Such rights must be flexible enough to account for the collective nature of cultural heritage, diverging from the Western-centric model that emphasizes individual ownership.

As policies are implemented, continuous monitoring and evaluation are crucial. Governance must remain agile, adapting to the effects of policies on the ground and recalibrating them as necessary. This iterative process is not merely bureaucratic due diligence; it is a commitment to the living heart of heritage preservation.

In the grand narrative of humanity, modern governance of ancient practices is not about imposing a static order but about fostering a dynamic equilibrium. It is about crafting policy frameworks that are as resilient and enduring as the traditions they seek to protect. In this endeavor, we become not just guardians of heritage but also architects of a future where the old and new harmoniously coexist, sustaining the diverse tapestry of human culture.


*- Balancing development and conservation*

In the heart of the modern governance matrix lies an ancient puzzle: how to honor the time-honored traditions of a culture while steering the ship of progress into the uncharted waters of the future. As the world accelerates into a digital, interconnected age, the guardians of heritage face a daunting task. They must decipher the delicate balance between development and conservation, ensuring that the march of modernity does not trample the sacred grounds of tradition.

At the core of this conundrum, there seems to be an inherent dichotomy. Modern governance often equates progress with innovation, infrastructure, and economic growth, metrics that are seemingly at odds with the preservation of ancient practices and cultural landscapes. Yet, upon closer examination, this dichotomy dissolves into a harmonic potential, a synergistic opportunity wherein lies the true art of contemporary governance.

Imagine a governance system where ancient practices are not only protected but are leveraged as living museums, educational resources, and even economic assets. Such a system does not just cage tradition in the confines of ritual and memory but rather allows it to breathe anew in the lungs of modern society. For instance, traditional agricultural methods, once thought to be inefficient relics, are now recognized for their sustainable and ecological advantages, offering lessons in the balance of ecosystems and the conservation of biodiversity.

The key to achieving this balance is an integrative approach that recognizes the multiplicity of values associated with cultural practices and heritage sites. These values—be they historical, spiritual, social, environmental, or economic—inform a governance framework that is flexible and adaptive. This framework must be capable of embracing modern technology and methods, such as using digital archives to preserve ancient texts or employing satellite imagery to protect archaeological sites from urban encroachment.

Yet, in harnessing modern tools, governance must also remain deeply rooted in the ethos and ethics of the communities it serves. It is through the lens of local knowledge and participation that the most effective conservation strategies emerge. By engaging with local custodians of tradition, governance becomes a collaborative process, a dialogue rather than a directive. In this dialogue, the voices of the past are not echoes fading into the silence of history but are active participants in the shaping of the present and the future.

Modern governance of ancient practices, therefore, is not a static policy but a dynamic dance—a dance that respects the rhythm of tradition while choreographing steps toward sustainable development. It is a governance that understands that the seeds of the past, when planted in the fertile soil of the present, can blossom into a future where development and conservation are not adversaries but allies in the quest for a harmonious world.

5.9 Media's Role in Cultural Continuity

- *Broadcasting heritage: radio, TV, and online platforms*

In a world suffused with digital currents, the media has burgeoned into an omnipresent force, shaping perceptions and narratives across the globe. It is the storyteller of our times, weaving the past into the present, and projecting visions of the future. As such, it holds an unparalleled capacity to act as a custodian of cultural heritage, a vessel that carries the essence of humanity's diverse traditions into the heart of modern society.

Radio waves, long considered the voice of the people, have the power to traverse physical and social barriers, bringing the melodies of ancient folk songs or the wisdom of oral traditions into homes and communities. In remote areas, where the tendrils of the internet have yet to reach, radio remains a lifeline, a beacon of cultural identity amidst the encroaching tide of homogenization. Programs dedicated to local languages, stories, and music foster a sense of belonging and pride, nurturing a lineage of customs that might otherwise fade into obscurity.

Television, with its vivid tableau, offers a canvas for the dramatization of historical epics, the reenactment of traditional ceremonies, and the detailed exposition of artisanal crafts. It is a visual conduit through which the vibrant hues of cultural festivals, the grandeur of architectural marvels, and the subtleties of age-old practices are broadcast into the collective consciousness. Through thoughtful programming, television can transcend mere entertainment, becoming an educational tool that solidifies the threads of heritage within the fabric of contemporary life.

The advent of online platforms has ushered in a new epoch of cultural dissemination, one that is interactive and boundless. Social media, streaming services, and virtual reality experiences break the constraints of time and space, allowing for an unprecedented exchange of cultural wisdom. Online archives and digital exhibitions make accessible the treasures of yesteryear, while forums and blogs offer spaces for discussion and the exchange of traditional knowledge. The internet has the potential to be a great democratizer, providing a stage where all voices can be heard and all stories told.

In this digital renaissance, the imperative is for media creators and curators to embrace their role as guardians of heritage. They must strike a delicate balance, harnessing the seductive pull of modernity while giving due reverence to the ancestry of the cultures they represent. It is through their lenses that traditions are not merely spectacles to be observed but living, breathing elements of contemporary society, deserving of both celebration and thoughtful integration.

To achieve this harmony, media entities must collaborate with cultural custodians—historians, artists, community leaders—to ensure authenticity and respect guide their narratives. Educational initiatives can equip media professionals with the sensitivities required to handle cultural content with the care it warrants. Ultimately, the media's portrayal of heritage will shape future generations' understanding and appreciation of their roots, sewing seeds for a unity that is rich with the diversity of its past.

Thus, we advocate for the preservation of heritage in the face of modernity and call for its active propagation through the most powerful channels available to us. The media, in all its forms, is a mirror reflecting society and a lantern illuminating the path to a future where every cultural thread is valued and woven into the tapestry of human civilization.

*- Social media as a tool for cultural expression*

In the digital age, the guardianship of heritage has found a new ally—social media. Platforms once relegated to the realm of personal updates and entertainment have morphed into vibrant tapestries showcasing the cultural expressions of communities worldwide. Social media plays an incredibly powerful role in cultural continuity, acting as a bridge between the ancient echoes of tradition and the pulsating beat of modern life.

The alchemy of social media lies in its democratization of voice and narrative. No longer are stories of cultural heritage confined to dusty archives or exclusive academic circles; they are now shared, liked, and commented upon by millions across the globe. The digital sphere has become a theatre of memory, where traditional dances are not just steps, but stories told in motion, captured in high-definition and available to an audience unconstrained by geography.

Take, for instance, the resurgence of indigenous languages, many on the brink of extinction. Social media campaigns have emerged as a beacon of hope, with hashtags becoming rallying cries for preservation efforts. Younger generations, armed with smartphones and a renewed sense of identity, broadcast their linguistic heritage, engaging with peers in a celebration of linguistic diversity that transcends borders.

Similarly, traditional artisans find in social media a marketplace without parallel. The intricate weaves of a handloom saree or the delicate brushstrokes of indigenous art are no longer confined to the village fair; they are now shared stories, with each post a thread in the larger narrative of cultural survival. Artisans and custodians of craft can directly connect with patrons and enthusiasts, fostering a sense of community and shared responsibility for heritage preservation.

Moreover, social media platforms have become critical in the fight against cultural appropriation. Communities can now assert ownership and educate a global audience about the significance of cultural symbols and practices, ensuring that respect and acknowledgment accompany any borrowing from cultural repositories.

Yet, the role of social media is not without its challenges. The risk of dilution of cultural practices for 'shareability', the potential homogenization of cultural expressions, and the commodification of heritage are pitfalls that must be navigated with care. Thus, the guardians of heritage must engage with social media judiciously, crafting content that is both engaging and respectful, ensuring that the essence of traditions is not lost in translation to the digital dialect.

In this era of connectivity, social media emerges as a tool of immense potential for cultural expression, a digital loom weaving the rich tapestry of humanity's heritage into the fabric of modern consciousness. As we scroll through our feeds, we are not merely consumers of content; we are witnesses to the unfolding narrative of human creativity and custodians of the legacy that it upholds.


## 5.10 Community Engagement in Heritage Conservation

*- Grassroots movements in heritage preservation*

In the heart of the city, nestled between the relentless march of progress and the shadows of towering skyscrapers, lies the old textile district—a tapestry of history woven into the very fabric of the community. It is here that we find the most poignant example of grassroots movements in heritage preservation, a testament to the power of community engagement in the conservation of our cultural legacies.

The textile district, once the bustling hub of the city's early industrial age, faced the threat of being erased from the urban landscape. Developers, fueled by visions of modernity and the relentless pursuit of economic growth, eyed the area with plans for gleaming office spaces and luxury apartments. But the community saw something else—a story that needed to be told, an identity that needed to be preserved.

It began with a small group of local historians and concerned citizens who recognized the value of the district beyond its old, brick-lined streets and fading facades. They saw the district as a living museum, a place where the trials and triumphs of the past could inform the future. With a passion fueled by the love for their city's heritage, they mobilized, forming the Textile Heritage Society.

The society's approach was multifaceted. They organized walking tours, inviting locals and tourists alike to step into the past and witness the enduring legacy of the textile workers' lives. They hosted seminars and workshops in the old weaver's cottages, teaching traditional crafts that once defined the district's economy. Through these events, they fostered a deep appreciation for the district's historical value, transforming apathy into a shared sense of responsibility.

On the political front, they lobbied tirelessly, advocating for the district's designation as a heritage conservation area. They presented well-researched proposals to the city council, highlighting the potential for heritage tourism and the economic benefits of preserving the historical character of the area. They partnered with local businesses, whose livelihoods were as woven into the district's identity as the threads of the textiles once produced there.

The society knew that every saved brick was a victory, every restored façade a triumph. They understood that modernity need not be a bulldozer to the past, but rather a careful architect that honors and incorporates it. Through their efforts, the textile district became more than a relic—it became a vibrant part of the city's contemporary life, a place where the past was not only remembered but also lived.

As our society continues to navigate the delicate balance between modernity and tradition, the Textile Heritage Society stands as a beacon of what can be achieved through community engagement. They are the guardians of heritage, proving that when citizens take ownership of their history, they can weave a future where cultural identity and modern life coexist in harmonious splendor.

*- Involving youth in guardianship of traditions*

In the quest to preserve the intricacies of our past, the youth emerge as the torchbearers of tomorrow's cultural legacies. The vibrant energy of younger generations, when channeled into the guardianship of traditions, can ignite a continuity of heritage that might otherwise flicker and fade in the winds of modernity. Let's explore the dynamic role that youth can play in heritage conservation and how their involvement can bridge the gap between time-honored practices and the pulse of the present.

It is essential to recognize that the very essence of heritage is not static; it is a living, breathing tapestry that evolves with each passing generation. To engage youth effectively, we must invite them to not merely be passive custodians but active participants in the narrative of cultural preservation. This involvement can take many forms, from incorporating traditional arts into the modern educational curriculum to fostering mentorship programs where elders impart ancestral knowledge to young minds eager to learn.

Digital platforms offer a fertile ground for youth engagement. Social media campaigns, interactive websites, and virtual reality experiences can bring the allure of heritage to the digital doorstep of the younger demographic. By showcasing the richness of traditional crafts, music, dance, and rituals in formats that resonate with a technologically savvy audience, we can kindle a sense of pride and ownership among the youth.

Engaging youth in heritage conservation must go beyond mere appreciation and into the realm of empowerment. Community-driven projects can provide the scaffolding for young individuals to take on leadership roles. Initiatives such as youth-led tours of historical sites, student-organized cultural festivals, and workshops on traditional craftsmanship allow young people to be at the forefront of heritage advocacy, fostering a sense of responsibility and community connection.

In cities and villages alike, heritage conservation can serve as a catalyst for intergenerational dialogue. By creating spaces where stories and skills are exchanged, we foster a continuum of knowledge that transcends age and time. In these dialogues, the wisdom of the past and the innovation of the future converge, crafting a shared vision for the preservation of our collective cultural memory.

The guardianship of traditions by the youth is not just about safeguarding relics of yesteryear; it's about instilling a consciousness that heritage is a living dialogue between the past and the future. When young people are involved in the stewardship of their cultural inheritance, they become the architects of a future where tradition and modernity coexist in a symphony of progress and reverence.

The engagement of youth in heritage conservation is an imperative for the survival and flourishing of our cultural landscapes. As such, it is the responsibility of governance, educators, and community leaders to lay down the pathways for youth participation in this sacred task, ensuring that our traditions are not only remembered but vibrantly alive within the hearts of tomorrow's guardians.

# 6. The People's Voice

*Voices rise as one,*
*Democracy's heart beats loud,*
*People's will is done.*

## 6.1 The Pillars of Participation

*- Defining participatory governance: core principles and values*

In the realm of participatory governance, the voice of the people is not a faint echo but the symphony to which the entire system orchestrates its movements. It is a form of governance tailored to fit the intricacies of human diversity, recognizing that the wisdom of the collective can be harnessed to chart a course for the common good. Here, we explore the core principles and values that stand as the pillars supporting the grand edifice of participatory governance.

The first pillar is inclusivity. Participatory governance is predicated on the idea that all voices, regardless of societal status, creed, or background, should have the opportunity to be heard. It is a commitment to dismantle the barriers that silence segments of society, ensuring that governance is not the exclusive domain of the elite but a common ground where each individual has a stake and a say.

Transparency is the second pillar. The mechanisms of decision-making must be as clear as crystal, enabling the populace to see through the processes that shape their lives. Transparency breeds trust, and trust is the currency of effective governance. When citizens can track the journey of their contributions from utterance to action, faith in the system is fortified.

The third pillar is responsiveness. A government that listens but does not act on the concerns of its citizens is like a play without an audience - an exercise in futility. Participatory governance demands that the feedback and inputs gathered from the public discourse translate into policies and initiatives that reflect the will and the welfare of the people.

Empowerment stands as the fourth pillar. To participate is to have not only a voice but also the power to influence. Participatory governance must equip its citizens with the necessary knowledge, resources, and platforms to effect change. It is about moving beyond token gestures to creating real levers of power that can be accessed by the ordinary citizen.

Sustainability is the fifth pillar. The participatory governance model must be designed to endure, to transcend the flickering moments of current affairs and root itself deeply in the culture of governance. It requires the cultivation of civic education, the building of institutions that can carry the torch of participation from one generation to the next, and the continuous evaluation and evolution of participatory processes.

By upholding these pillars—Inclusivity, Transparency, Responsiveness, Empowerment, and Sustainability—participatory governance breathes life into the concept of democracy. It transforms it from a static system into a living organism that grows and adapts with the heartbeat of its people. It is within this framework that governance can truly be of the people, by the people, and for the people, resonating with the diverse and harmonious melody of humanity.

*- Historical perspectives on people's participation in governance*

In the tapestry of human governance, the warp and weft of history have often been woven by the hands of a few, yet the most vibrant patterns emerge when the many contribute to the loom. To understand the future of participatory governance, we must first revisit the ancient assemblies where the seeds of democracy were sown.

The Athenian agora bustled not just with the commerce of goods, but with the exchange of ideas. Here, in the cradle of democracy, citizens gathered, their voices rising in a cacophony of debate and discussion. Participation was not merely a right; it was a civic duty, an act of responsibility towards the polis. The Athenian model, though far from inclusive by modern standards, as it excluded women, slaves, and foreigners, laid the foundational pillars of participation: direct engagement, public deliberation, and collective decision-making.

As the centuries turned, the Roman Republic refined these concepts, introducing representative elements through the Senate and the Tribal Assembly. The Roman approach echoed the voices of the many, albeit filtered through the elected few, setting the stage for a balance between direct and indirect governance that would resonate throughout the ages.

However, as empires rose and fell, the flame of participation often flickered and waned. It was not until the Enlightenment that the pillars of participation were rediscovered and re-energized. The American and French revolutions, though distinct in character and context, were united by a common thread—the assertion of the populace's sovereignty. The fundamental Enlightenment belief in the individual's capacity for reason led to the reinvigoration of participatory governance, with an emphasis on the protection of natural rights and the crafting of constitutions that enshrined the people's will.

The 19th and 20th centuries witnessed the gradual expansion of suffrage, a crucial pillar of participation that extended the franchise to previously disenfranchised groups: women, people of color, and the working class. This expansion was not merely a legal milestone but a profound cultural shift that acknowledged the intrinsic value of every voice in the governance process.

Today, we stand at a new crossroads where the digital agora has the potential to rekindle the ancient spirit of participation on an unprecedented scale. The pillars of participation—engagement, deliberation, and decision-making—are being reimagined in the context of a connected world. As we craft the inclusive governance structures of tomorrow, we must draw wisdom from the past. We must ensure that these pillars are not only preserved but also strengthened, recognizing that a harmonious world is built on the chorus of its citizens' voices, each one contributing a vital note to the symphony of society.

In the following pages, we will explore contemporary case studies and theoretical frameworks that illustrate the resurgence of participatory governance. We will investigate how historical principles are being applied and adapted to meet the challenges of a diverse humanity, seeking harmony through the active, informed, and passionate involvement of the people.


6.2 Digital Platforms for Engagement

*- E-governance and online decision-making tools*

In the digital age, the voice of the people resonates not just in the town squares and public forums of old but also through the vast and borderless expanse of the Internet. E-governance emerges as the modern-day agora, a digital commons where citizens can engage, deliberate, and contribute to the policymaking process with an immediacy and scale previously unimaginable.

The proliferation of online platforms for civic engagement has democratized political participation, enabling a broader spectrum of society to exert influence on the decisions that shape their lives. From social media campaigns to dedicated e-participation portals, these platforms harness the collective wisdom and diversity of the populace, fostering an inclusive atmosphere where every voice has the potential to be heard.

Yet, for e-governance to truly embody the principles of participatory governance, it must be more than just a digital suggestion box. It requires the careful integration of online decision-making tools that not only gather public input but also facilitate informed debate and translate popular sentiment into actionable policy.

One such tool is the electronic town hall meeting, an innovative approach to public consultation that combines live streaming with interactive polling and moderated discussion forums. Here, citizens can question their representatives, debate with their peers, and directly influence the direction of policy, all from the convenience of their digital devices.

Another key development in e-governance is the use of participatory budgeting platforms. These online systems enable residents to allocate a portion of the public budget to projects of their choosing, ensuring that community funds are spent in a manner that reflects the priorities of the people. The result is a tangible manifestation of democracy in action, as playgrounds, libraries, and public spaces materialize from the collective decision-making of engaged citizens.

However, the transition to digital governance is not without obstacles. Issues of digital literacy and access must be addressed to prevent the creation of a new divide wherein the less technologically adept are excluded from the democratic process. Furthermore, the integrity of these platforms must be safeguarded against misinformation and cyber threats, ensuring that the digital space remains a secure and trustworthy environment for civic engagement.

In this digital renaissance of democratic participation, we glimpse the contours of a future where governance is collaborative, transparent, and responsive. By embracing the potential of e-governance and online decision-making tools, we pave the way for a more dynamic and participatory model of governance—one that empowers citizens to shape the harmonious worlds they inhabit.


*- Case studies: Successful digital participatory initiatives*

The digital age has brought forth an era where the voices of citizens are not only audible but also actionable, provided the right platforms are in place to capture and translate them into policy. Here we explore several case studies of successful digital participatory initiatives that have empowered citizens and revitalized governance.

First, we turn to Estonia, a pioneer in e-governance. The Estonian government has harnessed digital technology to create a cohesive, secure, and highly inclusive digital environment known as e-Estonia. Through platforms such as e-Residency and the digital ID system, Estonians can vote, sign documents, and access public services online with ease. The digital engagement has led to increased participation rates and a more informed citizenry, actively contributing to the decisions that shape their society.

Across the globe, in Taiwan, the vTaiwan platform presents a beacon of digital democracy. In the wake of social unrest concerning the regulation of online alcohol sales, the government, led by digital minister Audrey Tang, turned to vTaiwan—a digital platform that allows for open dialogue and consensus-building among citizens, experts, and government officials. The platform's use of Pol.is, an AI-driven conversation tool, ensures that diverse voices are heard and that complex policy issues are distilled into actionable insights. The success of this initiative can be observed in its outcomes, such as the passing of the Digital Communications Act, which was heavily influenced by citizen input.

Another inspiring case is from Brazil with its e-Democracia project. The initiative invites citizens to contribute to the legislative process through online discussions and virtual forums. This inclusive approach has seen tangible results, such as the influence on the shaping of the Internet Bill of Rights, which received significant contributions from the public.

In Madrid, Spain, the Decide Madrid platform showcases how a local government can leverage digital tools to foster participatory budgeting and policy proposals. Citizens are given the power to propose and prioritize projects within their city, leading to democratic and community-driven improvements in public infrastructure and services. The platform has garnered widespread participation, with tens of thousands of proposals submitted and millions of votes cast, reflecting a vibrant and engaged community.

These case studies emphasize key factors for successful digital participatory initiatives: secure and user-friendly platforms, transparent processes, and a genuine commitment from government entities to consider and implement public input. By drawing on technology to amplify the collective voice, these examples provide a template for other regions seeking to revitalize their approach to participatory governance. The ultimate goal is a harmonious world where governance is not just top-down but also bottom-up, with citizens at the heart of every decision.


6.3 Inclusive Policy-Making

- *Strategies for including marginalized voices*

The lifeblood of any truly democratic system pulses with the voices of its citizens —all of its citizens. Yet, the path to achieving an inclusive policy-making process is riddled with historical inequities and entrenched power structures. Here, we explore the strategies that can bridge this gap and amplify those whispers that have been traditionally drowned out in the cacophony of governance.

To start, policy-making must move beyond the tokenistic inclusion of marginalized voices, where diverse representation is often merely symbolic. True inclusion requires a paradigm shift towards actively seeking, hearing, and valuing the insights and experiences of the marginalized. It is a commitment to the idea that every voice can contribute to a richer, more nuanced understanding of the collective needs.

One such strategy is the establishment of dedicated advisory councils composed of members from marginalized communities. These councils can serve as critical touchpoints between the government and underrepresented groups, ensuring that their perspectives are not an afterthought but a foundation upon which policies are built. This approach has been adopted in various forms, such as the Sami parliaments in the Nordic countries, which give the indigenous Sami people a platform to influence policies affecting their lands and culture.

Another avenue is the implementation of participatory budgeting, a process that empowers citizens to decide how to allocate a portion of public funds. From Porto Alegre in Brazil to New York City in the United States, participatory budgeting has allowed communities, including those that are marginalized, to directly shape the landscape of their neighborhoods, thereby fostering a sense of ownership and engagement in the political process.

Further, digital platforms can democratize access to policy-making. Through online forums and voting systems, those who might be physically unable to attend town hall meetings or rallies can still make their voices heard. However, this also necessitates addressing the digital divide, ensuring that the marginalized have the necessary tools and skills to engage in these digital spaces.

Language, too, plays a vital role in inclusion. Multilingual access to information and the availability of interpreters during consultations can remove barriers to participation for those who might otherwise be excluded due to language constraints.

Inclusive policy-making must be backed by education. Educational programs that teach civic engagement from an early age can empower future generations to participate actively in governance. Moreover, these programs must be designed to be inclusive themselves, taking into account diverse learning needs and cultural backgrounds.

Inclusive policy-making is not an end in itself but a continuous process of listening, adapting, and evolving. It is a commitment to the mosaic of humanity, a recognition that every piece, no matter how seemingly small, is vital to the integrity and beauty of the whole. If governance is to be truly for the people, it must be shaped by all the people. Only then can the symphony of the people's voice rise in harmonious accord, guiding the hand that steers the ship of state towards a more equitable and just horizon.

*- The role of civil society organizations in policy consultation*

In the tapestry of participatory governance, civil society organizations (CSOs) emerge as vibrant threads interwoven into the fabric of policy-making. These entities, ranging from non-profits and community groups to advocacy networks and think tanks, play a pivotal role in ensuring that the chorus of the people's voice resonates through the halls of power.

Inclusive policy-making is not merely a noble aspiration but a pragmatic approach to crafting robust and responsive governance. It demands a symphonic dialogue where the melodies of diverse stakeholders harmonize to shape decisions that impact the collective future. In this endeavor, CSOs act as the conductors orchestrating the ensemble of public opinion and expert knowledge.

The participatory model recognizes that effective policy-making is not confined within the rigid walls of governmental institutions. Instead, it spills into the public squares and digital forums where civil society vibrates with ideas and aspirations. CSOs facilitate this process by collecting, synthesizing, and channeling public sentiment into actionable intelligence that policymakers can leverage.

Consider a community facing the threat of environmental degradation due to industrial expansion. Local environmental CSOs, deeply rooted in the community's socio-ecological context, can gather data, mobilize local expertise, and articulate the population's concerns. Such organizations can then collaborate with governmental bodies, ensuring that environmental policies not only reflect scientific evidence but also resonate with the values and needs of the community.

Furthermore, CSOs serve as guardians of transparency and accountability. They monitor policy implementation, offer critical feedback, and advocate for course corrections when policies diverge from their intended outcomes. This feedback loop is essential for policies to remain relevant and effective amidst an ever-changing societal landscape.

However, the inclusion of CSOs in policy consultation does not come without challenges. It requires a culture of trust and openness from the government, an infrastructure that supports active engagement, and a commitment to overcoming barriers such as limited resources or political resistance. Moreover, CSOs must navigate the delicate balance of representing their constituencies without being co-opted by political agendas.

In the grand narrative of governance, the role of CSOs in policy consultation is a testament to the power of collective wisdom. Their inclusion is not just an addendum; it is a fundamental chapter in the story of a governance system that listens, learns, and adapts. It is through the vibrant participation of civil society that policies can be crafted with a kaleidoscope of perspectives, leading to a governance that is as inclusive as it is insightful.

The resonant voice of the people, channeled through the diligent work of CSOs, ensures that the symphony of governance is not a solo act but a harmonious ensemble, playing the music of progress for all to hear and partake in.


6.4 Deliberative Democracy in Action

*- The process and importance of public deliberation*

In the clamor of the modern world, the voice of the individual often drowns in the cacophony of mass opinion and polarized debate. Yet, the concept of deliberative democracy offers a chorus of hope—a means to harmonize the disparate voices within a society. Deliberative democracy is not merely about casting votes in isolation, but engaging in informed, respectful, and reflective discourse aimed at reaching a consensus that benefits the collective.

The process of public deliberation is both an art and a science. It begins with the creation of diverse forums where individuals from all walks of life can gather. These assemblies serve as microcosms of the broader society, spaces where every segment of the population is represented and every voice holds weight. In these forums, citizens are not passive recipients of top-down political decrees; they are active participants, contributors to the shaping of their own governance.

The art of deliberation lies in fostering an environment of mutual respect and open-mindedness. Participants are encouraged to listen attentively, to consider perspectives that challenge their preconceived notions, and to articulate their views without the fear of retribution or ridicule. It is through this process that the seeds of understanding are sown, allowing for the emergence of creative solutions that might otherwise have been overlooked.

The science of deliberation involves structuring these discussions in a way that promotes equality and inclusiveness. Facilitators play a crucial role, ensuring that the dialogue remains focused and productive, and that all participants have an equal opportunity to contribute. This may involve breaking larger groups into smaller circles, using technology to bridge geographical divides, or employing decision-making tools that help crystallize common ground.

Public deliberation shines in its ability to address complex and contentious issues. When citizens deliberate on matters such as healthcare, education, or climate change, they do more than just exchange opinions—they actively engage with the facts, wrestle with ethical implications, and weigh the long-term consequences of potential policies. This depth of engagement fosters a sense of ownership and responsibility for the decisions that are ultimately made.

Moreover, deliberative democracy has a transformative power. It can turn apathy into action, conflict into collaboration. It teaches the art of compromise and the grace of concession. It elevates the conversation from what is politically expedient to what is genuinely beneficial for the community. In doing so, it cultivates a culture of democracy that extends beyond the walls of the deliberative forum and into the everyday lives of its citizens.

The importance of public deliberation cannot be overstated. It is the beating heart of a participatory governance system—a system that thrives on the informed consent and active engagement of its people. It is through this rigorous and heartfelt process that governance transcends the mere exercise of power and becomes a harmonious expression of the collective will—a symphony of voices united in their diversity, shaping the melody of a just and inclusive society.


*- Examples of deliberative democracy from around the world*

Deliberative democracy, a process that engages citizens in the direct decision-making of policies, has been the subject of much theoretical discussion. However, there are several compelling real-world examples where deliberative democracy has been implemented successfully, creating a ripple effect of positive change across societies.

In the picturesque city of Porto Alegre in Brazil, an experiment in participatory budgeting marked a groundbreaking moment for deliberative democracy. Initiated in the late 1980s, this process involved regular citizens in the allocation of municipal resources. Residents gathered in assemblies to set priorities and allocate funds, a practice that not only improved infrastructure but also empowered the poorest citizens, giving them a direct say in their city's development.

Moving across the Atlantic to the continent of Europe, the country of Ireland stands as a testament to the transformative power of citizen assemblies. Faced with deeply contentious issues such as same-sex marriage and abortion, the Irish government convened a series of citizen assemblies composed of a representative sample of the population. These assemblies were tasked with deliberating on the matters at hand and advising the government on potential legislative changes. The recommendations of these assemblies led to historic referendums, which in turn resulted in sweeping changes to Irish law and society, demonstrating the potential of deliberative democracy to resolve even the most divisive of debates.

In the city of Madrid, the digital platform 'Decide Madrid' has been utilized to allow citizens to propose and prioritize projects for the city. The innovative use of technology in this instance has demonstrated how digital tools can enhance participatory governance, providing a scalable and accessible method for ensuring that the voice of the people is heard.

Further north, in the Scandinavian haven of Iceland, the nation turned to deliberative democracy in the wake of the 2008 financial crisis. A constitutional council, inclusive of randomly selected citizens, was formed to rewrite the nation's constitution. Despite the new constitution not being adopted due to political complexities, the process itself was a leap forward in inclusive governance, providing a blueprint for how nations can engage citizens in foundational acts of statecraft.

These examples are not mere isolated incidents but represent a growing trend in governance that seeks to reconcile the often-disparate voices of a diverse populace. They demonstrate that when citizens are engaged, informed, and empowered to participate in the decisions that affect their lives, governance can be conducted not only with the people but by the people, embodying the true spirit of democracy.

Deliberative democracy in action is a powerful force. It can heal divisions, invigorate civic life, and cultivate a sense of shared ownership and responsibility among citizens. By examining these examples, we glean valuable insights into the potential for crafting inclusive governance that does more than just pay lip service to the ideals of democracy—it lives them.


6.5 Citizen Assemblies and Councils

In the bustling agora of our modern world, the ancient practices of direct democracy, where citizens gathered to deliberate and decide upon the matters of state, seem a distant dream. Yet, this dream is not beyond our reach. Through the innovative use of citizen assemblies and councils, we can revitalize the participatory spirit of governance and breathe new life into the democratic process.

Citizen assemblies, the modern-day descendants of Athenian democracy, are structured to mirror the demographic and psychographic composition of the populace they represent. They are typically formed through a process of sortition, a random selection that ensures a microcosm of society is brought together, reflecting various ages, genders, ethnicities, and socioeconomic backgrounds.

These assemblies are given a clear mandate – to deliberate on a specific issue of public importance, such as climate change policy, healthcare reform, or urban development. To function effectively, they are typically organized into three phases: learning, deliberation, and decision.

During the learning phase, assembly members are provided with balanced and comprehensive information about the issue at hand. Experts and stakeholders are invited to present evidence and answer questions, equipping citizens with the knowledge required to make informed decisions.

The deliberation phase is the heart of the citizen assembly. It is here that the art of dialogue is practiced, with members discussing the issue in depth, challenging assumptions, and considering diverse perspectives. Facilitators, skilled in the craft of mediation, guide the process to ensure that every voice is heard and every concern is addressed.

Finally, in the decision phase, members develop recommendations or solutions, which are often put forward in the form of a report. These recommendations can be advisory, informing the wider public and policymakers, or, in some cases, they may carry the weight of a referendum, directly influencing legislation.

The function of citizen assemblies is manifold. First, they serve as a bridge between the public and the political sphere, translating the complex chorus of citizen voices into coherent and actionable advice. Second, they act as a forum for public education, not only for the members but also for the broader community as assembly proceedings are often made transparent and accessible. Third, they are a laboratory for social cohesion, where individuals from different walks of life come together to engage in the collective task of governance.

By embodying the principles of equality, deliberation, and representation, citizen assemblies offer a blueprint for a more engaged and informed citizenry. They signal a return to the roots of democracy, where governance is not just for the people, but by the people, and where the collective wisdom of the populace is harnessed to shape the future. Indeed, through these assemblies, we can construct a governance that resonates with the harmonious chorus of an inclusive and participatory society, ensuring that the tapestry of humanity is both preserved and celebrated.

*- Impact studies: The outcomes of citizen councils on governance*

In Ireland, the 2016 Citizen's Assembly on abortion rights stands as a testament to the power of inclusive discourse. Ordinary citizens, selected to represent the demographics of the nation, convened to examine the moral and legal complexities surrounding the issue. Their recommendations ultimately paved the way for a historic referendum, demonstrating that when given the platform, citizens can catalyze profound societal shifts.

Venturing northward to the Nordics, we observe the Finnish experiment with citizen councils shaping urban planning. These assemblies, composed of residents from various districts, addressed the gnarled question of sustainable city development. Their collaborative efforts yielded innovative solutions that harmonized environmental considerations with the needs of a growing population, crafting a blueprint for urban futures built on the bedrock of community consensus.

In Canada, the British Columbia Citizens' Assembly on Electoral Reform showcased the potential for citizen bodies to tackle intricate policy questions. The assembly's meticulous exploration of electoral systems, and its subsequent proposition for a single transferable vote mechanism, illustrated the capacity of lay individuals to engage with complex policy issues when supported by expert knowledge and a structured deliberative process.

These impact studies reveal several key outcomes on governance. First, citizen assemblies and councils have fostered a deeper sense of ownership and responsibility among participants. This empowerment has led to increased civic engagement, with citizens more likely to vote, volunteer, and partake in community activities. Second, the inclusion of diverse voices has enriched the policy-making process, infusing it with a multiplicity of perspectives that often go unheard in traditional political arenas.

Third, the transparency and deliberative nature of these councils have enhanced public trust in government institutions. By witnessing their peers partake in reasoned debate and informed decision-making, the larger populace gains confidence in the democratic process. Fourth, the recommendations emanating from these assemblies have often proven to be more innovative, sustainable, and socially just than those arising from conventional governance structures.

However, it's crucial to acknowledge the challenges. Scaling participation, ensuring the execution of proposals, and integrating these assemblies into the existing political framework are hurdles yet to be fully surmounted. Despite these challenges, the impact of citizen councils on governance cannot be overstated. They stand as beacons of what can be achieved when the chorus of democracy sings in harmony, and every voice finds its note in the grand symphony of participatory governance.

<u>6.6 Participatory Budgeting</u>

*- Fundamentals of community-based budgeting*

In the heart of participatory governance lies the cornerstone of democratic engagement: the power of the purse. Participatory budgeting, a novel yet increasingly embraced concept, stands as a testament to the principles of inclusion and collective decision-making. It marks a shift from the conventional top-down budgetary allocations to a more grassroots-level financial democracy, where communities have a direct say in how public funds are distributed and utilized.

The journey of participatory budgeting begins with understanding its fundamental premise, which is to democratize fiscal policy by involving citizens in budget allocation. This process transforms residents from mere spectators into active participants, enabling them to identify, discuss, and prioritize public spending projects in their communities. It is a radical re-envisioning of the traditional budgetary process, which often leaves citizens on the periphery of financial discourse and decision-making.

Imagine a community meeting, a convocation of diverse voices and perspectives, all gathered with a singular goal: to carve out a slice of the municipal budget for projects that resonate with their collective aspirations. From repairing the worn-out playground that echoes with the laughter of children to installing streetlights that promise safety in the velvet cloak of night, the projects are as varied as the lives they touch.

The process typically unfolds through several stages: ideation, proposal development, voting, and implementation. It commences with public forums that serve as breeding grounds for ideas. Citizens are encouraged to articulate their needs and visions for the community, laying the groundwork for project proposals. These proposals are then refined and transformed into actionable plans, often with the assistance of experts or public officials, ensuring that they are both feasible and impactful.

The magic of participatory budgeting unfolds during the voting phase. It is a profound moment of civic engagement, as residents, regardless of their social or economic status, cast their votes to determine which projects will receive funding. This act of collective decision-making is not only empowering but also serves as a catalyst for increased transparency and accountability in governance.

Finally, the implementation stage breathes life into the community's choices, as the winning projects are executed with public funds. This tangible outcome of the participatory budgeting process is a powerful illustration of democracy in action, a concrete manifestation of the community's will.

Yet, the beauty of participatory budgeting extends beyond the allocation of resources. It fosters a deeper sense of community ownership and responsibility, as residents become stewards of their shared spaces and advocates for their collective wellbeing. It also serves as an educational platform, acquainting citizens with the intricacies of budgetary constraints and governance challenges.

Crucially, participatory budgeting is not a panacea for all the ailments of public finance, nor is it devoid of challenges. It requires a cultural shift in governance, a willingness to embrace the messiness of democracy, and a commitment to nurturing civic education. But for those communities bold enough to embark on this democratic experiment, the rewards are multifold: more equitable public spending, enhanced civic participation, and a reinvigorated trust in the institutions of governance.

In essence, participatory budgeting is more than a method of allocating funds; it is a celebration of community spirit, an affirmation of democratic ideals, and a step towards the harmonious world we aspire to create. It is here, in the hands of the people, that the budget becomes not just a financial document but a tapestry woven with the threads of their collective hopes and dreams.

*- Outcomes and lessons learned from participatory budgeting experiments*

In the corridors of power, a transformation is taking hold, one fiscal decision at a time. Participatory budgeting, a democratic process in which community members directly decide how to allocate parts of a public budget, has been spreading across the globe like the early morning light that dispels the darkness of night. It is in the outcomes and lessons of these participatory budgeting experiments that we find the seeds of a more engaged and empowered citizenry, and the potential rejuvenation of the democratic spirit.

From Porto Alegre, Brazil, where participatory budgeting first took root in the late 1980s, to the bustling boroughs of New York City, the impact of this inclusive approach to governance has been profound. In Porto Alegre, the implementation of participatory budgeting saw an increase in access to sanitation and health services, as well as a dramatic rise in tax revenues—clear indicators of its success in aligning governmental action with the population's priorities.

Participatory budgeting has also proven to be a potent educational tool. It brings the budgetary process into the public square, demystifying financial jargon and illuminating the often opaque pathways through which public funds flow. Citizens, once passive spectators to the fiscal fate of their communities, become active participants, gaining a practical understanding of budgeting that transcends the theoretical confines of economics.

One of the key lessons learned from these experiments is the importance of accessibility. Inclusion means not just opening the doors but also actively inviting people in, ensuring that they have the necessary information and support to contribute meaningfully. Digital platforms have emerged as powerful enablers in this regard, bridging geographical divides and expanding the reach of participatory budgeting initiatives.

However, one must not overlook the challenges. Critics argue that without careful design, participatory budgeting can become a mere tokenistic exercise, or worse, an avenue for reinforcing existing power structures. The process must be structured to ensure that it is not dominated by a vocal minority and that the diverse tapestry of the community is truly represented in the decision-making.

Moreover, the process can be time-consuming and resource-intensive. It requires a substantial investment in public education and engagement to prevent disillusionment and fatigue. Nonetheless, the outcomes—increased civic engagement, improved public services, and a strengthened social contract —suggest that the investment is a worthwhile one.

In the tapestry of governance, participatory budgeting is emerging as an essential thread, binding the state to its citizens through the shared enterprise of budgetary decision-making. It encourages transparency, fosters trust, and empowers communities. As we continue to weave the fabric of democratic governance, the lessons learned from participatory budgeting experiments will guide us in crafting a pattern that is both beautiful and robust, reflective of the diverse voices that give it form and strength.


<u>6.7 Direct Democracy Mechanisms</u>

*- Referendums and initiatives: empowering direct voter input*

In the heart of participatory governance lies the concept of direct democracy, a system that extends beyond the mere act of voting for representatives—it allows the citizenry to become active legislators in their own right. This section delves into two pivotal mechanisms of direct democracy: referendums and initiatives, both of which empower citizens to have a tangible impact on policy-making.

Referendums are the instruments through which the electorate is invited to vote directly on particular issues or laws. These can be binding, where the outcome is enacted into law, or advisory, serving to guide legislators on the public's sentiment. The power of referendums is evident in their ability to bypass traditional political gatekeepers, placing decision-making power into the hands of the people. Referendums can be called forth by government bodies seeking public endorsement for policies (top-down), or, in some systems, they can be triggered by citizens themselves through a petition process (bottom-up), exemplifying the essence of grassroots activism.

Initiatives, on the other hand, are the purest form of citizen law-making. They allow a defined number of voters to propose legislation or amendments to the constitution, which are then submitted to a public vote. This tool enables citizens to shape the legal framework of their society directly, fostering a sense of ownership and responsibility over communal norms and standards.

However, the implementation of these mechanisms is an art as much as it is a science. It demands careful consideration to ensure that the will of the majority does not infringe upon the rights of minorities. The question of how to balance majority rule with minority rights is a recurring theme in the discourse on direct democracy.

Moreover, the practical challenges of crafting clear, concise, and unbiased referendum and initiative questions cannot be overstated. Language must be accessible yet precise, and the implications of each choice clearly articulated, to avoid confusion and misinterpretation among voters.

Education plays a critical role in the success of direct democracy. It is incumbent upon governance to provide citizens with the tools and information necessary to make informed decisions. This may involve civic education campaigns, public debates, and providing balanced informational materials about the issues at stake.

In the age of digital democracy, technology has the potential to streamline these processes further, making it easier for citizens to participate in referendums and initiatives. Digital platforms can facilitate the collection of signatures, dissemination of information, and even the voting process itself. However, such advancements must be navigated with caution to maintain the integrity of the vote and protect against manipulation or fraud.

Referendums and initiatives are potent mechanisms that enrich democratic governance by embedding the populace's voice into the legislative process. When implemented with diligence and foresight, they can strengthen the bonds between government and governed, fostering a more engaged and responsive political culture. They epitomize the spirit of a harmonious world, where each individual's voice contributes to the symphony of the whole.


*- Balancing direct democracy with representative governance*

In the tapestry of governance, the warp and weft of representative and direct democracy intertwine to create a resilient and responsive fabric. This section explores the delicate balance between the two, advocating for a participatory system that enhances the efficacy of governance while preserving the voice of the people.

The concept of direct democracy harkens back to the Athenian agora, where citizens would gather to make decisions about public policy. In today's digital age, we have the technology to facilitate such assemblies on a global scale, yet the question remains: how can we harness these tools to empower individuals without undermining the stability provided by representative institutions?

To answer this, we must first recognize the limitations of unbridled direct democracy. It can lead to decision-making that is reactive rather than reflective, swayed by the passions of the moment rather than the considerations of long-term impact. The complexity of modern governance also demands a level of expertise and continuity that transient public opinion might not always support.

Nevertheless, the benefits of incorporating direct democracy mechanisms are manifold. They serve to increase civic engagement, foster a sense of ownership in political processes, and can act as a corrective to representative bodies that may become detached from the electorate's will.

In the symphony of governance, direct democracy could be likened to the dramatic crescendos that energize the piece, while representative democracy provides the steady rhythm that holds the composition together. Innovations like participatory budgeting, referendums, and citizen assemblies can be the crescendos—the moments when the people's voice resounds clearly and decisively.

For example, participatory budgeting allows citizens to directly influence how a portion of public funds are spent, offering a tangible connection between civic participation and tangible outcomes. Referendums, while powerful, must be approached with caution, ensuring they are used to complement rather than circumvent the legislative process.

The key to harmonizing direct and representative democracy lies in creating structured opportunities for public participation that are both meaningful and manageable. Citizen assemblies, selected through sortition or stratified random sampling, can provide a microcosm of the electorate, gathering diverse perspectives to deliberate on complex issues. Their recommendations can then inform the decision-making of elected officials, ensuring policies are grounded in the lived experiences and insights of the populace.

Ultimately, the balance between direct and representative governance should not be static but dynamic—a living system that evolves with society's needs. It requires continuous calibration, a willingness to experiment, and an unwavering commitment to the principles of democracy. In such a balanced system, governance becomes not only a function of the state but a collective work of art, painted in the many hues of humanity's diverse voices.


6.8 Community Activism and Governance

- *Grassroots movements shaping public policy*

In the shadow of grand legislative halls and stately government buildings, there lies a potent force, often underestimated in its capacity to influence and reshape the landscape of governance. This force is community activism, a vibrant expression of participatory governance that breathes life into the democratic process from the ground up.

In the bustling neighborhoods, rural towns, and city streets, individuals come together, united by common causes and shared concerns. They are the unsung architects of change, the voices that call out for justice, equity, and representation. Their tools are not decrees or mandates, but dialogue, advocacy, and collective action. Through their efforts, grassroots movements have the power to capture the attention of policymakers and etch their agendas onto the public consciousness.

Consider the story of a small community grappling with the threat of environmental degradation. A local factory has been polluting the nearby river for years, and the consequences are dire. Fish populations are dwindling, and the water quality has deteriorated, affecting the health and livelihoods of the residents. Frustrated by governmental inaction, a group of concerned citizens band together, forming an environmental action committee.

Their journey begins with local meet-ups, where they share information, discuss strategies, and empower one another. They organize clean-up drives, bringing visibility to the issue while simultaneously taking tangible action. They reach out to local media, sparking interest and gaining coverage that turns a regional concern into a topic of national debate.

Through persistent lobbying and the power of social media, their message reaches the ears of decision-makers. They collect signatures, draft proposals, and attend council meetings. Their voices, once drowned out by the din of political machinery, now echo in the chambers where policies are made.

The result is a triumph not only for the environment but for democracy itself. The local government adopts new regulations to curb pollution, invests in sustainable waste management solutions, and begins regular inspections of industrial facilities. The community's activism has led to a tangible policy change, setting a precedent for other groups facing similar struggles.

This narrative is not unique. Across the globe, grassroots movements are influencing public policy by advocating for change in areas such as education reform, civil rights, and public health. They demonstrate that governance is not solely the domain of elected officials and bureaucrats; it is the right and responsibility of every citizen.

Community activism underscores the principle that governance should be an inclusive process, reflective of the society it serves. It is a testament to the power of collective action and the importance of amplifying the people's voice. In this age of participatory governance, there is a growing recognition that those who govern must not only listen but actively engage with the communities they represent.

The spirit of community activism challenges the status quo, proving that when citizens are engaged and empowered, governance can be transformed. It is a vital component of a harmonious world, where the chorus of diverse voices shapes the symphony of public policy.



*- The interplay between activism and institutional change*

In the bustling heart of a city, where the cacophony of daily life blends with the cries for change, lies the crucible of modern participatory governance: community activism. Let's delve into the vibrant interplay between grassroots movements and the evolution of institutional frameworks.

The most resonant of voices often emerge from the very pavements that bear the weight of a society's collective stride. It is here, on the street corners and in the public squares, that citizens gather, their hands clasped around banners and their breaths forging chants that pierce through the veil of bureaucratic inertia. This is the theater where the narrative of community activism unfolds, weaving a tale of empowerment and institutional metamorphosis.

Activism, in its most transformative expression, does not stand merely as a shout against the prevailing winds of governance but as a dialogue—a call and response with the structures that dictate the rhythm of public life. It is a dynamic force that demands attention, not only to the issues at hand but also to the mechanisms of governance that either facilitate or suppress the realization of the community's aspirations.

Through the lens of case studies and historical examples, we see how activism has carved pathways for change. The civil rights movement of the 1960s, the environmental protests of the 1970s, and the more recent digital advocacy campaigns that sweep across social media platforms—all are threads in the tapestry of participatory governance. They highlight how activism's most profound impact often lies in its ability to foster institutional change, prompting the adaptation of laws, the redirection of policies, and the reformation of governance structures to reflect the evolving will of the people.

Yet, the relationship between activism and governance is nuanced, a delicate dance of push and pull. While activism seeks to inject urgency and moral clarity into the public discourse, governance must balance these inputs with the practicalities and complexities of policy-making. The artful governance recognizes the vitality that activism brings to the democratic process, channeling its energy into sustainable and inclusive reforms.

Here, we explore various models of how this synergy can be harnessed. Participatory budgeting initiatives, citizen advisory boards, and co-governance arrangements all represent the fruits of activism's labor—concrete embodiments of a community's voice within the edifice of governance. The narrative weaves through stories of communities that have succeeded in translating protest into policy, demonstrating the potential for a new paradigm of governance that is not only responsive but also anticipatory of the needs and desires of its citizens.

We are reminded that the heartbeat of participatory governance is the persistent pulse of the people's voice. It is a testament to the power of collective action and the capacity of governance structures to evolve, ensuring that the harmonious world we envision is not a static utopia but a living, breathing organism shaped by the very individuals it serves.

## 6.9 Education for Civic Engagement

*- Educational programs fostering participatory skills*

In the fabric of a thriving democracy, the thread that often goes unseen, yet holds the pattern together, is civic education. It is here, in the classrooms and educational forums of our societies, that the seeds of participatory governance are sown. To create a citizenry not only capable but also enthusiastic about engaging in the democratic process, educational programs must evolve to foster participatory skills from a young age.

Imagine a curriculum that begins in the earliest years with the basics of empathy and cooperation. These foundational lessons are the bedrock of civic engagement, teaching children that their voices matter, and that they have a responsibility to listen to and understand the voices of others. As students grow, the curriculum expands to include critical thinking and dialogue skills, empowering them to navigate the complexities of differing viewpoints and the nuances of societal issues.

In middle and high school, the focus shifts to the mechanics of governance and the role of citizens within it. Programs like mock parliaments, student government, and debate clubs become essential, allowing youth to experience firsthand the intricacies of policy-making and the art of compromise. Through these simulated environments, students gain a profound understanding of the democratic process and the importance of active participation.

Universities and adult education programs continue this trajectory, offering courses on public policy, ethics, and leadership that are intertwined with practical experiences. Internships with government agencies, non-profits, and community organizations serve as the bridge between theory and the real world. This hands-on approach demystifies the workings of governance and cements the individual's role in the collective journey of civic life.

Yet, the most innovative educational programs go beyond traditional structures. They harness the power of technology to create virtual town halls, online platforms for policy discussion, and simulations of global diplomacy. Through these digital realms, students from diverse backgrounds engage with each other and with the world, breaking down barriers of distance and socio-economic status.

To be effective, these educational initiatives must be inclusive, ensuring that every individual, regardless of background, has access to the tools of civic engagement. This means not only equal opportunity but also tailored approaches that address the unique needs and perspectives of different communities.

Education for civic engagement is not a one-size-fits-all solution, but a tapestry of programs that must be as diverse and adaptable as the people they aim to serve. It is through this multifaceted educational approach that a culture of participation is cultivated—a culture where the people's voice is not only heard but resonates through the very halls of governance, shaping the world with the harmonious chorus of an engaged and informed citizenry.


*- The role of schools and universities in promoting civic involvement*

In the heart of a thriving democracy lies an informed and active citizenry. The bedrock of such an informed citizenry is education—an education that does not merely impart knowledge but fosters a deep sense of civic responsibility and engagement. In this section, we explore the crucial role that educational institutions play in shaping the citizens who will carry the torch of participatory governance into the future.

Schools and universities are not just centers for learning; they are the crucibles where the values of democracy are communicated, debated, and internalized. It is within these hallowed halls that young minds first encounter the grand narratives of their nation's history, the complexities of political theory, and the passionate dialogues that drive social change. However, to truly cultivate a culture of participation, these institutions must move beyond textbooks and lectures.

The first step is to integrate civic education into the curriculum from the earliest years. This education must be comprehensive, encompassing not only the structure of government and the rights of citizens but also the importance of community involvement and the skills necessary for effective advocacy. Interactive learning, such as debates, mock elections, and student councils, can bring these concepts to life. By engaging students in the democratic process on a microcosmic level, we can instill in them the confidence and understanding they need to participate in governance on a broader scale.

Universities, in particular, have a unique opportunity to advance civic engagement. They can serve as incubators for political thought and activism, encouraging students to apply their academic learning to real-world challenges. Service-learning programs, which combine volunteer work with classroom instruction, can bridge the gap between theory and practice, teaching students that their knowledge has the power to effect tangible change.

Beyond structured academic programs, educational institutions must also foster an environment where free speech and diverse perspectives are not just tolerated but celebrated. Encouraging open dialogue on controversial issues, supporting student-led initiatives, and facilitating connections with local government and community organizations can create a vibrant ecosystem where participatory governance thrives.

In this digital age, the role of education in civic engagement must also evolve. Digital literacy should be woven into the fabric of civic education, equipping students with the tools to navigate the complexities of online information and engage in digital democracy. Through blogs, social media, and online forums, young people can amplify their voices and join the global conversation on governance.

Ultimately, the goal of education for civic engagement is to create lifelong participants in the democratic process. By instilling in students an enduring commitment to the common good and the skills to contribute meaningfully to society, educational institutions can ensure that the flame of participatory governance burns bright for generations to come. It is through this commitment to education that we can build a harmonious world, one in which every citizen is both a learner and a leader in the endless pursuit of a more perfect democracy.


## 6.10 Overcoming Barriers to Participation

*- Identifying and addressing obstacles to citizen engagement*

In the quest to revitalize participatory governance, we must confront the barriers that prevent citizens from engaging fully in the democratic process. These barriers are varied and complex, rooted in historical, social, economic, and technological factors that can discourage or obstruct meaningful participation.

One of the most significant hurdles is the sense of disenfranchisement felt by marginalized groups. For too long, the voices of certain communities have been silenced or ignored, leading to a deep-seated mistrust in government institutions. To overcome this, we need to build inclusive platforms where every voice is not only heard but valued and acted upon. This means reaching out to underrepresented populations through community organizations, social networks, and local leaders who can bridge the gap between government and the people.

Another challenge is the lack of accessible information. Citizens can hardly be expected to engage with issues they don't understand or even know about. Therefore, it is imperative to invest in public education campaigns and provide clear, concise information about how governance works and why individual participation matters. Simplifying legal jargon, offering materials in multiple languages, and utilizing various media channels can demystify the process and empower citizens to take part.

Time and resources also pose significant barriers. Many individuals are consumed by the demands of daily life, with little left for civic engagement. Recognizing this, governments can create more flexible opportunities for participation, such as online forums, mobile voting, and after-hours community meetings. Additionally, providing resources like childcare during town halls or transportation to polling stations can remove practical obstacles that prevent people from engaging.

Moreover, the rise of digital democracy presents both an opportunity and a challenge. While technology can facilitate broader participation, there's a risk of excluding those without access to digital resources or the skills to use them. Bridging the digital divide is essential, requiring investments in internet infrastructure and digital literacy programs. It is also crucial to maintain traditional methods of participation to ensure no one is left behind as we transition to more tech-savvy approaches.

In addressing these barriers, we must be mindful not to create new ones inadvertently. Every solution must be scrutinized for potential biases and unintended consequences. For instance, while online platforms can increase accessibility, they may also expose users to data privacy concerns and misinformation. To mitigate these risks, robust cybersecurity measures and digital education are needed to create safe and reliable spaces for public discourse.

Overcoming barriers to participation is a multi-faceted endeavor that demands a thoughtful and persistent approach. By identifying and addressing the obstacles to citizen engagement, we can move closer to a model of governance that truly embodies the people's voice. It is through this collective effort that we can transform the ideal of participatory governance into a vibrant and enduring reality.


*- Case studies on reinvigorating participation in diverse communities*

As we navigate the complexities of participatory governance, we must acknowledge and address the barriers that impede the full engagement of all members of society. Different communities face unique challenges that require innovative and tailored approaches.

In the small coastal town of Mariposa, the local government initiated a project called the "Listening Booths." These booths were placed in various neighborhoods, equipped with recording devices where residents could voice their concerns and suggestions at any time. The anonymity of the booths encouraged participation from those who were traditionally reticent to speak in public forums, such as introverts or those fearing retribution. The recordings were then transcribed and presented at town hall meetings, ensuring that every voice was heard.

The city of Technopolis, known for its tech-savvy population, developed an app called "CivicEngage" to overcome barriers to participation. The app was designed to be accessible, with user-friendly interfaces in multiple languages, and featured voice-command functions for those with disabilities. CivicEngage allowed residents to vote on local issues, propose initiatives, and engage in community discussions. It became a vital tool for the disabled and working parents who found it difficult to attend in-person meetings.

Meanwhile, in the culturally rich but economically challenged neighborhood of Kaleidoscope, the barrier was not just technological but also cultural and linguistic. The local governance body formed a Cultural Ambassadors Group, comprising members from the diverse communities within Kaleidoscope. These ambassadors served as bridges between the government and their respective communities, facilitating understanding and encouraging participation in governance processes. They organized community gatherings where government representatives would listen to local concerns, and cultural nuances were respected and integrated into policy-making.

In each of these case studies, we observe the power of tailored, community-specific solutions in overcoming barriers to participation. In Mariposa, the anonymity of the Listening Booths was key. In Technopolis, leveraging technology was the answer. And in Kaleidoscope, the human touch of Cultural Ambassadors proved indispensable. These case studies serve as a blueprint for revitalizing participatory governance in diverse communities, highlighting the importance of creativity, inclusivity, and respect for the unique qualities that each community brings to the collective table.

By addressing and dismantling these barriers, we witness the reinvigoration of participation, the strengthening of democracy, and the formation of governance that is truly by the people, for the people. Through such endeavors, we craft a world where the whispers of the shy, the ideas of the busy, and the wisdom of the marginalized are amplified into a chorus that shapes our shared destiny.

# 7. The Art of Peace



## 7.1 The Roots of Discord

*- Understanding Historical Grievances*

In the dappled shade of history, the roots of discord run deep, gnarling through the soil of human experience with an almost insidious persistence. To comprehend the nature of contemporary conflict, one must first embark on an archaeological dig through the strata of past grievances, unearthing the relics of bygone eras that have fortified the ramparts of resentment and mistrust.

Let this serve as our time machine, transporting us to the battlefields of memory where the specters of injustice still haunt the present. Like the exhumation of a long-buried city, we delve into the sedimentary layers of human conflict, revealing how historical wounds have been passed down through generations like a bitter inheritance.

We begin by tracing the contours of ancient animosities, where empires clashed and cultures were subjugated. The conquests and defeats of these times did not simply fade with the turning of pages in history books; they transmuted into narratives of identity, fueling the engines of nationalism and sectarianism. The scars they left have become part of the collective psyche, etched into the very DNA of nations.

Moving forward to the colonial era, we encounter the arbitrary lines drawn by distant rulers, carving up continents into spheres of influence with little regard for the intricate tapestry of tribal and ethnic connections. These cartographic incisions would fester, erupting into conflicts whose ferocity was magnified by the pent-up pressures of imposed borders and the legacy of exploitation.

In the more recent past, ideological rifts born out of the Cold War have further complicated the landscape of conflict. Proxy wars and the strategic interests of superpowers have intertwined with local grievances, creating a labyrinthine web of alliances and enmities that defy simple resolution.

Yet, understanding these historical grievances is not an exercise in futility or a descent into despair. Rather, it is a foundational step in the art of peace. For it is only by acknowledging the full breadth and depth of these grievances that we can begin to address them. We must recognize the humanity in the histories of all parties, validating the pain while seeking pathways to reconciliation.

As we peel back the layers, we expose the raw nerve of historical trauma, and it is here that the potential for healing begins. By unraveling the tangled threads of the past, we can start to weave a new narrative, one that prioritizes dialogue over division and empathy over enmity. This is where the transformation from discord to harmony starts, in the fertile ground of understanding, where the seeds of peace may one day flourish.

*- Recognizing Cultural and Ideological Differences*

At the heart of many conflicts lie the twin specters of cultural and ideological differences. In a world that is both metaphorically shrinking due to technology and expanding through the recognition of a multitude of identities, these specters haunt the halls of governance with increasing regularity. Understanding the roots of discord is akin to a gardener understanding the soil before planting – it is the essential first step to nurturing peace.

Cultures are the intricate tapestries of societies, woven from the threads of history, language, traditions, and beliefs. Each culture possesses its unique patterns, and like any artwork, the beauty lies in its detail and complexity. However, when cultures intersect, the differences in these patterns can lead to friction. Governance systems, therefore, must become the curators of this global gallery, appreciating each piece's value while ensuring the exhibition coexists harmoniously.

Ideologies, on the other hand, are the prisms through which individuals and groups view the world. They shape perceptions of right and wrong, just and unjust, and their roots often delve deep into the bedrock of culture. Ideological differences are particularly thorny issues in governance, for they are not merely intellectual disagreements but often emotional and existential ones. A governance system that strives for inclusivity must not only acknowledge these differences but actively engage with them through dialogue and empathy.

The recognition of cultural and ideological differences requires a governance that is both observant and sensitive. This governance must foster environments where such differences can be expressed safely and constructively. It must also be vigilant against the forces of homogenization that threaten to erase the uniqueness of minority cultures or ideologies under the guise of unity.

In this section, we will explore how these differences become roots of discord, and how they are often exacerbated by competition for resources, historical grievances, and a lack of effective communication channels. We will also examine the role of education in cultivating understanding and the importance of creating spaces for cultural and ideological expression.

The art of peace, therefore, begins by recognizing that discord's roots are not in the differences themselves, but in how they are perceived and managed. It is the duty of inclusive governance to transform these roots from sources of division into foundations of strength—nurturing a garden of diverse flora that stands as a testament to the resilience and beauty of humanity's many faces.


## 7.2 The Psychology of Conflict

*- Cognitive Biases and Conflict Perpetuation*

In the labyrinth of human psychology, cognitive biases act like unseen puppeteers, influencing our perceptions and decisions, often without our conscious awareness. These biases can be particularly insidious in the context of conflict, where they can distort reality and perpetuate hostilities, sometimes across generations. Here we'll examine how understanding and mitigating cognitive biases is crucial for effective conflict resolution.

One of the most pervasive cognitive biases in conflict situations is the fundamental attribution error. This is the tendency to attribute others' actions to their character or disposition while attributing our own actions to external circumstances. In the realm of conflict, this means that we may view an adversary's aggressive actions as a reflection of their inherently hostile nature, while excusing our own similar actions as responses to provocation or necessity.

The impact of this bias is profound. It feeds a narrative of 'us versus them,' painting the other side as innately unreasonable or malevolent, and ourselves as righteous victims. The danger here lies in the simplicity of the narrative—it forgoes the complex web of motivations and circumstances that underlie most conflicts, making it difficult to empathize with the opposing side and find common ground.

Confirmation bias is another mental snare that can deepen the fissures of discord. It is our tendency to seek, interpret, and remember information that confirms our pre-existing beliefs. In a dispute, this means we are more likely to absorb evidence that supports our perspective and ignore or discredit evidence that contradicts it. This selective perception entrenches our stance and makes us impervious to alternative viewpoints, thus calcifying the conflict.

To break free from the grip of these biases, several strategies can be employed. One such approach is the practice of active listening, which requires us to attentively hear out the other party's perspective without immediately reacting or judging. This simple, yet powerful technique can reveal the shared human emotions and needs beneath the surface of the conflict, fostering empathy and understanding.

Another approach is the cultivation of intellectual humility, recognizing that our knowledge and understanding of the situation is inherently limited and that we may hold incorrect or incomplete assumptions. This attitude opens us up to new information and perspectives, which is essential for finding solutions that are acceptable to all parties involved.

Furthermore, conflict resolution mechanisms can integrate structured reflection periods, allowing parties to step back and examine their own thoughts and motivations. This pause provides an opportunity to identify cognitive biases and challenge them, leading to more objective and productive negotiations.

Incorporating these psychological insights into governance structures and peacebuilding initiatives can be transformative. It equips us with the tools to not only resolve existing conflicts but also to preempt potential future ones by fostering a culture of introspection, empathy, and open-minded dialogue. As we peel away the layers of cognitive biases, we inch closer to the harmonious worlds we aspire to create, where the art of peace is practiced with the finesse and precision it truly deserves.


*- Emotional Intelligence in Negotiations*

At the heart of every conflict lie the raw, often untamed emotions of the individuals involved. These emotions, if not understood or managed, can escalate disputes into enduring battles that leave deep scars on the collective psyche of societies. In this section, we delve into the subtle art of employing emotional intelligence within the sphere of conflict resolution, particularly in the context of negotiations.

Emotional intelligence, the ability to perceive, understand, and manage emotions, is a cornerstone of effective negotiation. It acts as a bridge between divergent perspectives, facilitating a dialogue that can withstand the tremors of discord. When we speak of negotiations, we typically envision a battle of wits and logic, yet it is the undercurrent of emotions that often determines the outcome.

To harness emotional intelligence, negotiators must first become adept at self-awareness. This means recognizing their own emotional triggers and understanding how these can affect their judgment. By achieving a heightened state of self-awareness, a negotiator can remain composed, even when the discussion veers into turbulent waters. Furthermore, self-regulation becomes a powerful tool; it allows negotiators to refrain from impulsive reactions that could jeopardize the process.

The second aspect of emotional intelligence is empathy, the ability to perceive the emotions of others. In the theater of conflict resolution, empathy is the lens through which we can view the world from another's vantage point. It is not simply about being kind or compassionate; empathy is a strategic element that provides crucial insight into the motivations and fears driving the opposing party. When a negotiator demonstrates genuine understanding, it can dissolve barriers and shift the negotiation landscape from antagonism towards cooperation.

Furthermore, adept negotiators use emotional intelligence to foster social skills that are conducive to building rapport. They are able to communicate effectively, listen actively, and send signals that encourage openness and trust. In doing so, they create an environment where all parties feel heard and valued, which is essential for collaborative problem-solving.

Motivation, another facet of emotional intelligence, plays a significant role in sustaining the momentum of negotiations. It involves the ability to keep sight of the larger goals beyond the immediate emotional entanglements. Negotiators with high emotional intelligence are driven by a purpose that transcends personal victory; they seek resolutions that benefit all parties, creating a sense of shared success.

In the realm of governance, where conflicts can range from local disputes to international standoffs, the application of emotional intelligence in negotiations is not merely beneficial—it is imperative. As leaders and policymakers engage with the complexities of an interconnected world, it is this emotional acumen that can steer them away from the precipice of conflict towards the fertile grounds of peace.

The harmonious worlds we envision can only be achieved through such understanding and management of the emotional landscapes that define human interaction. In the next sections, we will explore practical frameworks and case studies that illustrate the transformative power of emotional intelligence in resolving conflicts and building a unified, yet diverse, global community.

<u>7.3 The Landscape of Modern Warfare</u>

*- Cyber Conflicts and Their Global Impact*

In the digital age, the theater of war has expanded beyond the physical world into the vast expanse of cyberspace. In this section, we shall traverse the labyrinthine pathways of modern warfare, where battles are fought not with bullets and bombs, but with bits and bytes.

Cyber conflicts present a new paradigm of warfare that is silent yet potentially devastating. Unlike traditional warfare, the casualties of a cyber attack are often invisible at first glance, manifesting as disrupted services, stolen data, and compromised infrastructures. The global impact of such conflicts is profound, as they can affect economies, destabilize governments, and erode the trust between nations within the intricate web of international relations.

The art of peace in this new landscape requires a nuanced approach, with strategies that encompass diplomacy, technological prowess, and ethical considerations. To mitigate the risks of cyber warfare, nations must engage in collaborative efforts to establish international norms and agreements that define and limit the use of cyber weapons. The Geneva Convention of the digital age, if you will, must set boundaries to protect civilians and critical infrastructure from the silent strikes of cyber combatants.

Moreover, an inclusive governance approach to cybersecurity is imperative. It should encourage the participation of multiple stakeholders, including governments, private sector entities, and civil society organizations, to foster a shared responsibility for the cyber commons. The cultivation of a resilient cyber ecosystem, equipped with robust defense mechanisms and rapid response capabilities, is essential to withstand and quickly recover from cyber attacks.

At the heart of this effort lies the need to develop a culture of cyber peace that prioritizes cooperation over confrontation. Education plays a pivotal role here, as it empowers citizens to understand the complexities of cyber threats and the importance of cyber hygiene. It also lays the foundation for the next generation of peacebuilders, who will navigate the cyber terrain with a mindset geared towards constructive, rather than destructive, engagement.

The global impact of cyber conflicts challenges us to reconsider the very notion of warfare. As we move forward, our strategies for resolving such conflicts must evolve to address the ethical implications of digital weapons and the invisible scars they leave on societies. By fostering an environment of trust, transparency, and international cooperation, we can transform the landscape of modern warfare into a domain where peace is the principal victor, and the harmonious world we aspire to becomes an attainable reality.

*- The Rise of Non-State Actors*

In the foggy terrain of modern conflict, the traditional image of armies clashing on battlefields has become an anachronism. Today's warfare often involves a diverse array of non-state actors that operate within and across national borders, challenging the very notion of a state's monopoly on legitimate violence. These actors range from insurgent groups, private military corporations, terrorist organizations, to cyber collectives—all wielding significant influence on the geopolitical chessboard.

The rise of non-state actors has fundamentally altered the art of conflict resolution. In the tapestry of contemporary strife, these groups often hold objectives that are deeply rooted in ideology, religion, or ethnicity, rather than the political ambitions of nation-states. Their motivations are as complex as the societies from which they emerge, and thus, the strategies to engage with them must be equally nuanced.

For governments and international coalitions seeking peaceful resolutions, understanding the intricate web of these actors' relationships is crucial. A non-state actor's influence often transcends borders, drawing support through transnational networks and exploiting the interconnectedness of the global community. As a result, a conflict that appears local may have tentacles reaching far beyond its immediate environment, complicating the peacemaking process.

In this new landscape of warfare, diplomacy extends beyond the negotiation table of state representatives. It requires a multifaceted approach that engages with the diverse stakeholders involved in a conflict. This includes establishing back-channel communications with non-state actors, leveraging the influence of transnational advocacy networks, and fostering local community initiatives that can address the root causes of insurgence.

Furthermore, the digital age has equipped non-state actors with powerful tools for propaganda and recruitment, expanding their reach dramatically. Cyber collectives can disrupt national infrastructure without a physical presence, while social media allows for the rapid spread of ideological narratives. This requires conflict resolution strategies to be agile and responsive, countering not just physical threats but also combating the war of ideas in the digital realm.

At the core of this approach must be a commitment to understanding the grievances and aspirations that fuel these actors. Traditional conflict resolution methods often fall short as they are predicated on state-centric models of power and interest negotiation. To navigate the modern maze of non-state warfare, peacemakers must adopt a more holistic perspective, one that sees the human stories behind the unrest and seeks to weave a social fabric that can accommodate the disparate threads of human experience.

## 7.4 Principles of Peaceful Negotiation

*- Frameworks for Constructive Dialogue*

In the tapestry of governance, the threads of conflict resolution are among the most delicate yet vital to the strength and beauty of the whole. The art of peaceful negotiation hinges upon a symphony of principles that, when conducted with skill and empathy, can transform discord into harmony. Let's explore the frameworks for constructive dialogue that can guide fractured communities and nations toward a concordant future.

The first principle is the recognition of shared humanity. Before sitting at the negotiation table, participants must commit to seeing one another not as adversaries, but as partners in the quest for a mutually beneficial resolution. This requires a willingness to listen, to understand different perspectives, and to respect the intrinsic value of each voice in the conversation. By affirming the dignity of all parties, the stage is set for open, honest exchange.

Next is the pursuit of common ground. Conflict often arises from a belief that interests are diametrically opposed, yet this perspective overlooks the potential for commonality. Effective negotiators delve deeply to identify shared goals, values, or needs that can serve as a foundation for agreement. Whether it's the mutual desire for stability, prosperity, or simply the avoidance of further strife, these shared elements become the bedrock upon which agreements are built.

The third principle is the embrace of transparency. Peaceful negotiation is undermined by hidden agendas or deceit. It is essential for all parties to articulate their intentions, constraints, and concerns openly. This transparency fosters trust and demonstrates a commitment to finding solutions rather than exploiting vulnerabilities. It also ensures that any agreement reached is based on a clear and shared understanding, which is critical for lasting resolution.

Another core principle is the cultivation of empathy. To negotiate peace, one must be willing to step into the shoes of another, to feel the weight of their concerns and the urgency of their needs. This empathic bridge does not mean abandoning one's own position but rather enriching it with a broader perspective that encompasses the collective well-being. Empathy can turn the tide of negotiation, transforming it from a zero-sum game to a collaborative effort for the greater good.

The principle of creativity is indispensable. Traditional approaches to conflict resolution often fail because they are rooted in the very mindset that led to discord. Peaceful negotiation requires innovative thinking, a willingness to explore uncharted territories of compromise and solution. This creativity may manifest in unconventional agreements, novel governance structures, or the integration of diverse cultural practices into the resolution process.

These principles are not mere abstractions; they are the lifeblood of peaceful negotiation. In the intricate dance of dialogue, they guide us toward resolutions that are not only satisfactory but also sustainable and just. As we weave the future of governance, it is through frameworks such as these that we can construct a world where conflict gives way to concord, and diversity is the melody of humanity's most profound symphony.


*- Strategies for Mutual Gain*

In the quest for a harmonious world, the art of peaceful negotiation is akin to a delicate dance. It requires an understanding of rhythm, an appreciation of different styles, and a willingness to move together toward mutual gain. The principles of peaceful negotiation are not merely strategies but an ethos for a fractured world yearning for unity amidst diversity.

The first principle lies in the art of listening. True negotiation begins with the recognition that every voice has value. It is through active, empathetic listening that a shared understanding emerges—a common ground from which growth can sprout. To listen is to acknowledge the humanity of the other, to give space for their concerns, fears, and aspirations to surface.

Once the stage of mutual understanding is established, the second principle comes into play: the search for common interests. While positions might differ, the underlying interests often reveal areas of potential agreement. A community divided by the allocation of resources might discover that at the heart of their discord is a mutual desire for prosperity and well-being. In identifying these shared interests, the soil is prepared for seeds of agreement to be sown.

The third principle of peaceful negotiation calls for creativity in problem-solving. It is not enough to identify common interests; the challenge lies in crafting solutions that are innovative and inclusive. This requires stepping outside the bounds of traditional thinking, drawing from a diverse palette of cultural wisdom, and being willing to experiment with novel governance structures. The negotiators become artists, painting a new landscape of possibility.

The fourth principle is rooted in respect. To negotiate is to respect the other party's right to a different viewpoint and to honor the dignity of their position. This respect also extends to the process itself—acknowledging that negotiation is a journey rather than a battleground, a series of steps towards a more peaceful coexistence.

In practicing these principles, the fifth emerges almost naturally: building trust. Trust is the currency of negotiation, the invisible thread that weaves through every interaction. It is earned through consistency, transparency, and the honoring of commitments. With trust, even the most divided communities can begin to envision a shared future.

The final principle is that of sustainable agreements. The outcomes of negotiation must not only satisfy immediate interests but also endure the test of time. Agreements should be adaptable, allowing for the ebb and flow of change, and should be designed with the long-term health of the community in mind.

In the tapestry of governance, the fibers of peaceful negotiation are golden strands that strengthen the whole. As we weave these principles into the fabric of our societies, we create patterns of mutual gain, vibrant with the colors of cooperation and unity. It is through these strategies that governance can become a symphony of diverse voices, each contributing to a harmonious global society.


7.5 The Role of International Organizations

*United Nations Peacekeeping Operations*

Beneath the vast sky of international diplomacy, peacekeeping operations under the aegis of the United Nations represent an intricate ballet of negotiation, intervention, and reconciliation. This section delves into the pivotal role these operations play in the tapestry of conflict resolution within our fractured world.

At the heart of United Nations (UN) peacekeeping lies a philosophy of collective responsibility and international solidarity. It is a manifestation of the belief that peace is a communal asset and its guardianship requires the cooperation of nations. The blue helmets, as the peacekeepers are commonly known, serve as the physical embodiment of this ethos, their presence a testament to the commitment of member states to safeguard stability and foster a conducive atmosphere for peace.

UN peacekeeping operations are characterized by their multifaceted nature. They do not simply stand as neutral forces separating warring factions; they are the architects of environments where sustainable peace can be constructed. These operations work in concert with diplomatic efforts, helping to implement peace agreements, disarming combatants, supporting the return of refugees, and ensuring the delivery of humanitarian aid.

Through their work, UN peacekeepers often address the underlying causes of conflict. They provide a buffer that allows for the cooling of tensions, the rebuilding of trust, and the initiation of dialogue. However, the efficacy of these operations is contingent upon a nuanced understanding of the cultural, historical, and political landscapes they are deployed in. This involves a delicate balance between non-interference in the internal affairs of a sovereign state and the need to take action to prevent atrocities and protect civilians.

One of the most compelling examples of the impact of UN peacekeeping operations can be found in the transformation of conflict zones into arenas for democratic governance. In places where the rule of law has been eroded by conflict, peacekeepers have been instrumental in re-establishing legal frameworks and supporting the conduct of free and fair elections.

However, the road to peace is fraught with challenges. Peacekeeping operations often face criticism for their limitations and failures. The complexities of modern conflicts, with their non-state actors and transnational threats, demand adaptive strategies and robust mandates. Moreover, the success of these missions is heavily dependent on the political will of member states, the availability of resources, and the cooperation of host nations.

In our pursuit of harmonious worlds, we must recognize the contributions of UN peacekeeping operations while also acknowledging their imperfections. They are an essential tool in the international community's conflict resolution arsenal, yet they are but one piece of a larger puzzle. The quest for peace requires a comprehensive approach that combines peacekeeping with peacemaking and peacebuilding efforts, emphasizing the importance of prevention and addressing root causes of conflict.

The role of international organizations in peacekeeping is not only about managing the cessation of hostilities but also about weaving the fabric of a society where former adversaries can envision a shared future. It is an art form that demands patience, perseverance, and the collective endeavor of the global community, working harmoniously to turn the page from war to peace.

*- International Courts and Conflict Resolution*

In the labyrinthine corridors of international diplomacy, where the echo of unresolved conflicts often resounds, international organizations emerge as the architects of harmony—diligently crafting the scaffolding upon which peace can be restored. Their existence is a testament to our collective yearning for a world where justice serves as the cornerstone of societal edifices, regardless of the complexity of the conflict at hand.

The role of international courts in conflict resolution is particularly pivotal. These esteemed institutions, like the International Court of Justice and the International Criminal Court, strive to adjudicate disputes with impartiality and authority, providing a legal framework that transcends national boundaries. They serve as the arbiters of international law, seeking not retribution but resolution and reconciliation.

It is within the solemn chambers of these courts that the scales of justice weigh the grievances of nations against the imperatives of peace. Here, the voices of the aggrieved and the accused alike can be heard, and the tapestry of human rights is delicately repaired, thread by thread. In these halls, the rule of law is not an abstract concept but a living entity, shaping the very fabric of international relations.

Yet, the efficacy of international courts is not only measured by the verdicts they pronounce but also by their ability to deter future transgressions. Their presence serves as a sentinel, guarding against the specter of unbridled conflict by promoting a culture of accountability. Where once might have dominated right, these institutions herald the triumph of just over the unjust, ensuring that even the most powerful are not above the law.

Moreover, the success of international courts in fostering conflict resolution lies in their capacity to adapt to the evolving landscape of global disputes. As the nature of conflict metamorphoses—spurred by technological innovation, geopolitical shifts, and the growing complexity of international law—these courts, too, must evolve. They must embrace the challenge of remaining relevant and accessible to those who seek their intervention, ensuring that justice is not an elusive mirage, but a tangible destination.

In the grand tapestry of international governance, the role of international organizations and their courts is not merely supportive but foundational. They provide a forum where sovereign states can engage in dialogue, where justice is dispensed with a gavel that resonates across continents, and where the art of peace is meticulously crafted with the quill of jurisprudence. It is within this framework that nations, communities, and individuals can hope to find the harmonious resolutions to their discord—a symphony of justice that plays the melody of a more peaceful world.


<u>7.6 Localized Approaches to Peace</u>

*- Community-Based Reconciliation Initiatives*

In the shadow of grand political gestures and international peace accords lies the subtle, yet powerful, domain of localized peace efforts. Community-based reconciliation initiatives offer a canvas for the practice of peace in its most organic form, embodying the principle that harmony begins at the grassroots level.

The art of peace is not a monolith but a mosaic, composed of small pieces meticulously placed together by the hands of those who know their landscapes best—the local communities. In this section, we explore the transformative power of initiatives that rise from the soil of conflict-affected areas, where the heartbeats of their inhabitants dictate the rhythm of reconciliation.

Consider the story of Karamoja, a region in northeastern Uganda, where a history of inter-tribal conflict over resources and cattle rustling had sown deep divisions. Here, a community-led peace process emerged, driven by the elders' council, which had maintained the social fabric for generations. They understood the cultural nuances and historical grievances that no external peacekeeper could fully grasp. Through a series of dialogues and traditional ceremonies, the elders facilitated the return of stolen cattle and the exchange of symbolic gifts, gradually restoring trust where it had been eroded by years of animosity.

These localized initiatives often employ restorative justice practices rather than punitive ones. The aim is to heal relationships and address the underlying causes of conflict rather than merely punishing transgressors. This approach is evident in Rwanda's Gacaca courts, a participatory justice system that was revived to deal with the aftermath of the genocide. By engaging local populations in the process of truth-telling and reconciliation, these courts helped to mend the torn social fabric of Rwandan society, one community at a time.

In Colombia, too, after decades of civil war, peace is being woven through local initiatives. The "peace villages" concept, where settlements declare themselves neutral zones amidst the conflict, showcases the power of local determination. These villages, though diverse in their composition and strategies, share a common goal: to create spaces of peace and sanctuary, immune from the surrounding turmoil.

Yet, the success of community-based reconciliation initiatives hinges on certain conditions. They require respect for local autonomy, sustained support from broader governance structures, and the integration of diverse voices, particularly those of women and youth. They also depend on the willingness to embrace innovative and culturally sensitive methods of conflict resolution.

In the tapestry of global governance, these localized approaches to peace are vital threads. They remind us that, while the narrative of conflict is often written on a broad canvas, the story of peace needs to be painted with a finer brush—one community at a time. As we seek to craft inclusive governance for a diverse humanity, let us not overlook the profound impact of community-based reconciliation initiatives. They are the living embodiment of the belief that peace is not merely the absence of war, but the presence of justice, dialogue, and mutual understanding at the most fundamental level of society.

*- Empowering Local Leaders for Sustainable Peace*

In the tangled web of global conflict, the role of local leaders often remains overshadowed by the grandeur of international diplomacy. Yet, it is in the hands of these community stewards where the most enduring and impactful narratives of peace are woven. This section delves into the heart of localized approaches to conflict resolution, spotlighting how empowering local leaders can pave the way for sustainable peace.

The criticality of local leadership in peacebuilding cannot be overstated. After all, these are the individuals who understand the unique cultural, social, and historical context of their communities. They speak the language of the people, both literally and metaphorically, and hold within them the trust and legitimacy that outsiders might take years to build—If ever.

One exemplary case is the story of a small town in the volatile region of Karamoja, Uganda. Despite being marred by decades of tribal conflict, a transformation unfolded when local leaders spearheaded peace initiatives. They engaged in dialogue with rival factions, fostering a shared vision for the future that transcended tribal lines. Their intimate knowledge of clan dynamics enabled them to mediate disputes and promote reconciliation in ways external forces could not replicate. The result was a significant reduction in violence and a newfound sense of unity within the region.

Such localized approaches are not without challenges. Local leaders may face threats to their safety, struggle with limited resources, and navigate complex political landscapes. However, the potential rewards justify the risks. When local leaders are empowered, they can leverage their influence to initiate grass-roots movements, inspire community-driven development, and instill a sense of ownership among the people. This is the bedrock upon which the edifice of lasting peace is constructed.

Empowerment of local leadership requires a multi-pronged strategy. First, it calls for capacity building—providing leaders with the skills and knowledge necessary to navigate the intricacies of conflict resolution. This may involve training in mediation, negotiation, or governance. Second, it necessitates establishing networks of support, connecting local leaders with regional and international peers, as well as experts who can provide guidance and assistance. Third, it demands ensuring the safety and protection of these leaders, for their vulnerability could spell the vulnerability of the entire peace process.

Finally, and most crucially, it involves listening. To truly empower local leaders, we must tune in to their voices, respect their insights, and incorporate their perspectives into broader peacebuilding efforts. They are the composers of the symphony of peace, and it is through their baton that the harmonious potential of a fractured world can be realized.

As we turn the page on conflict, it is the localized approaches that offer the most authentic and sustainable path to peace. By championing and empowering local leaders, we can create a tapestry of harmonious worlds, each thread contributing to the strength and beauty of the whole.


7.7 Non-Violent Activism

- *The Legacy of Civil Disobedience*

In the delicate dance of human interactions, where grievances and aspirations often tangle in a complex choreography, the legacy of civil disobedience has emerged as a poignant and powerful form of non-violent activism. This tradition, rooted in the moral conviction that unjust laws and policies must be challenged through peaceful resistance, has been a transformative force throughout history.

The practice of civil disobedience is not merely a refusal to comply with certain laws, it is an affirmation of a higher ethical calling. It is about harnessing the power of collective non-compliance to spotlight inequities and spark change. This artful form of protest, when orchestrated with discipline and careful strategy, resonates deeply within the chambers of public conscience.

Consider, for instance, the serene yet insistent figure of Mahatma Gandhi, whose Salt March galvanized a nation against colonial oppression. Or the quiet dignity of Rosa Parks, whose refusal to relinquish her bus seat awakened the civil rights movement in America. These individuals, and many like them, did not raise arms in anger; instead, they armed themselves with an unwavering commitment to justice and equality.

In this section, we explore how the principles of civil disobedience have been employed to resolve conflicts and advance societal shifts. The art lies not in confrontation, but in the way these acts of defiance are designed to engage the broader public, to educate and ultimately to enlist society in the pursuit of a shared vision. It is about creating a spectacle that is impossible to ignore, one that forces the onlooker to question and, ideally, to act.

Modern governance must heed the lessons of civil disobedience, incorporating avenues for peaceful protest into the fabric of societal norms. It is imperative that governments recognize the value of dissent as a form of dialogue, a way for citizens to express pressing concerns and to hold those in power accountable. Inclusive governance, therefore, includes not only the structures of decision-making but also the spaces for opposition within the framework of law and order.

An effective and harmonious world acknowledges the need for such activism. It understands that the vibrancy of a democracy is measured not by the absence of conflict but by the presence of mechanisms to address and resolve it. Non-violent activism is the testament to a society's maturity, its ability to navigate the tumultuous seas of disagreement with a compass calibrated toward progress and peace.

As we forge ahead in our quest for inclusive governance, we must not forget the legacy of civil disobedience. It is a legacy that teaches us the power of peaceful resistance, the art of non-violent protest, and the imperative of moral courage. It is a legacy that continues to inspire, challenge, and guide us toward a more just and harmonious world.

*- Case Studies of Successful Peace Movements*

In the tapestry of human history, threads of non-violent activism have woven patterns of peaceful resolution that stand out against the backdrop of conflict. The strength of such movements lies not in their might but in their capacity to harness the power of unity, empathy, and moral fortitude. Here, we examine the intricate artistry of successful peace movements and draw lessons from their impact on governance.

The Salt March of 1930, led by Mahatma Gandhi, is a seminal example of non-violent activism that galvanized a nation. In defiance of the British monopoly on salt production, thousands marched 240 miles to the Arabian Sea to make their own salt. This act of civil disobedience was a masterstroke in political symbolism, illustrating the injustice of colonial rule and the power of collective action. The Salt March did not immediately dismantle British authority, but it was a pivotal moment that eventually led to India's independence. Its legacy is a testament to the effectiveness of non-violent strategies in challenging entrenched power structures.

Across the globe and decades later, the Velvet Revolution in Czechoslovakia painted another portrait of peaceful change. In 1989, after years of Soviet influence, a series of non-violent protests and demonstrations by students and dissidents culminated in a dramatic shift from communist one-party rule to a democratic government. Not a single shot was fired, yet the Velvet Revolution succeeded in rewriting the script of governance, demonstrating that the pen—or in this case, the collective voice of the people—was indeed mightier than the sword.

More recently, the peaceful resistance movement in Tunisia in 2010-2011, known as the Jasmine Revolution, sparked a wildfire of change across the Arab world. The self-immolation of a young street vendor protesting police corruption and economic hardship put a human face on the suffering of many. It ignited a flame of resistance that was fought not with weapons but with the relentless demand for dignity, human rights, and democratic governance. The revolution led to the ousting of a long-standing autocrat and inspired uprisings across the region, showcasing the domino effect of non-violent activism.

These movements, diverse in culture and context, share the brushstrokes of strategic non-violence and the unwavering pursuit of justice. They teach us that peaceful change requires both the audacity to imagine a different world and the patience to work steadfastly towards it. They also remind those in the realms of governance that legitimacy is derived from the consent of the governed and that authority, when misused, can be challenged through united, peaceful means.

As we navigate the complexities of modern governance, these case studies serve as blueprints for constructing a world where conflicts, inevitably arising from diversity, are resolved not through violence but through the courageous art of peace.


7.8 Economic Incentives for Peace

*- Post-Conflict Economic Reconstruction*

The ashes of conflict hold the potential for new growth, a phoenix-like rebirth of societies that have endured the ravages of division and strife. In this crucible of reconstruction, economic incentives emerge as one of the most potent tools for crafting durable peace. The narrative of renewal is not merely one of rebuilding infrastructure but of reweaving the social fabric torn asunder by conflict.

It is within this context that we explore the transformative power of post-conflict economic reconstruction. The journey from discord to harmony requires more than just a cessation of hostilities; it necessitates a comprehensive strategy to address the underlying economic disparities that often fuel unrest. Economic reconstruction presents a unique opportunity to rectify past injustices and create a shared prosperity that underpins lasting peace.

Governments and international bodies must prioritize initiatives that stimulate economic activity and provide tangible benefits to all segments of society. One of the most effective approaches is the implementation of employment programs focused on rebuilding critical infrastructure. These programs serve a dual purpose: they repair the physical damage wrought by conflict and provide employment to individuals, many of whom may otherwise be susceptible to the siren call of lingering unrest.

Investing in local entrepreneurship is another vital strategy in the post-conflict economic landscape. By providing microfinance opportunities and business training, communities can nurture homegrown enterprises that contribute to the local economy and empower individuals with the agency to shape their future. Such initiatives not only promote economic diversification but also help to restore a sense of normalcy and hope.

Furthermore, economic reconstruction must be inclusive, ensuring that marginalized groups— women, ethnic minorities, and displaced persons—are integral to the rebuilding process. Their participation ensures that the dividends of peace are equitably distributed, thereby reducing the risk of renewed grievances that could jeopardize stability.

International partnerships are crucial in this endeavor, with foreign investment and aid playing a supportive role. However, the goal should always be to foster self-sufficiency, rather than creating dependency. Aid must be structured in a way that builds local capacity and aligns with national priorities, ensuring that the benefits of reconstruction are sustainable and aligned with the community's needs.

In the grand tapestry of peacebuilding, economic reconstruction serves as both a thread and a needle, mending the torn fabric and creating a pattern of interwoven interests and shared success. As communities emerge from the shadow of conflict, the collective endeavor of rebuilding can unite former adversaries in a common cause, transforming the economic landscape into fertile ground for a harmonious future.

Economic incentives for peace are not just about monetary gain; they are about crafting a narrative of collective growth, shared prosperity, and a commitment to a future that honors the dignity of every individual. In the art of peace, the canvas of economic reconstruction becomes a masterpiece of human resilience and a testament to the power of unity in diversity.

*- Trade Agreements as Peace Tools*

In the tapestry of global interactions, the threads of economy and peace are inextricably woven together, each influencing the other in profound ways. It is within this context that trade agreements emerge not merely as economic tools but as instruments of peace. In this section, we shall delve into the artful crafting of trade agreements that serve the dual purpose of fostering economic interdependence and nurturing the fragile blooms of peace in conflict-ridden soils.

Economic incentives for peace are rooted in the understanding that when nations are bound together by the mutual benefits of trade, the costs of conflict rise steeply, tipping the scales in favor of cooperation. A well-architected trade agreement becomes a canvas on which nations can paint a future of shared prosperity, reducing the likelihood of conflict by aligning their interests towards common goals.

Consider, for example, the historical narrative of a region rife with skirmishes over resources. As these nations enter into a trade agreement, a transformation begins. They start to see the resources not as bones of contention but as shared assets, the optimization of which could benefit all. The agreement stipulates terms that allow for equitable access, joint ventures, and shared infrastructure, turning a battleground into a collaborative industrial zone.

This approach requires a delicate balance—designing trade agreements that are not only economically sound but also equitable enough to address underlying grievances that may have fueled past conflicts. It involves incorporating clauses that support development, provide for the transfer of technology and skills, and establish dispute resolution mechanisms that are perceived as fair by all parties.

At the core of such agreements is the principle of economic interdependence, a concept that can make the prospect of renewed hostilities less attractive. As trade flows increase and economies become entwined, the cost of disrupting these flows becomes a deterrent against aggression. The art lies in creating a system where the benefits are so tangible and the costs of disturbance so clear that peace becomes the most lucrative option on the table.

Moreover, trade agreements can be designed to include provisions that directly promote peace initiatives. For instance, portions of the revenue generated from the trade could be earmarked for a fund dedicated to peace education or rebuilding efforts in post-conflict zones. Such tangible commitments enshrined in the fabric of trade agreements signal a shared commitment to not only economic growth but also to the flourishing of peace.

In this grand design, it must be acknowledged that trade agreements alone cannot magically resolve deep-seated animosities or replace the need for diplomacy and dialogue. However, when crafted with vision and care, these agreements can serve as powerful peace tools, providing economic incentives that pave the way for a more harmonious world. They become, in essence, not just contracts between nations, but covenants for a future where the dividends of peace are enjoyed by all humanity.

## 7.9 Education for Reconciliation

*- Curriculum Reform for Peace Education*

The corridors of learning have long echoed with the potential to transform societies, to mend the torn fabric of communities, and to heal the fissures wrought by conflict. Within these halls, a movement takes root – one of curriculum reform aimed at instilling the principles of reconciliation and peace In the minds of the young. This section delves into the heart of peace education, an artful blend of knowledge and empathy, history and hope.

Peace education does not merely present an alternative curriculum; it reimagines the pedagogical landscape. It is an approach that transcends traditional academic boundaries, fostering a culture of non-violence, mutual respect, and social justice. This transformative journey begins with the acknowledgment of past grievances and the recognition of the narrative of the 'other'.

Curriculum reform for peace education involves the meticulous crafting of syllabi that include historical perspectives from all sides of a conflict. It seeks to replace the myopic and often nationalistic views of history with a more nuanced, multi-faceted understanding. Textbooks are rewritten, not to erase history, but to broaden its scope, to include stories of cooperation and coexistence alongside accounts of strife and division.

Classroom discussions become safe spaces where students can navigate the complexities of identity and heritage. Educators are not just conveyors of knowledge but facilitators of dialogue, trained in the delicate art of guiding conversations that may tread on sensitive ground. They encourage critical thinking and empathy, allowing students to step into the shoes of others and view the world through a lens not clouded by bias or hate.

Projects and activities within this reformed curriculum are collaborative, designed to dissolve the invisible barriers that separate students along ethnic or religious lines. The classroom becomes a microcosm of a more harmonious society, where cooperation and interdependence are not just taught but practiced.

Moreover, peace education extends beyond the walls of the school. Community service initiatives become an integral part of the learning experience, engaging students with their communities in meaningful ways that build bridges and foster a sense of shared humanity. Through service, young minds learn the value of giving back, of contributing to the healing of their societies, and of playing an active role in the creation of a more peaceful world.

Let's explore the case studies from diverse regions where curriculum reform has made tangible strides in reconciliation. In these models, we witness the dawning of an enlightened approach to education – one that does not shy away from the scars of the past but instead uses them as lessons for a more hopeful future. Here, we find a clarion call for educators and policymakers alike: to weave the threads of peace into the very fabric of our educational systems, to nurture generations of peacemakers, and to lay the foundations for a world where governance is not just inclusive but compassionate, not just fair but just.

The path towards a harmonious world is long and fraught with challenges, but the seeds of reconciliation, once sown in the fertile minds of the young, promise a harvest of lasting peace. The art of peace begins with education, and the canvas of change is the curriculum from which the leaders of tomorrow will learn the timeless values of coexistence and respect.


*- Youth Engagement and Conflict Prevention*

In the shadowed corners of conflict-ridden societies, the flickering light of hope often manifests in the eyes of the young. It is in the classrooms, on the playgrounds, and within the safe havens of educational institutions that the seeds of peace find fertile ground. The art of peace is a subtle craft, requiring not only the hands of skilled diplomats but also the minds of informed and empathetic youths. In this section, we explore the transformative power of education as a tool for reconciliation and conflict prevention.

Education, when wielded with care and foresight, serves as a bridge between divided communities. It imparts not only knowledge but values; not merely skills but understanding. By integrating conflict resolution training and peace education into school curricula, we cultivate a generation better equipped to navigate the intricacies of a fractured world.

Imagine a classroom that serves as a microcosm of society. Here, students from diverse backgrounds come together, their narratives intermingling and forming a mosaic of shared experiences. A curriculum that emphasizes empathy, critical thinking, and the appreciation of cultural diversity teaches these young citizens to view the world through a lens of understanding and respect.

Youth engagement in peace-building activities is pivotal. Through role-playing exercises, debates, and collaborative projects, students learn to articulate their views while recognizing the validity of others'. They develop the ability to listen —a skill often underrated but essential for reconciliation. As they engage in dialogue, they learn the art of compromise and discover the strength in finding common ground.

Projects that encourage interaction with different community groups can break down the walls of isolation that often surround marginalized populations. Through service-learning opportunities, young people can contribute to community development, fostering a sense of investment in the collective well-being. Here, the classroom extends to the streets, the fields, the town halls— wherever the pulse of the community beats.

As part of a holistic approach to education, storytelling and the arts play a significant role. The sharing of personal stories can transform abstract conflicts into tangible narratives of human experience. Theatre, music, and visual arts provide outlets for expression and can communicate messages of reconciliation in ways that transcend language barriers.

Preventative measures in education are as crucial as the content itself. Schools must be vigilant in creating environments where bullying and discrimination are not tolerated. These behaviors are the microcosms of larger societal conflicts and if left unchecked, can perpetuate cycles of violence. By addressing these issues at their root, educational institutions lay the groundwork for a culture of peace.

In this harmonious world we envision, education does not simply inform; it inspires. It does not merely instruct; it ignites. As custodians of the future, our youths hold the power to dismantle the legacies of division that have long plagued humanity. Through education for reconciliation, we empower them to turn the tides of conflict and to chart a course toward a world where peace is the most cherished lesson learned.


## 7.10 Technology's Double-Edged Sword

*- Social Media in Mobilizing for Peace*

In the labyrinth of today's digital society, social media emerges as a potent force, wielding the power to unite or divide with the mere tap of a screen. Its influence in the realm of conflict resolution is particularly paradoxical, serving simultaneously as a catalyst for discord and a beacon for peace.

As we delve into the dichotomous nature of this modern-day agora, we must recognize that social media platforms have become the digital incarnation of the public square. Here, voices that were once stifled by oppressive regimes or geographic isolation can now echo across the world, galvanizing communities into action and shining a light on injustices that may have otherwise remained shrouded in shadow. The potential of these platforms to mobilize grassroots movements, foster solidarity across borders, and amplify calls for peace is a testament to their power.

However, to harness this power effectively, we must be cognizant of the delicate balance that needs to be struck. Social media can just as easily be the harbinger of misinformation and the amplifier of hate speech, exacerbating tensions and inflaming conflicts. The speed at which information—and disinformation—spreads is staggering, with the potential to reach millions in a matter of seconds. Thus, while social media can organize peace rallies, it can also mobilize rioters, propagate extremist ideologies, and perpetuate cycles of violence.

To navigate this double-edged sword, we must cultivate a digital ecosystem that encourages constructive dialogue and critical thinking. The establishment of digital literacy programs within educational curricula is fundamental, equipping individuals with the skills to discern fact from fiction and engage in informed debate. Furthermore, peacebuilding initiatives must integrate social media strategies that promote empathy, understanding, and collaboration. This could involve the creation of online forums that connect conflicting parties, moderated discussions that facilitate reconciliation, and campaigns that celebrate shared human values.

In conjunction, governance structures must work in tandem with technology companies to create frameworks that mitigate the risks of online incitement without stifling free expression. This delicate act of balancing involves developing algorithms that flag and filter hate speech while ensuring transparency and accountability in their operations. It also requires a commitment to upholding international human rights standards, ensuring that voices calling for peace are not unjustly silenced under the guise of security.

In this intricate dance of technology and governance, the vision of a harmonious world hinges on our collective ability to wield social media not as a weapon of war but as a tool for peace. It is a platform that, if steered with wisdom and foresight, can transform the cacophony of a fractured world into a symphony of reconciled differences, a testament to humanity's enduring quest for harmony amidst diversity.


*- Misinformation and Its Challenges to Resolution*

As we navigate the labyrinthine pathways of the digital age, we are confronted with the paradox of technology: while it has the power to connect us, it also holds the potential to divide us with the spread of misinformation. In this section, we delve into the heart of the digital quagmire where misinformation lurks, threatening the fragile tapestry of peace that we strive to weave.

Misinformation—false or inaccurate information that is spread, regardless of intent to deceive—has become the modern hydra; for every head cut off, two more seem to sprout. In an era where information can circumnavigate the globe in seconds, the virality of misinformation presents a formidable obstacle to conflict resolution. It fuels distrust, hardens biases, and escalates tensions, often with alarming speed and reach.

The proliferation of social media platforms has democratized content creation and dissemination, allowing anyone with an internet connection to broadcast their narrative. While this has empowered voices that were traditionally marginalized, it has also created fertile ground for the spread of unverified and deceptive content. In conflict scenarios, this means that each side can entrench itself behind a fortress of its own facts, impervious to dialogue or compromise.

To constructively address and untangle the web of misinformation, we must first recognize its impact on the psychological terrain of the populace. Misinformation exploits cognitive biases, such as the confirmation bias, where individuals favor information that confirms their preexisting beliefs. In the context of conflict, this can calcify opinions and reduce the openness required for resolution.

The battle against misinformation is multifaceted and requires a concerted effort from governments, technology companies, and individuals. Governments can legislate to hold platforms accountable for the content they host, but such regulation must be carefully crafted to avoid infringing on free speech. Technology companies, for their part, have a responsibility to develop algorithms and tools that promote credible sources and flag questionable content, while also respecting user privacy and the diversity of opinion.

But perhaps most critically, individuals must cultivate digital literacy. By learning to critically evaluate sources, question the veracity of information, and understand the manipulative nature of certain content, citizens can become the first line of defense in the battle against misinformation.

In the realm of conflict resolution, mediators and negotiators must now be as skilled in navigating digital landscapes as they are in traditional diplomacy. They must be adept at identifying and countering misinformation, employing digital tools to disseminate facts, and building narratives that foster common ground rather than division.

The digital age has indeed presented us with a double-edged sword; it offers unprecedented opportunities for connection and understanding, but also challenges us with the specter of misinformation. It is only by wielding this sword with wisdom, balance, and a commitment to truth that we can hope to cut through the discord and carve out a path to peace.

# 8. Educating Citizens

*Knowledge's seeds grow,*
*In the minds of tomorrow,*
*Enlightened winds blow.*

<u>8.1 The Purpose of Education in Governance</u>

*- Instilling Democratic Values*

In the heart of an enlightened society lies the education of its citizens, a process not merely confined to the acquisition of knowledge and skills but also to the inculcation of democratic values. The role of education in governance is to forge individuals who are not only well-informed and capable of critical thinking but who also embody the principles of democracy: equality, justice, and respect for diversity.

The classrooms of today are the cradles of future governance. Here, young minds must learn the importance of participation in public life and the value of their voice in the chorus of democracy. The curriculum must extend beyond the traditional subjects to include lessons on civic rights and responsibilities, the workings of government, and the significance of active engagement in the political process.

To foster a citizenry that is both knowledgeable and morally attuned to the tenets of democratic society, education systems must emphasize dialogue and debate. Students should be encouraged to question, to challenge, and to express their views within a respectful and open environment. They must learn to listen as much as they speak, to understand differing perspectives, and to appreciate the pluralism that characterizes their world.

This educational foundation equips individuals with the tools necessary to participate effectively in governance. It creates a populace that is not only prepared to vote but is also willing to stand for office, to advocate for community interests, and to hold their leaders accountable. In essence, education becomes a means of empowering citizens, granting them the capacity to shape the policies and decisions that affect their lives.

Moreover, schools must act as microcosms of the larger society, embodying the very principles of inclusivity and collaboration that they seek to promote. This means creating learning environments that are free from discrimination, where all students, regardless of their background, can flourish. It requires educators who model democratic behavior and who are committed to the principle that every student has an equal right to succeed.

Education not only informs but forms citizens. We must delve into pedagogical strategies that can instill a sense of civic duty, mutual respect, and a commitment to the common good. We must examine successful models where education has acted as a transformative force in governance, inspiring individuals to become active contributors to their society's well-being.

The purpose of education in governance extends beyond creating a workforce or advancing economies. It is about shaping the guardians of democracy, the stewards of justice, and the architects of a harmonious world. As such, the true measure of a nation's educational success is not found in test scores or graduation rates, but in the quality of its democracy and the character of its governance.


*- Fostering Civic Responsibility*

In the soft glow of dawn, as the world stirs awake to the rhythms of life, there is a quiet revolution taking place within the hallowed halls of education. Far beyond the rote memorization of facts and figures, education in its most enlightened form serves as the bedrock of governance, for it is here that the seeds of civic responsibility are tenderly sown and nurtured to blossom.

This is a sacred contract between knowledge and power. Education shapes the citizens who will one day wield the reins of governance, or indeed, critique and hold it accountable.

Education, when envisioned as a cornerstone of governance, transcends the mere acquisition of skills for economic utility. It becomes an alchemy that transforms the individual, instilling a profound understanding of their role within the tapestry of society. The ultimate aim of education is to cultivate informed, critically-thinking individuals capable of engaging in the democratic process with wisdom and insight.

The classroom is the crucible where the values of democracy, equality, justice, and freedom are not only taught but also lived and experienced. Through the study of history, students witness the ebb and flow of governance systems, the pendulum swings between tyranny and liberty, and the ever-present struggle for human rights. Through literature, they explore the diverse narratives and lived experiences of their fellow humans, building empathy and a deep appreciation for the pluralism that strengthens the fabric of society. Science and technology courses teach them not just the 'how' but also the 'why,' empowering them to make decisions that will foster sustainable progress.

The role of education in governance is to ensure that every individual understands their rights and responsibilities as a citizen. It teaches them to question, to debate, to listen, and to contribute constructively to the public discourse. It is in the classroom where the abstract principles of governance are made tangible through discussions on current events, ethical dilemmas, and simulations of democratic processes.

Educators are the unsung heroes in this narrative, serving as guides, mentors, and role models. They do not only impart knowledge but also inspire a lifelong passion for learning and civic engagement. Their classrooms are the incubators of future leaders, policymakers, activists, and informed voters.

Through education, individuals learn to discern truth from falsehood, to stand firm against the tides of misinformation, and to appreciate the delicate balance of checks and balances that ensure the vibrancy of a democratic society. They are taught to understand not just the machinery of governance but also the philosophical underpinnings that justify its existence.

The purpose of education in governance is multifaceted. It fosters civic responsibility, nurtures the skills necessary for participation in a democratic society, and engenders an enduring commitment to the common good. For a society to flourish, its citizens must be both enlightened and engaged, and education is the powerful catalyst that makes this possible.

## 8.2 Curriculum Development for Civic Engagement

*- Integrating Civics into Education*

In the orchestration of a symphony that is inclusive governance, education is the maestro, wielding the baton that shapes the minds and hearts of citizens. As we delve into the nuances of curriculum development for civic engagement, we find ourselves in the workshop where citizens are crafted, not merely educated. Here we explore how integrating civics into education creates the foundation for enlightened governance, a place where each individual is not just a resident but an active participant in the democratic process.

To foster a populace that is both informed and involved, educational institutions must prioritize civics within their curriculum. Civics education is not simply about understanding the mechanics of government but about instilling a sense of communal responsibility and the skills necessary for participation in public life. It must be dynamic, engaging, and, above all, relevant to the challenges of our times.

A curriculum rich in civic engagement must begin with the basics of governmental structure and the rights and responsibilities of citizenship. However, it must not end there. The heart of civics education lies in its ability to connect the theoretical underpinnings of democracy with the lived experiences of its students. It should be a springboard for discussion and debate, encouraging critical thinking about current events, social justice issues, and the very nature of governance itself.

Hands-on experiences, such as community service projects, mock elections, and student councils, are vital. They provide students with a laboratory where theories of governance and citizenship can be tested and applied. Such experiences empower students to see the tangible outcomes of civic participation and understand the significance of their contributions to the community tapestry.

Equally important is the integration of technology into civics education. In an era where digital platforms can significantly amplify voices, understanding how to navigate and utilize these tools for civic engagement is paramount. Digital literacy becomes a cornerstone of modern civics education, equipping students with the ability to discern credible information, engage in online discourse, and harness the power of social media for social change.

As we sculpt this curriculum, we must also ensure it is inclusive, reflecting the diversity of society. Every student, regardless of background, should see themselves and their potential role in governance. Civics education should celebrate cultural differences while highlighting the shared values and goals that bind us as a community and a nation.

The end goal of integrating civics into education is the creation of a populace that is not only equipped with knowledge but also with the will and the skill to use that knowledge for the betterment of society. It is about nurturing the seeds of participatory democracy so that they may bloom in every corner of our shared garden.


*- Encouraging Critical Thinking and Debate*

Education for civic engagement must move beyond the rote memorization of historical dates and legislative processes. It should ignite a passion for active participation and provide the analytical skills necessary for discerning the veracity of information in an era where misinformation is rampant. Curriculum development thus becomes a creative and strategic art, shaping the minds that will shape the future.

A cornerstone of this curriculum is the encouragement of critical thinking. Students must be taught to question, to analyze, and to challenge the status quo. This is not to foster dissent for dissent's sake but to instill a sense of responsibility towards the continuous improvement of our governance structures. Classrooms should become forums for debate and discussion, where diverse perspectives are not only tolerated but welcomed and examined.

To achieve this, educators must integrate real-world issues into their teaching, making the connection between theory and practice explicit. Case studies of governance successes and failures can be dissected, allowing students to understand the complex factors that influence policy outcomes. By engaging in simulations of democratic processes, such as mock elections or legislative debates, students can experience firsthand the challenges and triumphs of governance.

Additionally, the curriculum must be inclusive, reflecting the diversity of voices and experiences within the society. It should highlight the contributions of various cultures and groups to the political landscape, thereby fostering a sense of unity and shared destiny among the student body. In doing so, the curriculum becomes a mirror reflecting the society it aims to serve, teaching respect and appreciation for the myriad threads that weave the tapestry of our collective existence.

Here, we argue that such a curriculum is not a utopian ideal but a pragmatic necessity. By weaving critical thinking and debate into the fabric of education, we prepare a generation not only to inherit governance but to reinvent it continually. This is the hallmark of a civilization that does not merely endure but evolves, a civilization capable of harmonizing the myriad voices of its people into a symphony of progress.

As students learn to engage with complex ideas and navigate the intricacies of differing viewpoints, they lay the groundwork for a society that values dialogue over division, and informed consensus over impulsive contention. It is through this rigorous practice of thought and discussion that the seeds of enlightened governance are sown, promising a harvest rich with the fruits of a truly democratic life.


8.3 Role of Educators in Political Socialization

- *Teachers as Role Models for Democratic Participation*

Teachers, the architects of young minds, hold a profound responsibility that extends far beyond the impartation of academic knowledge. They are the custodians of democracy, instilling in their pupils the principles of civic duty, critical thinking, and the importance of active participation in the political processes that shape their lives and communities. The classroom is a microcosm of society, a laboratory where the ideals of inclusiveness, debate, and the search for common ground are not just taught but practiced.

Educators weave threads of political awareness into the fabric of their teaching. Through the careful selection of curricula that includes diverse perspectives, they foster an environment where students learn to appreciate the multiplicity of voices that make up a democratic society. As role models, teachers demonstrate the essence of democratic participation through their own engagement with community issues and governance, thus providing a living example to their charges.

There are myriad ways in which educators can encourage students to become informed citizens. From organizing mock elections to facilitating student-led community projects, teachers can create experiential learning opportunities that resonate with the real-world application of governance. These experiences are not merely academic exercises; they are rehearsals for the responsibilities these young citizens will one day assume.

Moreover, educators are uniquely positioned to identify and dismantle the barriers that might prevent full participation in democratic processes. By championing initiatives that address disparities in access to information and resources, teachers can empower students from all backgrounds to claim their rightful place in the political landscape.

In the gentle ebb and flow of classroom discussion, the seeds of future governance are sown. As educators model respectful dialogue and encourage the peaceful resolution of conflicts, they are imparting the skills necessary for the art of compromise and consensus-building. These are the hallmarks of effective and inclusive governance, and they are being nurtured daily in the fertile ground of education.

This section is a tribute to the educators who realize the gravity of their role. It is an affirmation of the belief that within the four walls of their classrooms, they are shaping not just students, but future voters, leaders, and architects of a harmonious world.

*- Facilitating Discussions on Governance and Ethics*

In the fertile grounds of the classroom, educators stand as the vanguards of political socialization, cultivating the seeds of tomorrow's governance. It is through their guidance that students first encounter the complex tapestry of political ideologies, governance structures, and ethical quandaries that shape our world. The role of educators in this process is pivotal, for they are tasked with the delicate art of opening minds without imprinting biases, guiding thought without dictating conclusions.

To achieve this, educators must embrace the role of facilitators, creating an environment where discussions on governance and ethics are not only encouraged but are foundational to the learning experience. The classroom can be transformed into a microcosm of society, a safe space where diverse opinions are aired and respected, and where the principles of democracy are not just taught but practiced.

Such discussions are not confined to the realms of civics or political science courses. They permeate every discipline, for governance and ethics are intrinsically linked to all aspects of human endeavor. In literature classes, for instance, students can explore the societal implications of a character's actions and the governance systems within fictional worlds. Science lessons can pivot to address the ethical considerations of new technologies and the role of government in regulating advancements for the public good.

Educators must also encourage critical thinking, pushing students to question and analyze the status quo. By examining case studies of different governance models, students can identify the strengths and pitfalls of various systems, understanding that no one model is perfect and that governance is an ever-evolving beast, shaped by the will and the voice of the people it serves.

Moreover, educators should foster a sense of global citizenship, highlighting the interconnectedness of today's world. Discussions should not be confined to local or national governance but should extend to international institutions and agreements. Students must recognize that in a world where borders are increasingly porous, the actions of one nation can have far-reaching impacts on the global community.

In a society where fake news and polarized media can skew perceptions, educators have the responsibility to teach students how to discern fact from fiction, to research effectively, and to develop informed opinions. They are the custodians of enlightenment, tasked with the mission to produce not just scholars, but engaged, ethical citizens who are equipped to contribute thoughtfully to the governance of their communities and beyond.

The educator, then, is not merely a disseminator of knowledge but a moderator of dialogue, a mentor in ethical reasoning, and an advocate for active participation in the democratic process. In their hands lies the potential to shape a generation of citizens who are knowledgeable, empathetic, and committed to the pursuit of harmonious governance built on a foundation of shared ethical principles. It is a role of monumental importance and one that holds the promise of a more enlightened and inclusive future.


## 8.4 School Governance as a Learning Model

*- Student Councils and the Miniature Governance Experience*

In the hallowed halls of academia, where the minds of tomorrow are sculpted, lies a microcosm of governance that mirrors the greater societal structures we inhabit—the student council. Often overlooked as merely a rite of passage or an extracurricular activity, student councils provide a foundational experience for the practical application of inclusive governance. These miniature governments serve as a critical pedagogical tool, offering students firsthand insights into the workings of democracy, the responsibilities of leadership, and the intricacies of policy-making.

Within the ecosystem of school governance, student councils are not just symbolic entities but powerful platforms for initiating change, reflecting student voices, and instilling a sense of agency. The lessons learned through these institutions are profound. Students engage in elections, giving them a taste of the electoral process and the significance of informed voting. They learn to campaign responsibly, to articulate their visions for the future, and to debate with respect and openness.

The council itself, once elected, becomes a vessel for the intersection of diverse viewpoints. Here, students from varying backgrounds and beliefs come together to negotiate, compromise, and reach consensus—skills that are essential in the broader context of national and global governance. They experience the delicate balance between advocating for their own agenda and recognizing the needs of their peers, developing empathy and a deeper understanding of collective well-being.

Moreover, student councils act as a laboratory for policy experimentation. They tackle issues pertinent to their constituents—be it school lunch quality, dress code policies, or the allocation of funds for student projects. Through such initiatives, they grapple with budget constraints, stakeholder interests, and the evaluation of policy outcomes, mirroring the complexities faced by governments at all levels.

This miniature experience of governance also extends to the faculty and administration, who must relinquish a degree of control to allow for authentic student leadership. In doing so, they endorse a model of education that values democratic participation and the development of critical thinking skills. It's an exercise in trust and an acknowledgment that the students of today will be the policymakers of tomorrow.

Significantly, the student council experience does not stand in isolation. It is complemented by a curriculum that integrates civics education, encouraging students to understand their rights and responsibilities as citizens. The council's activities provide context to theoretical knowledge, breathing life into the concepts that define enlightened governance.

By providing a real-world governance framework scaled to the student experience, schools foster a generation of citizens who are not only knowledgeable but also equipped with the practical skills necessary to navigate and shape the societal structures they will inherit. It is in these formative years, within the microcosm of school governance, that the seeds of enlightened leadership are sown, cultivating the bedrock of a harmonious and inclusive future.


*- Participatory Decision-Making in Educational Institutions*

The walls of the classroom have long been acknowledged as the nurseries of our future society. Within these incubators of intellect and character, the principles of governance can find fertile ground, not just in theory but in actionable practice. By integrating participatory decision-making into the governance of educational institutions, we begin to cultivate the seeds of enlightened governance from an early age.

Participatory decision-making in schools is a microcosm of the larger democratic process, providing a hands-on experience of governance to students. When students are involved in making decisions that affect their learning environment, they develop a sense of ownership and responsibility towards their institution and the community it supports. It's through these small, but significant, exercises in democracy that students learn the value of their voice, the power of collective action, and the importance of compromise and consensus-building.

The application of participatory governance in schools takes various forms. Student councils are the most visible embodiment of this concept. With elected representatives, these councils give students a platform to express their views and influence school policies. When student council suggestions are taken seriously and result in tangible changes, it reinforces the notion that democratic participation can lead to positive outcomes.

Beyond student councils, the classroom itself can serve as an arena for democratic engagement. Teachers can incorporate group decision-making into lesson plans, allowing students to guide the direction of discussions or projects. Such involvement strengthens critical thinking, encourages active engagement, and fosters a sense of collective responsibility.

Furthermore, when school governance committees include student members, they bring fresh perspectives to the table, reminding administrators and teachers that the core purpose of educational institutions is to serve the needs and aspirations of the students. These committees can oversee various aspects of school life, from the development of extracurricular activities to the crafting of anti-bullying policies.

In this participatory model, an important lesson is imparted: that governance should not be a distant and abstract concept, but a living, breathing aspect of everyday life. It teaches that for governance to be truly effective, it must be inclusive, considering the voices of all stakeholders, regardless of their age.

The journey towards enlightened governance begins with the realization that each individual, no matter how young, has a role to play in shaping their community. By embedding participatory decision-making within the school governance structure, we are not merely educating students; we are empowering them to become engaged, informed, and responsible citizens. This is the bedrock upon which a harmonious world can be built, one where governance is not imposed, but rather grown from within the very heart of its constituency.


<u>8.5 Lifelong Learning and Continuous Citizenship</u>

*- Adult Education and Ongoing Civic Engagement*

In the heart of the city, a vibrant community center bustles with activity. Here, adults of all ages gather, united by a shared commitment to lifelong learning and the betterment of their society. This is the modern agora, a place where the principles of continuous education and civic engagement are not just spoken of but lived.

Here, we explore the transformative power of adult education as it intersects with the ongoing practice of citizenship. The ancient Greeks believed that a democracy was only as strong as the education of its citizens. It is upon this bedrock that enlightened governance must be built, for a populace that ceases to learn is a body politic that stagnates and withers.

Adult education initiatives have surged in response to the evolving demands of the 21st-century world. Technology, global interconnectedness, and rapid societal changes necessitate a model of education that extends far beyond the traditional classroom years. Adults must be encouraged to acquire new skills, absorb fresh ideas, and critically evaluate the world around them. It is through this continuous intellectual growth that citizens remain equipped to contribute meaningfully to the governance of their communities.

The role of adult education is not limited to vocational training or practical skills alone. It encompasses a wider spectrum, including political literacy, ethical considerations, and cultural awareness. Through seminars, workshops, and online courses, adults are exposed to a range of perspectives and are taught to navigate the complexities of modern governance with discernment and a sense of shared responsibility.

Civic engagement, the active participation in the political life of one's community, is the natural companion to this educational journey. As adults engage in learning, they are simultaneously called to put their knowledge into action. Whether it be through voting, community organizing, or public debate, the educated adult is a citizen who does not shy away from the mantle of civic duty.

Adult education fosters an environment where continuous citizenship flourishes. In such a society, governance is not seen as a distant or abstract concept, but rather as a tangible expression of the collective will and wisdom. Here, the citizen is both student and teacher, learner and leader, forever evolving in the pursuit of a more harmonious world.

As we delve deeper into this subject, we come to understand that the true measure of governance is found not in the grandiosity of its institutions but in the empowerment of its people. Lifelong learning and ongoing civic engagement are not merely pillars of enlightened governance; they are its very lifeblood, ensuring that the state and its citizens move forward together in a perpetual dance of progress and participation.


*- Online Platforms for Citizen Education*

The digital age has ushered in an era of unprecedented access to information, transforming the traditional paradigms of education and citizenship. In this landscape, online platforms emerge as vital arenas for lifelong learning, shaping a new generation of informed, engaged, and continuously evolving citizens.

Enlightened governance understands that the education of citizens does not end with a diploma or degree; it is an ongoing process that adapts to the changing tides of society and the individual's lifecycle. To this end, governments, non-profit organizations, and private enterprises have begun to cultivate online ecosystems where learning is not only accessible but also tailored to the needs of a diverse populace.

These platforms offer a plethora of resources ranging from open online courses on civic duties and rights, to interactive simulations that allow users to experience the complexities of policy-making first-hand. They are the virtual agoras of our time, where dialogue and debate flourish, and where the citizenry can hone the critical thinking skills necessary for robust democratic engagement.

One such platform, 'CivicEd', has become a beacon for those seeking to deepen their understanding of governance and their role within it. Its modular approach allows users to engage with content that spans constitutional law, economic theory, and environmental stewardship. Through a gamified experience, users earn badges and certifications, incentivizing participation and mastery over the topics that underpin an effective governance system.

Moreover, these platforms do not exist in isolation. They are interconnected with social media, news outlets, and academic institutions, creating a rich tapestry of knowledge exchange. They facilitate connections between citizens and their representatives, enabling real-time feedback and fostering a culture of transparency and accountability.

'PolicyCraft', another innovative platform, bridges the gap between knowledge and action. It provides a sandbox environment where users can draft mock legislation, budget for public projects, or even run virtual campaigns. By simulating the challenges faced by officials, it demystifies the governing process and empowers users to become more active participants in their actual communities.

At the heart of these online initiatives is the recognition that an educated citizenry is the bedrock of enlightened governance. Continuous citizenship is a call to be ever-vigilant, ever-curious, and ever-committed to the collective well-being of society. It is a commitment that transcends age, occupation, or background, embracing the idea that learning is a lifelong quest pivotal to the health and evolution of democracy.

As we venture further into the 21st century, these platforms will play an instrumental role in fostering a culture of learning and engagement. They are the digital forums where citizens can come together to build a more harmonious world, one click, one lesson, one informed decision at a time.


## 8.6 Educational Technology and Democratic Participation

*- Digital Literacy for Informed Citizenship*

In a world where information cascades through digital avenues and civic engagement is often mediated by screens, the role of educational technology in fostering democratic participation cannot be overstated. The crux of enlightened governance lies not just in the availability of information, but in the ability of citizens to critically engage with, understand, and utilize this information to make informed decisions.

Digital literacy, therefore, becomes a cornerstone of modern citizenship. It equips individuals with the skills to navigate the vast seas of data, discerning fact from fiction and meaningful discourse from noise. This section of the book delves into how educational technology, when thoughtfully integrated into curricula, can cultivate a citizenry adept in digital literacy.

The art of governance in diverse societies hinges on the participation of an informed public, capable of contributing to the policymaking process and holding leaders accountable. Educational institutions must adapt to this reality by embedding digital literacy into their teaching methods. Interactive platforms and online tools can simulate the environment of digital democracy, allowing students to practice the skills they need to participate effectively in e-governance initiatives.

Moreover, the use of educational technology in classrooms can democratize the learning process itself. Students from various backgrounds can access high-quality resources, engage in collaborative projects, and gain exposure to different perspectives. This inclusive approach to education fosters a sense of community and shared responsibility, essential ingredients for harmonious governance.

Through exercises that encourage critical thinking, such as evaluating the credibility of online sources or engaging in debates on digital forums, learners can hone the faculties necessary for robust democratic participation. Furthermore, by integrating technology into the learning process, educators can bridge the gap between the theoretical aspects of governance and the practical realities of participating in a digital society.

In this digital age, an enlightened citizen is one who can responsibly wield the power of technology. By fostering digital literacy, educational technology not only prepares individuals to navigate the complexities of the information age but also empowers them to be active, informed participants in the democratic process. As we educate the citizens of tomorrow, we must ensure that they are not only consumers of digital content but also shapers of the digital polity. Through this, governance becomes not a distant mechanism operated by the few but a living, breathing entity shaped by the many, in pursuit of a harmonious world.

*- E-Government and the Accessibility of Political Information*

In the digital age, the nexus between educational technology and democratic participation has become increasingly pronounced. The proliferation of e-government platforms marks a transformative shift in the way citizens interact with and influence their governing bodies. These platforms have the potential to serve as a cornerstone for enlightened governance, where informed and engaged citizens are integral to the political process.

At the heart of this transformation is the accessibility of political information. E-government enables a seamless flow of information from government repositories to the palms of citizens. Through carefully curated digital portals, individuals can access legislative updates, policy discussions, and a wide array of public services with unprecedented ease. This immediacy not only demystifies the workings of government but also empowers citizens to partake knowledgeably in the democratic process.

However, the efficacy of such platforms hinges on the integration of educational technology that is inclusive and user-friendly. It is here that the art of crafting e-government interfaces becomes crucial. They must be designed to accommodate diverse levels of digital literacy, ensuring that all citizens, regardless of their proficiency with technology, can benefit from this digital empowerment.

Consider the example of a virtual town hall, which utilizes video conferencing technology to allow citizens to participate in live debates and discussions. Here, educational modules can be embedded to guide users through the functionalities of the platform and the topics at hand. By doing so, the virtual town hall becomes not just a forum for discussion but also a classroom where civic education is continuously imparted and refined.

Moreover, e-government platforms can serve as repositories of educational resources, providing citizens with the knowledge necessary to understand complex policy issues. Interactive infographics, explainer videos, and gamified learning scenarios can transform dry policy documents into engaging educational experiences. This not only nurtures a more informed citizenry but also fosters a culture of lifelong learning, wherein citizens regularly update their understanding of governmental functions and their role within the democratic framework.

The harmonious world we envision, where governance is inclusive and balanced, is contingent upon an electorate that is both enlightened and engaged. Educational technology, when thoughtfully intertwined with e-government initiatives, can bridge the gap between government transparency and citizen participation. It is through this marriage of technology and education that we lay the bedrock for enlightened governance—a governance that is not only for the people but also shaped by an informed, empowered populace.

## 8.7 Bridging the Socioeconomic Divide in Education

*- Equal Access to Civic Education*

In a world where the gulf between wealth and poverty can be as wide as the ocean, the bridge of education offers a path to a more egalitarian society. Nowhere is this truer than in the realm of civic education, the cornerstone of an enlightened governance system. Civic education is not merely an academic pursuit; it is the nurturing ground for future leaders, conscious citizens, and the guardians of democracy.

To bridge the socioeconomic divide in education, we must first recognize that equal access to civic education is fundamental to the health of our governance. In this pursuit, it is essential to dismantle the barriers that hinder children from less affluent backgrounds from receiving the same quality of education as their more privileged peers. Such barriers are not just physical, such as the distances some must travel to reach school or the dilapidated state of educational facilities in poorer areas, but also ideological, rooted in low expectations and a lack of culturally responsive pedagogy.

An inclusive approach to civic education requires curriculum that reflects the diversity of experiences and values within a society. It should not only impart knowledge of governmental institutions and legal frameworks but also foster critical thinking and a sense of agency. Students from all walks of life must see themselves as part of the narrative, understanding their role and potential impact on the governance structures that shape their world.

Technology, when harnessed thoughtfully, can be a powerful equalizer in this domain. Digital platforms can democratize access to information and learning resources, transcending geographical and socioeconomic barriers. Through online courses, forums, and simulations, students can engage with civic concepts and participate in virtual communities that mirror the democratic processes of governance.

Moreover, civic education should extend beyond the classroom. Community-based programs can provide practical experience and foster a spirit of volunteerism. Partnerships between schools, local governments, and non-profit organizations can facilitate internships and service-learning opportunities, allowing students to apply their knowledge in meaningful ways that benefit their communities.

Active measures are also needed to ensure that teachers are adequately trained to deliver civic education in a way that resonates with all students. Professional development should equip educators with the tools to create an inclusive environment where every voice is heard and valued.

By investing in equal access to civic education, we sow the seeds of a more informed and engaged citizenry. This is the bedrock of enlightened governance, where power is not hoarded by a privileged few but shared among the many. It is an investment in the very fabric of democracy, ensuring that each citizen, regardless of their socioeconomic status, can partake in the governance of their society. It is an affirmation that every individual has a role to play in the symphony of governance, contributing to the harmonious world we all strive for.

*- Addressing Educational Disparities and Voter Turnout*

In the shadowed hallways of dilapidated schools and the gleaming corridors of privileged institutions, the disparity in educational resources paints a stark contrast. This division not only determines the fate of individual students but also shapes the contour of our democratic processes. It is in the crucible of education that citizens are forged, and it is here that an enlightened governance must begin its work.

The correlation between education and civic engagement is undeniable. A well-educated electorate is the bedrock of a vibrant democracy, for it is within the classroom that citizens learn to question, to evaluate, and to participate. Yet, when education is skewed by socioeconomic status, so too is the democratic voice that arises from its teachings. This imbalance leads to a diminished voter turnout in lower-income populations, a silent forfeiture of the right to shape society.

To bridge this socioeconomic divide in education, we must view schools as more than just knowledge dispensaries. They are the breeding grounds of future policymakers, voters, and leaders. The government's role in equalizing educational opportunity is paramount. Initiatives must be launched to ensure that every child, regardless of zip code or family income, receives a quality education that imparts not only academic knowledge but also civic responsibility.

Investment in early childhood education, teacher training, infrastructure improvement, and technological access in underfunded schools are immediate steps toward rectifying disparities. Moreover, integrating civic education into curricula across all socio-economic spectrums will prepare students to engage actively in the democratic process. This education should not merely touch on the mechanics of government but also inspire a commitment to the common good and a readiness to participate in governance at all levels.

Further, educational institutions must partner with community organizations to create programs that encourage political participation among the youth. Simulations of legislative processes, voter registration drives, and open debates on current issues can transform theoretical knowledge into practical engagement. By empowering the younger generation with the confidence to voice their opinions and the understanding to make informed decisions, we build a foundation for higher voter turnout and a more inclusive democracy.

As we strive for harmonious worlds, we must remember that the path to enlightened governance is paved with equitable education. It is through the eradication of educational inequities that we can nurture a populace well-equipped to cast their ballots, not out of mere obligation, but from a place of informed conviction and hope for a better future. Only then can we boast of a governance that truly reflects the diverse voices of its constituents, a symphony of ideas and aspirations playing in concert towards a more just and prosperous society.


8.8 Global Citizenship Education

- *Understanding Global Interdependence and Governance*

In the heart of enlightened governance lies a promise – to cultivate a generation of individuals who are not only well-informed and skilled but also deeply aware of their role within the larger tapestry of humanity. This is where Global Citizenship Education (GCED) emerges as a torchbearer, illuminating the path toward a more harmonious world.

The concept of GCED transcends the traditional confines of geography and national identity. It is an educational paradigm that fosters an understanding of global interdependence and the complexities of global governance. By instilling values of empathy, respect for diversity, and a sense of shared responsibility, GCED equips learners with the mindset needed to navigate and shape a world where the local and the global are inextricably linked.

Pillars uphold the edifice of GCED. Firstly, the role of intercultural competencies. In a classroom that mirrors the vibrancy of a global village, students engage with multiple worldviews, challenging their assumptions and expanding their horizons. They learn to communicate across cultural and linguistic barriers, fostering a sense of solidarity that transcends borders.

Secondly, critical thinking and problem-solving skills. As students grapple with complex global issues such as climate change, economic inequality, and social justice, they are encouraged to think creatively and collaboratively. Through project-based learning and simulations of global negotiations, they gain insights into the workings of governance structures, from local councils to international organizations.

Thirdly, participatory learning. GCED is not a passive receipt of knowledge; it is an active engagement with the world. Students are called to become agents of change, participating in community service projects, and advocacy campaigns. They learn that their voices matter, that they can influence policy and contribute to the common good.

In a world fraught with ethical dilemmas, global citizens must navigate the murky waters of moral decision-making. Through GCED, students confront these challenges head-on, engaging in debates and discussions that hone their ethical compasses. They emerge not only as knowledgeable individuals but as moral beacons in the quest for inclusive and effective governance.

We must weave together the strands of knowledge, skills, values, and attitudes that GCED instills. We imaging a future where every individual is a custodian of the planet, an advocate for justice, and a participant in the grand symphony of global governance. In this vision, education is not merely a tool for personal advancement but a sacred duty to the collective well-being of humanity.

Through the lens of GCED, we see a world where governance is no longer a distant, abstract concept but a lived reality, a shared responsibility, and a common journey toward a harmonious world.

*- Promoting International Law and Human Rights Awareness*

In the tapestry of global governance, the threads of international law and human rights are golden strands that weave through the fabric of nations, providing shimmering glimpses of what humanity can achieve when it works in concert. Global Citizenship Education (GCE) is the loom upon which this fabric is crafted, a pedagogical approach that not only instructs but also inspires, connective in its essence and transformative in its potential.

GCE fosters an understanding of the nuanced complexities of international law, encouraging students to grasp the delicate balance of sovereignty and cooperation that underpins our modern world. By illuminating the architecture of treaties, conventions, and resolutions, GCE demystifies the principles governing inter-state relations and the mechanisms designed to uphold peace and justice on a global scale.

However, GCE's mission extends beyond the mere dissemination of knowledge. It seeks to instill a sense of shared responsibility and collective identity among the world's citizens. It envisions a generation that not only comprehends the Universal Declaration of Human Rights but lives and breathes its tenets, championing dignity, equality, and respect across all borders.

Through interactive lessons, role-playing simulations, and engagement with real-world case studies, students are not passive recipients of information but active participants in a global dialogue. They are encouraged to debate, to question, and to propose solutions to the pressing human rights issues of our time. This critical engagement is the crucible in which enlightened governance is forged.

Imagine a classroom where children from diverse backgrounds learn about the International Criminal Court (ICC) not as a distant entity, but as a symbol of their collective commitment to justice. Picture a seminar where young adults from various countries collaborate to draft their own mock resolutions, fostering a spirit of diplomacy and mutual understanding.

Moreover, GCE positions environmental stewardship within the context of human rights, underscoring the right to a healthy environment as fundamental to the wellbeing of all peoples. Students are thus equipped with the knowledge and ethical framework to advocate for sustainable policies, recognizing that their local actions have a ripple effect on the global stage.

Armed with an awareness of international law and human rights, GCE graduates emerge as ambassadors of a new world order, one where governance is not a top-down directive, but a chorus of voices, each singular, yet harmonizing in pursuit of a more just, peaceful, and sustainable world. They are the stewards of the future, the architects of a global society that respects the rule of law, cherishes human rights, and thrives upon the rich soil of cultural diversity. In this vision, education is not merely a pillar of governance; it is its very heart, pulsing with the promise of a more harmonious world.


## 8.9 Evaluating the Impact of Educational Policies on Governance

*- Longitudinal Studies on Education and Civic Participation*

In the verdant landscape of enlightened governance, education stands as the mighty oak whose roots delve deep into the soil of civic participation. Over the decades, longitudinal studies have shed light on the profound relationship between the educational policies of a society and the health of its governance. These studies, examining the trajectories of individuals from various backgrounds over extended periods, provide a panoramic view of the ripple effects educational interventions can have on the broader political and social fabric.

One seminal study, stretching over thirty years, began with a simple hypothesis: that students exposed to civic education that emphasizes critical thinking, debate, and democratic engagement would be more likely to participate actively in governance processes. The results were telling. Participants who had engaged in such education displayed a markedly higher level of involvement in community activities, were more likely to vote, and were more knowledgeable about political issues compared to those who had experienced a more traditionalist, rote-learning approach.

These findings corroborate the idea that when students are taught not just the mechanics of governance but also the values of pluralism, dialogue, and responsibility, they emerge as citizens better equipped to contribute positively to the democratic process. Civic education, therefore, is not just about understanding the structure of government but fostering the skills needed for negotiation, empathy, and collective decision-making.

Furthermore, longitudinal studies highlight the importance of starting early and being consistent. Educational policies that integrate civic education throughout the schooling years yield individuals who are more resilient to the vagaries of political winds. They are less likely to be swayed by demagoguery and more likely to hold onto the principles of fair and just governance.

However, the impact of educational policies is not uniform across all demographics. For instance, studies show that marginalized groups often benefit exponentially more from policies that target their inclusion. When such groups are provided with resources and opportunities that recognize and address historical disparities, the effect on governance is multiplicative. These individuals not only participate more fully in the democratic process but also bring a diversity of perspectives that enriches the tapestry of governance.

As we traverse the intricate nexus of education and governance, what becomes abundantly clear is that our educational policies are not merely preparatory steps for future engagement. They are the crucible in which the metal of our governance is forged, the loom on which the fabric of our civic society is woven. Longitudinal studies on education and civic participation are the telescopes through which we observe the stars of our democratic constellation align, revealing patterns and insights that can guide us toward a more harmonious world, where each citizen is both an architect and a pillar of enlightened governance.

*- Policy Feedback Loops and Adjustments*

In a world where education is the keystone of society, the governance of nations must be intricately linked to the nurturing of informed, critical, and engaged citizens. It is through the lens of education that individuals can view the complexities of governance, understand their role within it, and act to shape it. Thus, educational policies are not merely a facet of governance; they are the crucible in which future governance is forged.

The feedback loops between educational policies and governance are dynamic and multifaceted. When a policy is implemented, it sends ripples across the entire governance structure, influencing not only the immediate educational sphere but also broader socio-political landscapes. To evaluate the impact of these policies, we must delve deeper into the layers of interaction that define the relationship between education and governance.

Firstly, consider the curriculum and its contents. A curriculum that emphasizes critical thinking and civic engagement instills in learners the capacity to analyze governance structures critically. Students who engage with political philosophy, economics, and social studies in a manner that encourages questioning are more likely to become active participants in their governance systems. As these individuals enter the public sphere, they bring with them a heightened awareness and a willingness to contribute to the evolution of their political and social environments. Governance that is receptive to these educated voices becomes more dynamic, more inclusive, and more responsive.

Secondly, the methodology of education itself can reflect and reinforce democratic principles. Classrooms that mimic democratic forums, where students are encouraged to voice diverse opinions and engage in collaborative decision-making, serve as microcosms of ideal governance. When students experience the impact of their voices in the educational setting, they are more likely to perceive their potential influence on governance. This experiential learning embeds democratic values and practices, which can later translate into higher levels of civic engagement and voter turnout.

However, to truly understand the efficacy of these policies, it is crucial to establish mechanisms for feedback and adjustment. Educational policies should be subject to rigorous, ongoing evaluation to gauge their real-world impact on governance. This requires a commitment to longitudinal studies that trace the trajectories of individuals from their school years into their adult participation in governance. It also necessitates a willingness to adapt educational strategies in response to shifting societal needs and the evolving landscape of governance.

Adjustments to policy must be informed by extensive data collection and analysis. Surveys, interviews, and case studies can provide insights into how educational experiences shape citizens' attitudes towards and participation in governance. Feedback from educators, students, and policymakers should feed directly back into the policy-making process to refine and enhance educational initiatives.

In this harmonious world we envision, a virtuous cycle emerges: enlightened governance supports comprehensive education, which in turn perpetuates enlightened governance. As we look towards this ideal, we must recognize that education is not static; it is a living, breathing entity that evolves alongside the society it serves. Thus, the governance of tomorrow is quietly taking shape in today's classrooms, and it is our collective responsibility to ensure that the educational policies we enact today are capable of fostering the inclusive, informed, and engaged citizens of tomorrow.

8.10 Innovative Approaches to Educating Future Leaders

*- Case Studies of Successful Youth Engagement Programs*

In the heart of the Scandinavian Peninsula, a remarkable program has taken root, blossoming into a beacon of progressive youth engagement. The Swedish "Leaders of Tomorrow" initiative, launched two decades ago, has since redefined the landscape of leadership education. It stands as a testament to the power of innovative pedagogy in shaping the minds that will govern the future.

The program's core philosophy is simple yet profound: leadership is not a privilege bestowed upon the few, but a skill to be cultivated in the many. From the bustling cities to the tranquil rural areas, "Leaders of Tomorrow" operates on the principle of accessibility for all. It bridges the gap between academic instruction and real-world application, immersing students in interactive learning environments that simulate the complex dynamics of governance.

Case studies form the backbone of the curriculum, encouraging critical thinking and ethical decision-making. However, the most striking feature is the program's annual "Youth Parliament" session. Here, students from diverse backgrounds step into the roles of lawmakers, debating bills and crafting policies on issues ranging from climate change to digital privacy. The experience is not merely academic; it is a profound exercise in empathy, cooperation, and civic responsibility.

Crossing the Atlantic, another pioneering effort emerges in the "Civic Seedlings" project of Costa Rica, a country renowned for its environmental stewardship and democratic stability. This initiative plants the seeds of civic engagement early, targeting elementary school children with a curriculum that integrates environmental science, social studies, and ethics.

Students embark on a journey that begins in the classroom and extends into their communities, where they undertake projects like neighborhood clean-ups and biodiversity surveys. These young citizens are not passive recipients of knowledge but active participants in their communities' well-being. The "Civic Seedlings" project has shown that when governance principles are instilled early, they take root and grow into a lifelong commitment to the public good.

The common thread weaving through these programs is the belief in youth as not just future leaders but as vital contributors to contemporary governance. By engaging them in the process early, they are endowed with a sense of ownership over their communities and a clearer understanding of the practical challenges of leadership. It is a model that has produced alumni who are more than just well-versed in governance—they are passionate, informed, and ready to take on the mantle.

These case studies offer a glimpse into the possibilities that arise when education systems break free from traditional confines. By fostering environments where young minds can engage with the complexities of governance in a hands-on, meaningful way, we lay the groundwork for a more enlightened and proactive citizenry. It is in these innovative approaches that the seeds of harmonious worlds are sown, nurtured by the promise of inclusive and dynamic governance for all.

*- Preparing the Next Generation for Complex Governance Challenges*

The crucible of governance is poised at the intersection of knowledge and wisdom, where the education of future leaders becomes a paramount concern. In the labyrinthine corridors of power, it is not enough to be merely well-informed; tomorrow's leaders must be sculpted with the acumen to navigate complexities and the sagacity to harmonize the cacophony of global voices. Innovative approaches to education are not just desirable; they are essential in preparing the next generation for the intricate governance challenges that lie ahead.

One such approach is the 'Global Stewardship Curriculum,' an educational framework that infuses traditional disciplines with a nuanced understanding of global interdependencies. This curriculum stretches beyond the confines of national history and geography, embracing a planetary perspective that instills in students a sense of belonging to a broader human polity. Subjects like 'Comparative Governance' and 'Sustainable Development Studies' become mainstays, teaching students the intricate dance between environmental stewardship and societal progress.

In tandem, experiential learning programs are crafted to transport students from the safety of the classroom into the unpredictable world of policy-making and diplomatic negotiation. Virtual reality simulations, for instance, plunge future leaders into crisis management scenarios where they must broker peace, respond to ecological disasters, or navigate economic downturns. These immersive experiences are not mere games; they are crucibles for character, honing the resilience and adaptability necessary for contemporary governance.

Moreover, mentorship initiatives partner seasoned statespeople with the youth, fostering a transgenerational dialogue that bridges the wisdom of experience with the innovation of youth. These mentorship channels serve as conduits for ethical grounding and leadership training, ensuring that moral compasses are not dulled in the cutthroat arena of politics.

To address the technological dimension, 'Digital Civics' becomes a staple, equipping students with the tools to comprehend and harness the power of technology in governance. From understanding the implications of artificial intelligence in decision-making to mastering digital platforms for citizen engagement, future leaders are taught to be as fluent in code as they are in the language of diplomacy.

In this forge of innovative education, the pedagogy is collaborative and adaptive, mirroring the dynamic nature of governance itself. It emphasizes critical thinking, cross-cultural communication, and ethical leadership. Diverse perspectives are not just welcomed; they are essential, mirroring the kaleidoscopic array of human experience.

Through such pioneering educational paradigms, we prepare our future leaders not only to face the known challenges of governance but also to anticipate the unknown, to navigate the uncharted waters of the future with foresight and grace. In this way, education becomes the bedrock of enlightened governance, ensuring that the leaders of tomorrow are not only adept and knowledgeable but also wise and humane stewards of the global community.

# 9. Health as a Political Pillar



## 9.1 The Fundamentals of Health-Centric Governance

*- Defining Health in Policy Making*

In the labyrinth of governance, where the architecture of policy intersects with the lived reality of citizens, the pursuit of health often becomes an afterthought —a line item on a budget or a platform promise easily deferred. Yet, as we unfold the pages of history and examine the tapestry of thriving civilizations, one thread stands out luminous and strong: the prioritization of public health.

The Fundamentals of Health-Centric Governance begins with an axiom: Health is a multidimensional construct that transcends mere absence of disease. It is the bedrock of societal prosperity, an enabler of economic stability, and a precondition for personal fulfillment. To define health in policymaking is to embrace a vision that is at once holistic and granular, a vision that acknowledges the intricate dance between individual well-being and collective resilience.

In this dance, the role of governance is not to lead or to follow, but to choreograph—a subtle yet powerful guide, ensuring that every step, every policy movement, contributes to the flourishing of the populace. A health-centric approach to governance demands the infusion of public well-being into the DNA of decision-making, from urban planning to environmental regulations, from education to economic reform.

Consider the urban planner, who must see beyond the concrete and steel. When the blueprint for a city incorporates green spaces, pedestrian pathways, and communal areas, it does more than create aesthetic appeal—it weaves the very fabric of physical and mental wellness into the urban sprawl. Similarly, when an environmental policy limits emissions, it not only protects the atmosphere but also reduces the burden of respiratory illnesses that can cripple a community.

Economic policies, too, must bear the stamp of health. A labor law that mandates reasonable working hours and supports parental leave is not just an economic instrument; it is a declaration that the health of workers is a pillar of a robust economy. An inclusive healthcare system, unfettered by barriers of wealth, is both a moral imperative and a strategic investment, for a healthy workforce is the engine of innovation and productivity.

Health-centric governance also manifests in the realm of education, where the seeds of lifelong well-being are sown. Nutritious school meals, physical education, and mental health curricula are not ancillary benefits but foundational elements of an enlightened educational policy. They prepare young citizens not just for the workforce but for a life of healthful vitality.

In defining health within the realm of policymaking, we must chart a course that is both bold and precise. It requires the mapping of intricate interdependencies and the crafting of policies that are as preventive as they are curative. It is a journey that demands foresight, compassion, and an unwavering commitment to the principle that the health of the individual is inseparable from the health of the collective.

As we venture further into this chapter, we will explore how nations across the globe have integrated health into the core of their governance, examining the strategies that have succeeded and the lessons learned from the challenges they have faced. For in the end, a governance that places health at its heart is one that not only heals but also elevates, transforming the very notion of what it means to govern and be governed.


*- The Historical Evolution of Public Health in Governance*

The journey of public health as a cornerstone of governance is as ancient as civilization itself. From the aqueducts of Rome to the quarantine stations of the Middle Ages, the nexus of health and governance has been instrumental in shaping human societies. In this section, we explore the historical evolution of public health in governance and how it has come to be recognized as a fundamental political pillar.

As we cast our gaze back to the earliest societies, we find that the essence of communal living was often predicated on public health measures. In ancient civilizations like Egypt and Mesopotamia, the state's role in water management and sanitation was crucial for preventing disease and ensuring the populace's well-being. These endeavors were not merely practical; they were entwined with the spiritual and moral fabric of society, where rulers often assumed the divine responsibility for their people's health.

The advent of the Roman Empire brought with it a sophistication of public health systems. The Romans understood that the health of the individual was directly linked to the health of the Republic. Their legendary aqueducts, which supplied clean water to the cities, and their vast network of sewers, were marvels of engineering and public policy that exemplified this understanding. Public baths, clean streets, and even the earliest forms of food regulation were hallmarks of a governance system in which public well-being was paramount.

Fast forward to the medieval era, and we encounter the birth of quarantine measures in response to the plague. Governments began to understand that controlling epidemics was as much a matter of isolating the sick as it was caring for them. These practices laid the groundwork for modern epidemiology and the notion that public health was a collective responsibility that required coordinated governance.

The Industrial Revolution introduced new challenges as urbanization and factory work led to overcrowded cities and increased the spread of disease. It was during this period that the concept of public health as a science began to crystallize. In the 19th century, figures like Edwin Chadwick in England championed the cause of public health reform, linking poor sanitary conditions to disease and economic hardship. This marked a turning point where health considerations started to influence urban planning, labor laws, and the creation of public health institutions.

In the 20th century, the establishment of international health organizations signified the recognition of health as a global governance issue. The founding of the World Health Organization (WHO) in 1948 was a landmark moment, embodying a commitment by nations to collaborate in the pursuit of worldwide health security. This period saw health initiatives become more encompassing, targeting not just infectious diseases but also chronic conditions, mental health, and the social determinants of health.

Today, health-centric governance must address a kaleidoscope of challenges, from pandemics to healthcare inequality, and from bioterrorism to the health impacts of climate change. The COVID-19 pandemic has underscored the critical importance of resilient and adaptive health governance systems, capable of rapid response and rooted in scientific expertise.

In examining the historical evolution of public health in governance, we witness the unmistakable truth that the health of the polity is inseparable from the health of its citizens. As we continue our journey towards harmonious worlds, the lessons of the past must inform the governance models of the future, ensuring that public well-being remains a steadfast political pillar.

*- National Campaigns and Programs*

In the grand tapestry of governance, few threads bear as much significance as the health of its citizens. It is a reflection of a nation's values, its priorities, and its commitment to the well-being of the populace. In this context, the role of government is not merely reactive—to step in during times of crisis—but fundamentally proactive. This section explores the innovative national campaigns and programs that serve as bulwarks against the encroachment of disease and as catalysts for a healthy society.

Governments across the globe have increasingly recognized that health promotion is a long-term investment with profound social and economic returns. In Norway, the "Frisklivssentraler" initiative—literally "Healthy Life Centres"— has been pioneering in this respect. These centres offer tailored health advice, physical activity, and dietary guidance to prevent non-communicable diseases, effectively curtailing the long-term costs to the healthcare system. Such programs are not just about individual well-being; they are about creating a resilient public health infrastructure that can withstand and adapt to future challenges.

In Japan, the "Health Japan 21" campaign is an exemplary model of comprehensive health promotion. It targets an array of lifestyle diseases through education, encouraging regular health check-ups, and fostering environments that make healthy choices easier for citizens. It's a national project that not only extends life expectancy but also improves the quality of life, setting a precedent for the globe.

Moving westward, we find Chile's "Elige Vivir Sano" (Choose to Live Healthy) program, which integrates health into various governmental policies. By reforming food labeling laws, improving urban green spaces, and subsidizing sports activities, the government has taken a holistic approach to health promotion, tackling the issue from multiple angles.

In the United States, the "Let's Move!" campaign, initiated by former First Lady Michelle Obama, made significant strides in addressing childhood obesity. By partnering with schools, local governments, and even the private sector, the campaign worked to provide healthier food in schools and improve physical education programs. Such collaborations highlight the power of cross-sectoral partnerships in promoting public health.

These examples are beacons of what is possible when governments place health at the forefront of their political agenda. They illustrate a fundamental shift from a paradigm of health as a personal responsibility to health as a collective endeavor, a shared goal that is inextricably linked to the fabric of society. National campaigns and programs, when thoughtfully crafted and implemented, have the power to cut across cultural, economic, and social divides, uniting citizens under the common cause of a healthier future.

As we consider the myriad ways in which governance can shape the health of societies, it becomes clear that these national campaigns are not mere initiatives; they are declarations of a nation's dedication to its citizens. They are the embodiment of the belief that a healthy society is the cornerstone of a stable, prosperous, and harmonious world.


*- Partnerships with Non-Governmental Organizations*

In the labyrinth of modern governance, health promotion emerges as a beacon of hope, a testament to a government's commitment to its citizens. It is a domain where the state's protective cloak converges with the spirited fervor of non-governmental organizations (NGOs), manifesting a symphony of collaborative effort aimed at uplifting public well-being.

Imagine a world where governments and NGOs dance in harmonious partnership, each step choreographed with precision to bolster the health of the populace. NGOs, with their agile structures and deep roots in local communities, possess a unique capability to navigate the social landscape, identify the needs of the underserved, and foster trust. Governments, wielding policy-making prowess and resource allocation, have the power to amplify the reach and impact of health initiatives on a grand scale.

Here we delve into the quintessential role of governments in endorsing and harnessing the potential of NGOs to spearhead health promotion. It posits that these partnerships, when molded with careful consideration and mutual respect, can become the cornerstone of a robust political pillar dedicated to public well-being.

For instance, imagine a local NGO that has developed an innovative approach to combating malnutrition in a remote village. By itself, the NGO's impact is limited to its immediate sphere of influence. However, when the government steps in to endorse this method, providing logistical support and integrating it into national health policies, the result can be transformative. The NGO's approach is disseminated across regions; its efficacy multiplied, and its vision realized on a scale that was once but a distant dream.

Moreover, such partnerships can serve as a crucible for policy experimentation and reform. NGOs often operate on the frontlines, directly engaging with health crises and, as such, are rich repositories of experiential knowledge. Governments can tap into this wellspring, adopting evidence-based practices and tailoring policies to meet the evolving challenges of health care delivery.

Yet, for these alliances to flourish, governments must foster an environment that encourages transparency, accountability, and reciprocal communication. It requires a paradigm shift—a reorientation away from hierarchical models of governance towards a more inclusive and participatory framework. This is a world where NGOs are not mere executors of government programs but equal stakeholders in the health promotion discourse.

There are many case studies where government-NGO partnerships have led to significant health outcomes. From the vaccination drives that turned the tide against infectious diseases to mental health initiatives breaking the shackles of stigma, these narratives are a testament to what can be achieved when the collective might of governance and civil society is channeled towards a common goal.

The vision is clear: a future where health is not merely an individual concern but a collective endeavor, where governments and NGOs unite under the banner of public well-being, crafting a society that is not just surviving, but thriving.


9.3 Healthcare Accessibility and Equity

- *Eliminating Barriers to Access*

In a world where the chasm between the haves and have-nots often dictates the quality of life and longevity, ensuring equitable access to healthcare is not just an ethical imperative but a fundamental pillar of inclusive governance. Let's explore the intricate tapestry of Initiatives and policies necessary to dismantle the barriers that hinder access to healthcare services, shining a light on the path toward a society where every individual, irrespective of their socioeconomic standing, can claim their right to wellness.

The cornerstone of this noble edifice is the recognition that healthcare is not a commodity to be traded in the marketplace of privilege but a universal right that must be safeguarded with the same zeal as the rights to freedom and security. To achieve this, governments must embark on a journey of transformation, where public health is not an afterthought in policymaking but the very bedrock upon which the edifice of governance rests.

One of the most significant impediments to healthcare accessibility is the cost barrier. For far too many across the globe, the prospect of illness is conflated with the fear of financial ruin. To surmount this barrier, innovative models of healthcare financing must be explored and implemented. These may include universal health coverage, subsidized insurance plans for low-income individuals, or even a radical rethinking of healthcare as a publicly funded service, free at the point of delivery.

Beyond financial constraints, geographical disparities can also impede access to health services. In rural hinterlands and urban slums alike, the scarcity of healthcare facilities and professionals creates deserts of care, parched of the healing touch of medicine. Bridging this gap requires a concerted effort to bolster healthcare infrastructure in underserved areas, perhaps through mobile clinics, telemedicine, or incentivizing healthcare providers to practice in these regions.

Cultural competence is another pivotal element in the quest for healthcare equity. A governance model attuned to the nuances of cultural diversity ensures that healthcare providers are trained to be sensitive to the beliefs and practices of the communities they serve. This not only fosters trust between caregivers and patients but also ensures that healthcare advice is heeded, and treatments are followed through.

Moreover, governance must seek to eliminate discrimination in healthcare, whether based on race, gender, sexual orientation, or disability. Legal frameworks must be fortified to protect against such biases, and healthcare systems must be audited for disparities in care and outcomes. It is also imperative to invest in education and awareness campaigns that challenge stereotypes and promote inclusivity within the healthcare profession and society at large.

In the grand tapestry of governance, threads of various hues and strengths are interwoven to create an inclusive health system that is resilient, responsive, and compassionate. It is a system that not only heals but also empowers individuals and communities, fostering a state of holistic well-being that is the truest measure of a society's prosperity.

As we envision a future where health is hailed as a political pillar, we must collectively strive to realize a world where the barriers to healthcare are relics of a bygone era, and every individual, regardless of their circumstances, has the assurance that their health is a priority safeguarded by the very fabric of their governance.

*- Addressing Socioeconomic Disparities*

In the heart of a just society, healthcare stands as a towering pillar, unwavering in its purpose to uphold the well-being of every citizen. However, the shadow of socioeconomic disparity often casts a long and oppressive shade, where the rich bask in the light of abundant care, and the poor languish in the penumbra of neglect. As we delve into the quest for healthcare accessibility and equity, we must recognize that the health of the collective is intrinsically tied to the health of the individual, and thus, to the health of the most marginalized among us.

Here, we venture into the labyrinth of structural inequalities that have historically hindered the fair distribution of healthcare. We examine the chasms carved by income gaps, the walls erected by social status, and the bridges burned by systemic bias. To navigate this labyrinth, we must arm ourselves with the compass of compassion and the map of meticulous policy design. It is a journey not for the faint of heart, for the challenges are many and the stakes are high.

We propose a threefold strategy to vanquish the hydra of healthcare inequity. Firstly, universal healthcare coverage must be embraced not as an idealistic dream but as a fundamental right. It is a clarion call to governments worldwide to ensure that every individual, regardless of wealth or want, can access the same quality of care. This is the bedrock upon which a harmonious world may be built, where health is a shared treasure, not a hoarded commodity.

Secondly, we must weave a safety net of social services that support the underprivileged, ensuring that healthcare is not a solitary pillar but part of an interconnected structure of well-being. Nutritional programs, housing stability, and education must intertwine with medical services, recognizing that the determinants of health are manifold and complex. When a child is nourished, educated, and secure, they are poised to become a healthy adult, contributing to the vitality of society.

We advocate for the formation of community health ecosystems, where local knowledge and cultural competences are harnessed to tailor healthcare to the mosaic of humanity's varied needs. In these ecosystems, caregivers and patients speak a common language — not just linguistically, but in the shared vernacular of cultural understanding and respect. It is in these crucibles of care that trust is forged and disparities dismantled.

Healthcare accessibility and equity are not merely policy goals; they are the golden threads in the tapestry of inclusive governance. By addressing socioeconomic disparities with a bold and compassionate hand, we can stitch a pattern of health that is both beautiful and just, a testament to our collective resolve to nurture a world where every life is valued, and every person is cared for. Let us then, with unwavering dedication, turn the pages of history toward a chapter where health is the shared language of humanity and equity the unwavering ethos of our governance.


9.4 Preventive Healthcare Strategies

*- Education and Community Outreach*

In an era where healthcare is often reactionary, the pivot to preventive measures becomes a cornerstone of enlightened governance. The political pillar of health rests not just on the treatment of illnesses, but also—and crucially—on the prevention of ailments before they take root. It is here that education and community outreach emerge as twin beacons guiding the way to public well-being.

The harmonization of health education across diverse populations begins in the classroom. From the earliest years of schooling, curricula infused with lessons on nutrition, exercise, and mental health can lay the groundwork for lifelong habits of wellness. Such education, however, must be adaptable, reflecting the cultural contexts and lived experiences of the students. A child growing up in the green valleys of rural landscapes will resonate with different health messages than one navigating the concrete mazes of urban environments.

But education must extend beyond the walls of formal institutions. Here, we explore the vital role of community outreach in fostering preventive healthcare. Community centers, local health fairs, and public workshops become the crucibles within which individual empowerment is forged. They serve as hubs where citizens can access information about vaccinations, screenings, and lifestyle changes that can preempt disease and disability.

Moreover, technology plays a pivotal role in expanding the reach of preventive healthcare. Telemedicine initiatives, health apps, and online platforms offer avenues for individuals to receive personalized advice, track their health metrics, and engage with support networks. In tech-savvy societies, these tools can democratize health education, making it accessible to those who might otherwise be marginalized by geography or socioeconomic status.

However, the success of these strategies is contingent on their inclusivity. Governance that prizes diversity must ensure that preventive health resources are available in multiple languages and tailored to various cultural beliefs. This means employing healthcare professionals who can communicate effectively with the communities they serve and who understand the nuances of cultural health practices.

We should examine case studies of successful preventive healthcare initiatives. We see the transformation in communities where local leaders, healthcare providers, and educators collaborate to create a culture of health. These stories are not just narratives of success; they are blueprints for replication across the fabric of humanity's diverse tapestry.

The journey toward a healthier society is ongoing, and it is one that requires the collective effort of educators, policymakers, healthcare professionals, and community activists. By emphasizing preventive healthcare through education and community outreach, governance can create a foundation for a future where the political pillar of health stands strong—a testament to a society that values the well-being of every citizen.

*- Incentivizing Healthy Lifestyles*

In the tapestry of governance, the strands of health care are interwoven with the vibrancy of community life and the resilience of national systems. The emphasis on preventive healthcare is not merely a policy choice but a reflection of a society that values its citizens' well-being and understands the economic implications of a healthy populace. Within this framework, incentivizing healthy lifestyles emerges as a cornerstone strategy, one that promises to reduce the burden on healthcare systems while enhancing the quality of life for individuals.

Imagine a society where the air is clean, the parks are plentiful, and the cities are designed to encourage walking and cycling. Here, the government doesn't just advise its citizens to lead healthier lives; it actively shapes the environment to make healthy choices the easiest options. Urban planning that prioritizes green spaces and community gardens isn't a utopian dream—it's a deliberate governance decision to foster wellness. These spaces serve not only as lungs for the city but also as hearts for communities, beating with the rhythm of shared activities, from yoga classes to farmers' markets brimming with local produce.

Incentivizing healthy lifestyles extends to the workplace. Companies receive tax benefits for implementing wellness programs that range from subsidized gym memberships to mental health days. This initiative recognizes that the mental well-being of citizens is just as crucial as their physical health. When employees are healthy, they are happier and more productive, creating a positive feedback loop that benefits both the economy and individual livelihoods.

The government also plays a vital role in nutrition, not by merely issuing guidelines, but by making nutritious food more accessible and affordable. Subsidies are redirected from processed foods to organic farms, and junk food taxes are implemented, creating a fiscal landscape where healthier food choices cost less. This is not a punitive measure but a pragmatic one, aiming to gently steer consumption habits towards more beneficial patterns without stripping away personal freedoms.

Education about health begins early, woven into the fabric of schooling. Children learn not only about the food pyramid but also how to cook simple, healthy meals. They understand the value of exercise not as a chore but as a joyous part of daily life. This educational approach demystifies health and empowers individuals from a young age to take control of their well-being.

The results of these strategies are striking. Healthcare costs decline as fewer people require treatment for conditions linked to unhealthy lifestyles, such as diabetes and heart disease. Life expectancy rises, but more importantly, so does the quality of those extra years. Citizens lead fuller, more vibrant lives, unburdened by preventable ailments.

By prioritizing preventive healthcare and incentivizing healthy lifestyles, governance does more than care for the sick; it nurtures the well-being of all, fostering a society where health is not just an individual concern but a collective triumph.


<u>9.5 Funding Public Health Initiatives</u>

*- Allocating Budgets for Health*

In the intricate dance of governance, the allocation of funds to public health initiatives is a step that cannot be missed. It is the silent music that underlies the grand performance of a society's well-being. The art of allocating budgets for health is a critical aspect of ensuring the vitality and longevity of a population.

To craft a budget that truly prioritizes public health is to embrace the notion that every individual's well-being is a brick in the edifice of a robust society. It is to acknowledge that health is not an expense, but an investment - one that yields dividends in the form of a productive workforce, reduced healthcare costs, and a happier citizenry.

Imagine a world where every budgetary decision is made through the lens of its impact on public health. Here, the questions asked are not merely "How much does it cost?" but "How many lives can it improve?" and "What is the long-term benefit?" This is the heart of a proactive, rather than reactive, approach to health governance.

In this envisioned world, funding is not just a matter of allocation, but of innovation. Traditional line-items expand to include community wellness programs, mental health support services, and preventative care initiatives that are accessible to all, regardless of socioeconomic status. Technology is leveraged to streamline healthcare delivery, making telemedicine available in remote areas and utilizing data analytics to predict and prevent outbreaks before they occur.

Moreover, the budget reflects a commitment to addressing the social determinants of health. It is well understood that health outcomes are often a reflection of environmental, educational, and economic conditions. Therefore, funding is also channeled into safe housing, pollution control, nutritional education, and programs that mitigate the effects of poverty.

In this harmonious world, the budget is a canvas on which the values of society are painted in bold strokes. It demonstrates a belief in the dignity of each life and the potential of every person to contribute meaningfully to the community. Governments act with the conviction that a healthy populace is the cornerstone of a stable and prosperous nation.

As with any masterpiece, the process of budget allocation requires collaboration. It calls for the collective insight of economists, healthcare professionals, community leaders, and, most importantly, the citizens themselves. Each voice contributes to the symphony of decisions that shape the allocation of resources, ensuring that the budget not only serves the needs of the present but also anticipates the challenges of the future.

Funding public health initiatives is an art form that demands both vision and pragmatism. It requires a delicate balance between immediate needs and long-term aspirations, between fiscal responsibility and moral imperative. For when governance places health at the forefront of its political agenda, it weaves a fabric of society that is not only resilient but also vibrant with the colors of life and the promise of well-being for all.


*- Innovative Financing Models*

In the quest for harmonious worlds, public health emerges as a cornerstone of enlightened governance. It is a domain where the symbiotic relationship between a government and its constituents is most palpable, where policy decisions can ripple through the fabric of society with profound immediacy. But the grand vision of a robust public health system is perennially confronted by the daunting task of securing adequate funding. Traditional budget allocations, while essential, are often insufficient to meet the escalating demands of public well-being in the face of novel health crises and the persistent burden of chronic diseases.

Enter the realm of innovative financing models, where creativity and fiscal acumen converge to forge new pathways for funding public health initiatives. We stand at the precipice of a new era, one that demands not only our ingenuity but also our collective will to invest in the health of our societies.

One such model is the harnessing of social impact bonds, a mechanism that invites private investors to fund public health projects with the promise of returns contingent upon the achievement of defined outcomes. This bonds the public sector's objectives with the private sector's efficiency, all the while focusing on measurable health improvements. It is a daring dance between profit and public service, where success is shared and failure is a burden collectively shouldered.

Another avenue is the introduction of sin taxes, levied on commodities that are detrimental to health, such as tobacco, alcohol, and sugar-laden products. These taxes serve a dual purpose: they discourage consumption of harmful substances while channeling much-needed funds into health promotion and disease prevention programs. It's a strategy that intertwines fiscal prudence with moral foresight, nudging societies toward healthier choices through the levers of taxation.

Philanthropy, too, has a pivotal role to play. Charitable foundations and wealthy benefactors, motivated by altruism and social responsibility, can provide the seed funding for experimental initiatives that might struggle to find government support. These philanthropic ventures act as incubators for innovative ideas, often serving as proof-of-concept that can later attract larger scale investment from more risk-averse entities.

Crowdfunding, a child of the digital age, offers yet another avenue for funding. By harnessing the collective financial power of the masses through online platforms, public health projects can tap into the global community's reservoir of goodwill. It is a democratic approach to financing, where the micro-donations of many can fuel significant change, enabling grassroots initiatives to flourish.

In this harmonious vision of the future, funding public health is not seen as a mere line item in a government's expenditure but as an investment in the very bedrock of society's prosperity. Innovative financing models are the tools through which we can sculpt a reality where public health initiatives are not only imagined but realized, ensuring that every individual, regardless of their socio-economic standing, is endowed with the opportunity for a healthy life.

In the grand tapestry of governance, the health of the population is a thread that weaves through every aspect of societal well-being, and it is our duty to ensure it is both strong and vibrant.


9.6 Health in the Workplace

*- Promoting Wellness in Employment Policies*

The modern work environment is a crucible where the pressures of productivity often clash with the needs of the human spirit. Yet, it is within this very crucible that an opportunity arises—a chance to forge policies that do not merely prevent illness but actively promote wellness. Health in the workplace transcends the provision of healthcare benefits or compliance with safety regulations. It encompasses the creation of a holistic environment that nurtures the physical, mental, and social well-being of every individual.

In the intricate tapestry of employment policies, wellness initiatives have begun to emerge as vibrant threads, signaling a transformation in how organizations perceive their role in the health of their employees. These policies are not simply add-ons to a benefits package; they are integral to a company's ethos, a statement that the well-being of its people is central to its success.

To illustrate, consider the integration of flexible work hours and the option for remote work. This flexibility acknowledges the varying rhythms of life outside the office, allowing employees to balance work with personal health needs, family responsibilities, and leisure activities. It is a recognition that a rested and contented worker is more engaged and productive.

Furthermore, the provision of mental health support through counseling services or stress management workshops reflects an understanding that mental well-being is as critical as physical health. A workplace that destigmatizes mental health issues and offers support is one that empowers its workforce to seek help without fear of judgment, creating a culture of openness and care.

Nutrition also plays a vital role in workplace health policies. Companies are now reimagining cafeterias and vending machines as sources of nourishment that offer healthy, wholesome food options. By making nutritious choices readily available, employers can subtly influence better eating habits, which in turn can lead to improved employee health outcomes.

On-site fitness centers or subsidized gym memberships are yet another example of health-centric initiatives. They not only encourage regular exercise but also foster community and camaraderie among colleagues as they engage in collective health pursuits.

But promoting wellness in employment policies is not confined to these tangible provisions. It also involves training leaders and managers to recognize the signs of burnout, to lead by example in prioritizing health, and to champion a work culture that values the individual beyond their labor.

As these policies become ingrained in the organizational fabric, they create a ripple effect. Healthy, satisfied employees are likely to carry these positive habits into their communities, thereby extending the reach of wellness beyond the workplace. Thus, companies do not merely contribute to the health of their workforce; they invest in the health of society at large.

We posit that the ideal governance structure is one that views public health as a political pillar, indispensable and inextricable from the pursuit of a thriving, dynamic society. The workplace, as a microcosm of society, is a critical frontier in this quest. By championing health-promoting employment policies, organizations can become partners in governance, contributing to a more resilient and harmonious world.


*- Corporate Responsibility and Workers' Health*

The clatter of keyboards, the low hum of office chatter, and the occasional ring of a phone are the familiar soundscapes of the modern workplace. Yet, beneath this veneer of normalcy, there lies a hidden narrative—one that speaks of the health of the workers who inhabit these spaces day after day. It is time to turn our gaze to the silent yet crucial aspect of governance that is health in the workplace.

Corporate responsibility for workers' health extends beyond the obligatory health insurance and annual flu shots. It encompasses a holistic approach to the physical, mental, and emotional well-being of employees. A harmonious workplace is not a mere utopian ideal; it is a realistic and achievable goal that serves as the bedrock of sustainable governance.

Consider the open-plan office, a design that once promised transparency and collaboration but often fell short, compromising privacy and increasing stress levels. Enlightened governance would advocate for workspaces that are thoughtfully designed to cater to diverse needs, balancing open areas for collaboration with quiet zones for deep thought and concentration. The inclusion of green spaces, ergonomic furniture, and natural lighting are not luxuries—they are investments in the workforce's vitality.

Mental health, a once-taboo subject, now demands its rightful place in corporate responsibility. The culture of relentless productivity has fostered an environment where burnout is often worn as a badge of honor. Governance within the corporate sphere must dismantle this outdated badge and replace it with policies that encourage work-life balance, provide mental health days, and offer access to counseling services. In crafting such an inclusive governance model, we foster a workforce that is not only healthier but also more engaged and productive.

In the face of a globalized economy, we must also confront the physical challenges of an interconnected world. The rise of telecommuting has blurred the lines between professional and personal life, while the threat of pandemics has underlined the importance of preventative health measures in the workplace. Progressive governance involves the implementation of flexible work arrangements and the readiness to adapt to public health guidances swiftly, ensuring that the health of workers is never compromised for the sake of economic gain.

Corporate governance must evolve to recognize that the health of its workers does not exist in a vacuum—it is a reflection of societal values. When companies lead by example, championing health and well-being as core principles, they contribute to a culture that values each individual's contribution to the collective mosaic. By weaving health into the fabric of workplace governance, corporations can set the stage for a future where the pursuit of profit and the nurturing of human capital are not conflicting aims but are harmoniously intertwined.

Let us envision a world where every boardroom agenda includes a steadfast commitment to health, where every policy decision is weighed against its impact on workers' well-being. In this world, health in the workplace is not just a corporate responsibility—it is a cornerstone of inclusive governance, a testament to our collective investment in a diverse and thriving humanity.


<u>9.7 Mental Health as a Policy Priority</u>

*- Integrating Mental Health Services*

In the labyrinthine corridors of governance, where the tangible—infrastructure, economy, and defense—often overshadows the intangible, it is the responsibility of enlightened leadership to illuminate the path towards a more holistic approach to public well-being. Within this framework, mental health emerges not as an adjunct concern but as a foundational pillar, essential to the structural integrity of a society's wellness.

Historically, mental health has been relegated to the shadows, whispered about in hushed tones and treated with a mix of apprehension and neglect. Yet, as our understanding deepens, we recognize that the mind is the wellspring of individual potential and collective prosperity. Therefore, it is imperative that governance systems integrate mental health services, treating them with the same urgency and importance as physical health.

In charting this course, our first endeavor is to dismantle the stigma that shrouds mental health issues. This begins with education and honest dialogue. Schools, workplaces, and public forums must become arenas of openness, where mental health education is embedded into curricula and policies, fostering an environment that encourages seeking help as a sign of strength, not weakness.

Governments must also ensure that mental health services are accessible to all, irrespective of socioeconomic status. This requires a multi-faceted approach, including but not limited to, the provision of subsidized care, the expansion of community mental health programs, and the integration of mental health services into primary health care systems.

The proliferation of digital technology offers unprecedented opportunities to extend the reach of mental health support. Telepsychiatry, e-therapy, and mobile health applications can bridge gaps in service delivery, especially in remote or underserved areas. However, technology must be harnessed thoughtfully, ensuring that it complements, rather than replaces, the irreplaceable human element of empathy and understanding intrinsic to mental health care.

Crucially, as we integrate mental health services into the fabric of governance, we must adopt a preventive stance. Investment in early detection and intervention programs can mitigate long-term personal and societal costs. In addition, creating supportive communities and fostering resilience can shield against mental health crises, laying the groundwork for a more robust population.

The interrelationship between mental health and other policy areas cannot be overstated. From the stress of unemployment to the trauma of social injustice, the tendrils of mental health weave through every aspect of governance. Thus, an inclusive governance model that prioritizes mental health is one that recognizes the interconnectedness of all policies and their impact on the human psyche.

The integration of mental health services into governance is not a mere addition to the roster of public services—it is a reimagining of the very notion of well-being. By elevating mental health to a policy priority, we can cultivate a society where every individual is empowered to not only survive but thrive, and in doing so, we forge a path toward a truly harmonious world.


*- Destigmatizing Mental Health Issues*

In the intricately woven fabric of public health policy, the thread of mental health has long been overlooked, its colors fading into the background. Yet, as we venture deeper into the 21st century, the imperative to bring mental health to the forefront of political discourse is not just evident—it is urgent. Here, we explore the transformative potential of destigmatizing mental health issues and establishing them as a policy priority.

For far too long, mental health has been shrouded in a veil of misconceptions and societal stigma, creating barriers to care and understanding. This must change. The call for destigmatization is not merely a compassionate plea but a strategic move towards a more robust and resilient society. It is within the power of governance to lift this veil by normalizing conversations about mental health and integrating mental wellness into the very core of public policy.

Imagine a society where mental health is not an afterthought but a cornerstone of political agendas. In this society, mental health education begins early, with school curricula incorporating lessons on emotional intelligence, mindfulness, and the importance of self-care. The knowledge that mental health is as crucial as physical health becomes a universally accepted truth.

Public campaigns play a vital role in reshaping perceptions. They celebrate recovery stories, spotlight the realities of living with mental health conditions, and honor the strength of those who seek help. Such campaigns not only educate but also cultivate empathy, challenging age-old stereotypes and fostering a community spirit of support and acceptance.

Healthcare systems are redesigned, with mental health services becoming as accessible as those for physical ailments. The integration is seamless, with primary care providers trained to recognize and address mental health concerns, and referral pathways to specialized care clear and efficient. Mental health professionals are valued and their numbers bolstered, ensuring that no one must endure lengthy waits to receive the help they need.

In the workplace, mental health policies are standard, with employers recognizing the link between well-being and productivity. Work environments are transformed into spaces that prioritize psychological safety, offering support systems such as counseling services, mental health days, and flexible work arrangements.

Governmental investment in mental health research and innovation is significant, propelling the development of new therapies and treatments. Mental health is recognized not as a burden but as an opportunity for societal advancement—a chance to unlock the full potential of each citizen.

In destigmatizing mental health issues, governance takes on the noble task of crafting a society where every individual is empowered to seek well-being without fear of judgment. This is a society that understands the intricate dance of the mind and the heart and acknowledges that within every person lies a universe of thoughts and emotions deserving of respect and care.

The harmonious world we strive for is one where mental health is a policy priority, a world that sees the mind as a garden to be tended to with the same diligence as we tend to the body. It is a world where the stigma once associated with mental health is but a relic of the past, and the future is one of hope, healing, and holistic health for all citizens.


## 9.8 Technology and Healthcare Efficiency

*- Digital Health Records and Data Sharing*

In an age where the pulse of healthcare beats to the rhythm of technological innovation, the implementation of digital health records stands as a testament to our progress. The journey toward a harmonious world is incomplete without the robust incorporation of health as a political pillar, and central to this endeavor is the efficient management of health information.

The digitalization of health records heralds a new era of healthcare efficiency. It is a canvas where the strokes of data meet the palette of care, creating a portrait of patient history that is accessible with the click of a button. These records, once locked away in the dusty recesses of filing cabinets, are now alive in the digital ether—safe, secure, and readily available to those who hold the key: healthcare professionals.

The art of governance in this arena lies not only in the adoption of digital systems but in the careful choreography of data sharing. For a patient, the health journey often involves a myriad of specialists, general practitioners, and hospitals. In the traditional scheme, this could lead to a fragmented narrative, with each caretaker holding a separate piece of the puzzle. Digital health records change the game by allowing for a unified, comprehensive view of the patient's medical history. This synergy enables practitioners to make informed decisions, reduce errors, and provide care that is both timely and tailored to the individual.

Yet, the brush with which we paint this future must be dipped in the ink of caution. Data sharing, though a boon to efficiency, comes hand-in-hand with concerns of privacy and consent. Governance structures must, therefore, be artful in crafting policies that protect patient information while facilitating the necessary flow of data. Encryption, access controls, and patient consent protocols become the guardians of this sacred trust, ensuring that only authorized eyes survey the sensitive landscape of personal health information.

Furthermore, interoperability—the ability of different systems to communicate seamlessly—is the linchpin of this digital revolution. It is not enough for records to be digital; they must speak a common language, allowing for a fluid exchange of data across platforms and borders. This is a call to action for governments, technology providers, and healthcare institutions to collaborate, setting global standards and fostering an environment that supports integration.

In the grand tapestry of governance, the thread of healthcare is woven with particular care, for it touches the very essence of life. The embrace of digital health records and data sharing is a bold stride toward a future where the well-being of citizens is placed at the heart of political endeavor. It is a future where health disparities are narrowed, outcomes are improved, and the pulse of humanity beats in unison, guided by the harmonious rhythm of inclusive and efficient governance.


*- Telemedicine and Remote Healthcare Services*

In the ripening orchard of modern healthcare, technology has burgeoned as a vital branch, extending the healing touch of medicine across the vastness of space. The advent of telemedicine and remote healthcare services has transfigured the landscape of public health governance, planting seeds of efficiency and accessibility in soil once thought barren.

Imagine, if you will, a world where the geography of need and the geography of care are seamlessly bridged. In this world, a farmer in a remote village grasps the power of a smartphone to consult with a cardiologist hundreds of miles away. A mother, cradling her feverish child in the dead of night, finds solace in the soft glow of her tablet as a pediatrician guides her through the necessary steps to alleviate the child's discomfort. These are not mere fragments of wishful thinking but the living fruits of a symbiotic relationship between technology and healthcare, nurtured by inclusive governance.

Telemedicine has emerged as a cornerstone of equitable health policy, transcending the limitations of traditional in-person consultations. Video conferencing, remote monitoring, and electronic health records have become the conduits through which medical expertise flows, unimpeded by the physical constraints of clinic walls. This digital embrace, however, is not without the need for careful orchestration. As stewards of the public good, governments must ensure that the infrastructure for such advancements is not only available but also equitable. The digital divide, which cleaves the populace into the haves and have-nots of technological access, must be bridged with the same urgency as any physical ailment.

The efficiency of telemedicine extends beyond mere connectivity; it is the heartbeat of a robust healthcare system. Remote healthcare services can drastically reduce waiting times and eliminate the need for unnecessary travel, conserving both patient energy and system resources. In emergencies, the swift digital delivery of medical advice can mean the difference between life and death. Chronic disease management, too, is revolutionized as continuous monitoring devices feed vital data to healthcare professionals, enabling timely interventions and personalized care plans.

Yet, let us not be blind to the challenges that lie in the shadow of progress. Privacy concerns, data security, and the need for a compassionate human element within the digital interface are but a few of the obstacles that governance must navigate. The integration of telemedicine into mainstream healthcare requires not only legislative foresight but also a concerted effort to educate both providers and patients about the potential and the limitations of these burgeoning technologies.


## 9.9 Emergency Preparedness and Response

*- Infrastructure for Epidemics and Natural Disasters*

We reach a critical juncture: the need for a robust infrastructure to confront the inevitable emergencies of our time—epidemics and natural disasters. The pulse of civilization itself depends on how swiftly and effectively a society can pivot from the rhythm of everyday life to the urgent cadence of crisis response.

The preparation for such events is an art as much as it is a science, a choreography that involves countless players from various sectors working in harmony. To create this infrastructure, one must envision a lattice of resilience, a network of systems and protocols that can withstand the tremors of unforeseen calamities.

In the heart of this infrastructure is the concept of 'surge capacity'—the ability to scale up services rapidly in the face of a crisis. This capacity must be embedded in hospitals, where the sudden influx of patients can overwhelm standard operations. It must also extend to the digital realm, where information systems can track the spread of disease or the impact of a natural disaster in real-time, enabling swift decision-making and resource allocation.

The architecture of emergency preparedness is not confined to the physical and digital alone; it requires a cultural framework as well. A society's readiness is reflected in the education of its citizens, the drills that are practiced, and the awareness campaigns that instill a collective sense of responsibility and knowledge of the actions required when disaster strikes.

In such an infrastructure, communication is the lifeblood. Clear, transparent, and frequent communication from governance structures to the public is essential to maintain trust and ensure compliance with emergency protocols. It's a delicate dance between providing enough information to prepare and not inciting panic, requiring nuanced messaging and a deep understanding of the societal pulse.

Cementing all these elements together is the role of leadership. During a crisis, the public looks to their leaders for direction and reassurance. Thus, governance must not only prioritize the development of emergency infrastructure but also nurture the leadership skills that can navigate the stormy seas of a disaster with composure and empathy.

However, the true measure of this infrastructure's efficacy is in its inclusivity. It must serve the most vulnerable populations—those who, even in times of calm, face the brunt of inequity. Emergency preparedness and response systems must be designed with a lens of compassion, ensuring that when the waves of calamity wash over us, they do not erode the foundations of social justice that have been so painstakingly built.

We are reminded that the robustness of our emergency response is not merely a matter of policy, but a reflection of our collective humanity. It is a testament to our ability to come together under the most trying of circumstances, to extend a hand to those in need, and to rebuild, not just structures, but trust, community, and the very essence of a harmonious world.

*- Training and Capacity Building*

We find ourselves peering into the realm of emergency preparedness. It is here, in this labyrinth of planning and reaction, that a society's resilience is truly tested, and where the art of governance reveals its most poignant flourishes.

To speak of emergency preparedness and response is to speak of a dance – a choreography that involves countless participants, each moving in synchronized anticipation of the other's steps. It is the embodiment of a paradox: the meticulous planning for chaos, the structured response to the unforeseen.

Training and capacity building are the twin pillars supporting this dance. Governments must not only envision the broad strokes of disaster response but must also instill the finesse and agility needed within the individuals and institutions responsible for carrying out these plans. This section, therefore, proposes a framework that is both prescriptive and poetic, ensuring that when the tempest comes, the fabric of society does not unravel, but rather, bends and sways in harmonious survival.

Training, the first pillar, must be comprehensive and continuous. It is a commitment to never-ending improvement, a journey with no final destination. Governments should foster programs that simulate crises in their myriad forms, from natural disasters to pandemics, ensuring that responders can navigate the complex emotional terrains of those afflicted while executing their duties with precision.

Capacity building, the second pillar, is akin to the deepening of roots, allowing the tree of governance to stand tall against gales and floods. It is essential to invest in infrastructure that can weather the storm, in communication systems that remain robust amidst chaos, and in supply chains that can operate when the ordinary flows of commerce are disrupted.

One must not forget the role of the community in this grand design. For it is in the hands of the people that true resilience is forged. Training exercises must extend beyond the officialdom, reaching into the heart of communities, empowering citizens with knowledge and tools to protect themselves and assist their neighbors. It is through this collective empowerment that a symphony of preparedness echoes across the land, and when the sirens sound, a harmonious response ensues.

The true art of governance in public well-being lies not in the avoidance of emergency but in the graceful embrace of its possibility. It is the preparation for the storm that ensures the calm, and the readiness for darkness that preserves the light.


9.10 Evaluating and Improving Health Policies

- *Metrics for Success in Health Initiatives*

In the grand tapestry of governance, the thread of public health is woven with a luminous urgency, paramount to the well-being of every citizen. As we unfold the fabric of health policies, the intricate patterns of success must be discerned with clarity and precision. It is within this realm that we explore the metrics for success in health initiatives, the guiding stars by which we navigate the vast ocean of governance.

We must consider the lifeblood of any health policy: accessibility. The measure of a policy's effectiveness is its reach to those in need. A metric of success is the reduction in disparities in healthcare access, including the availability of essential services across urban and rural divides, socioeconomic strata, and vulnerable populations. This metric is not merely quantitative but qualitative, for true accessibility embraces not only the presence of facilities but also the cultural and linguistic receptiveness that makes healthcare genuinely inclusive.

Another vital metric is the outcome-based evaluation. This involves tracking the progression of health indicators post-implementation. The decrease in morbidity and mortality rates, improvements in chronic disease management, and the rise in average life expectancy serve as tangible markers of a policy's impact. In this pursuit, we must be wary of surface-level improvements and seek sustained progress that endures beyond the initial glow of novel interventions.

Preventative measures form another cornerstone of effective health governance. The success of vaccination programs, public health campaigns, and early detection screenings can be measured by the decline in preventable diseases and the heightened awareness of health risks among the populace. These efforts reflect a governance model that does not merely react to health crises but anticipates and circumvents them through proactive measures.

Cost-effectiveness is an inescapable facet of policy evaluation. Investments in health must yield returns not only in the currency of longevity and quality of life but also in economic terms. This includes reductions in healthcare expenditures for both individuals and the state, as well as the broader economic benefits of a healthier workforce.

Engagement and satisfaction levels of citizens are subjective yet powerful indicators of a policy's resonance. Surveys and feedback mechanisms that capture the public's trust in health systems, their comfort in interactions with healthcare providers, and their overall satisfaction with services rendered, provide invaluable insights that can guide the refinement of health initiatives.

In the crucible of governance, policies are perpetually forged and reforged. The metrics for success in health initiatives thus serve as our anvil and hammer, tools with which we shape robust and resilient health policies. A policy that scores highly across these metrics is one that not only heals but also harmonizes, fostering a society where the health of each individual is the bedrock of collective prosperity.

The pursuit of excellence in health governance is relentless and requires the constant recalibration of strategies based on these metrics. It is a journey marked by the belief that the health of the polity is the wealth of the nation, a conviction that shapes our vision for a future where every citizen thrives in the embrace of a harmonious world.


*- Continuous Policy Review and Adaptation*

In the realm of public health governance, the aphorism 'prevention is better than cure' is a guiding principle. Yet, it is not the prevention of disease alone that must command our attention, but the prevention of policy stagnation. Health policies, like the very organisms they aim to protect, must be dynamic—evolving entities capable of adapting to the changing epidemiological landscape. It is in this spirit that we delve into the crucial process of continuous policy review and adaptation.

In the health governance tapestry, each thread—be it legislation, regulation, or education—must be regularly scrutinized for efficacy and relevance. The first step in this evaluation is the collection of data. Not merely quantitative statistics of morbidity and mortality, but qualitative feedback from the communities directly affected by these policies. Only with a robust evidence base can we begin the work of reflection and reform.

Once data is gathered, it is imperative that an interdisciplinary team of experts and stakeholders convene to interpret the findings. This coalition should include epidemiologists, health economists, clinicians, patient advocacy groups, and, crucially, representatives from marginalized communities who often bear the brunt of inadequate health policies. Together, they must ask: Are the current policies achieving their intended outcomes? Who is being left behind? What unintended consequences have arisen?

These questions lead to the iterative process of policy adaptation. It is here that the artful dance of governance unfolds, requiring a delicate balance between swift action to address immediate concerns and the meticulous crafting of long-term sustainable solutions. Policies may need to be recalibrated to account for new health threats, such as emerging infectious diseases, or to incorporate innovative health technologies.

Moreover, health policies must be viewed through the prism of social determinants of health. As such, policy adaptation may necessitate a foray into seemingly unrelated sectors—education, housing, and employment—to foster the conditions for a healthy populace. This holistic approach ensures that health governance does not exist in a silo but is interwoven with the broader socio-economic fabric.

In this continuous cycle of review and adaptation, communication with the public is key. Transparency in the policy-making process builds trust and ensures that the populace is not only informed of changes but understands the rationale behind them. This engenders public buy-in, which is essential for the successful implementation of health policies.

Health governance must embrace innovation, not only in technology but in policy-making itself. Adaptive policies may include novel funding mechanisms, such as health impact bonds, or the use of artificial intelligence to predict public health needs. The potential for creative governance solutions is as boundless as the challenges they seek to address.

Health governance is a living process, a continuous quest for societal well-being that demands both vigilance and vision. It is a journey we embark upon not merely as stewards of the present but as architects of the future, laying the foundations for a world where health is not a privilege but a shared, cherished commodity.

# 10. Adaptive and Resilient Governance



<u>10.1 Reflecting on the Journey</u>

*- Summarizing the governance challenges discussed*

As we draw the curtains on this profound exploration of governance, it is imperative that we pause to reflect on the journey we have undertaken together. We ventured into the heart of what it means to govern a world as diverse and intricate as ours, a world where each individual carries a universe within themselves, yet is inextricably linked to the larger cosmos of humanity.

We began our odyssey by painting a vision of global governance that both celebrates diversity and seeks unity. Here, we confronted the paradox of our times: how to craft systems that are robust enough to manage the collective needs of a planet, yet delicate enough to honor the myriad cultural nuances that define us. We recognized that governance cannot be a monolithic entity, but rather a mosaic of voices, each contributing to a symphony of organized society.

In the digital democracy segment, we peered into the future, imagining a world where technology empowers every voice, where the digital agora becomes the fulcrum of civic engagement. This dream, however, comes with its own set of challenges, including digital divides, privacy concerns, and the specter of misinformation. We grappled with these issues, seeking pathways that leverage technology for greater transparency and participation without sacrificing the sanctity of truth and personal liberty.

Our narrative then meandered through the green pastures of environmental governance. Here, the imperative of sustainable practices was not merely discussed as an ideal but as a necessity for survival. The challenge laid bare was how to transform governance to account for the environment not as a resource to be exploited, but as a partner to be respected, ensuring that our ecological footprint does not outweigh the earth's capacity to heal.

In examining economic equality, we delved into the heart of human disparity. The governance systems of tomorrow must strive to dismantle the fortresses of privilege and build bridges to prosperity for all. This means reimagining economic models that prioritize people over profit, ensuring that the wealth generated by collective human endeavor is shared equitably.

Through the lens of cultural heritage, we recognized the need to protect the tapestries of tradition while weaving in the strands of modernity. Governance must become the curator of history, ensuring that progress does not come at the cost of cultural amnesia but rather as a process of evolution that honors our ancestral legacies.

Participatory governance and conflict resolution chapters reminded us that the strength of a society lies in its ability to involve its citizens in decision-making and to navigate the turbulent waters of discord. Here, the challenge is to foster a culture of dialogue and consensus, where differences are not just tolerated but are the very fuel for innovation and growth.

Education emerged as a cornerstone of governance, with the power to shape the minds and hearts of future citizens. The challenge, then, is to create educational policies that are not just about imparting knowledge but about nurturing the values of empathy, critical thinking, and civic responsibility.

Public health governance stood as a testament to the belief that the well-being of the individual is inextricably bound to the health of the collective. The challenge is to build systems that prioritize prevention as much as they do cure, recognizing that a healthy populace is the bedrock of a thriving society.

We come to understand that adaptive and resilient governance is not a destination but a continuous process. It is a perpetual quest to balance the scales of justice, to harmonize the diverse melodies of human existence, and to ensure that as the world changes, our systems of governance are equipped not just to withstand the gales of change but to sail forth into the horizon of possibility.

Herein lies the essence of our journey: governance is the art of nurturing a society that can weather the storms of disparity, the droughts of discord, and the floods of change, all the while growing stronger, more inclusive, and harmonious. It is a journey that we must all undertake, for the world we govern today is the legacy we leave for the generations to come.


*- The evolution of governance in a diverse world*

It is worth pausing to reflect upon the journey that governance has undertaken throughout human history, and the pivotal junctures that have led us to this moment of potential transformation. The evolution of governance in a diverse world is not a narrative of linear progression, but rather a complex tapestry woven from the threads of countless human experiences, trials, and innovations.

In the earliest societies, governance was an intimate affair, where decisions were made around tribal fires, in village squares, or within the confines of city walls. The rulers and the ruled, often indistinguishable, navigated their collective destiny through direct dialogue and consensual, if not always equitable, decision-making processes.

With the dawn of empires and nation-states, governance structures became more hierarchical and centralized, a response to the challenges of maintaining order in expanding territories and diverse populations. These systems, while effective in some respects, often struggled to accommodate the richness of human diversity, sometimes suppressing it in favor of uniformity and control.

The Industrial Revolution introduced a new set of governance challenges, with rapid urbanization and technological advancements outpacing the ability of existing systems to adapt. It was during this era that the seeds of modern democracy were sown, as citizens demanded a voice in the decisions that were reshaping their lives in profound ways.

Now, in our present age, we stand at yet another crossroads. The digital revolution has democratized information and reshaped our social fabric. We have more tools at our disposal than ever before to create inclusive governance structures that can truly reflect and serve the diversity of humanity.

Yet, as we have seen, the path forward is not without obstacles. The specter of climate change, economic inequality, cultural erosion, and political polarization threatens to unravel the progress we have made. It is clear that our governance systems must not only be adaptive but resilient—able to withstand the shocks and stresses of a rapidly changing world.

To build such systems, we must lean into the diversity that defines us, harnessing it as a source of strength rather than a cause for division. We must draw from the well of collective wisdom, blending tradition with innovation, and embracing a plurality of voices. Our governance structures must be fluid, capable of evolving with the needs and aspirations of their constituents.

As we look to the future, let us remember that governance is not merely a mechanism for maintaining order or administering services. It is the very means by which we, as a species, navigate our shared existence on this planet. It is the canvas upon which we paint our dreams for a harmonious world—a world where every individual has the opportunity to thrive, contribute, and be heard.

May this understanding serve as a beacon, guiding us toward that future, inspiring us to build governance systems that are as vibrant and inclusive as the human spirit itself.


<u>10.2 Lessons from the Past</u>

*- Historical governance systems and their adaptability*

In the tapestry of time, the weave of governance systems across the world presents a rich mosaic of trial and error, of successes and failures. To construct adaptive and resilient governance structures for our future, we must first look to the lessons offered by the annals of history.

Consider the Roman Republic, an ancient beacon of governance, which thrived on a system of checks and balances long before the term entered the modern political lexicon. The Republic was a symphony of voices, from the Patricians to the Plebeians, each contributing to the legislative process. Yet, it was not immune to decay; as wealth and power concentrated, the Republic faltered, falling into autocracy. The lesson here is clear: adaptability in governance must be coupled with vigilance against the centralization of power that can lead to systemic rigidity.

Moving forward in time, the Iroquois Confederacy stands as a testament to a different kind of resilience. Its Great Law of Peace was a constitution that united six indigenous nations, fostering peace and cooperation that lasted centuries. This governance model was sustainable and participatory, with a profound respect for the environment. The Confederacy's downfall came not from within but from external forces unable to recognize and respect its value. Thus, history reminds us that governance systems must also be resilient against external pressures and the dangers of isolation.

The Venetian Republic offers another historical model, where nimble adaptability was key to its survival. Its maritime empire required constant innovation in both commerce and governance. The Venetians perfected the art of diplomacy and trade, leading to great prosperity. However, when new trade routes emerged and the geopolitical landscape shifted, Venice struggled to reinvent itself quickly enough. Adaptability, therefore, is not a static goal but a continuous process, requiring governance systems to evolve with changing circumstances.

As we pivot to our present and future challenges, the historical panorama instructs us to build governance systems that are inherently flexible, systems that distribute power widely and encourage active participation from all sectors of society. These systems must be designed to anticipate change, both from within and without, fostering a culture of perpetual innovation and learning.

Moreover, the environmental foresight of the Iroquois and the economic agility of the Venetians are of particular relevance today. As we face unprecedented global challenges, our governance structures must prioritize ecological stewardship and economic resilience, ensuring sustainability for generations to come.

History is not merely a repository of bygone eras but a wellspring of wisdom for the architects of tomorrow's governance. By embracing the adaptability and resilience of past systems while learning from their shortcomings, we can forge a path toward harmonious worlds, where governance is as dynamic as the diverse humanity it serves.

*- Learning from past failures to inform future resilience*

We must not overlook the historical panorama that has sculpted the contours of governance and its many transformations. It is by gazing into the rearview mirror of history that we glean the most valuable insights for constructing adaptive and resilient governance systems.

The tapestry of human civilization is rife with examples of governance structures that crumbled under the weight of their inflexibility. The rigid hierarchies of ancient empires, the draconian enforcement of colonial powers, and the insular policies of totalitarian regimes serve as cautionary tales, reminding us that the failure to evolve and adapt can lead to societal stagnation and collapse.

One of the most poignant lessons from the past is the fall of the Roman Empire. An entity that once stood as a colossus of civilization succumbed to a combination of internal decay and external pressures. The Roman experience teaches us that maintaining a complex governance system requires vigilance in the face of corruption, the ability to integrate diverse populations, and the foresight to reform institutions before they ossify.

Similarly, the democratic experiments of the 18th and 19th centuries—though revolutionary in their break from monarchical rule—revealed the perils of exclusionary practices. The initial denial of voting rights to women and minorities in many nascent democracies underscores the importance of inclusivity in governance. Modern systems must learn from these omissions and strive to amplify all voices within the polity.

Furthermore, the environmental catastrophes that have punctuated history, from the Dust Bowl of the 1930s to the Chernobyl disaster in 1986, starkly illustrate the consequences of neglecting ecological considerations in policy making. These events serve as somber reminders that the health of our governance systems is inextricably linked to the health of our planet.

In the realm of economic governance, the Great Depression of the 20th century and the more recent Global Financial Crisis of 2008 demonstrate the need for regulatory mechanisms that prevent the excesses of unfettered markets and ensure economic stability. They also highlight the importance of social safety nets to protect the vulnerable during times of economic upheaval.

As we forge ahead, drawing from a wellspring of historical knowledge, we must embrace a governance model that is both a tapestry and a mosaic—interwoven with the threads of collective experience yet composed of distinct, resilient pieces capable of withstanding the pressures of change. This model will recognize the cyclical patterns of history while remaining agile enough to innovate and disrupt those patterns when necessary.

Crafting governance that learns from past failures requires a commitment to ongoing education, reflection, and course correction. It demands that we equip our institutions with the tools to anticipate challenges and respond with alacrity. By infusing our governance structures with the wisdom of history, we can erect bulwarks against the repeating tides of past mistakes, ensuring that our systems are not just enduring, but eternally evolving.


<u>10.3 The Role of Technology in Adaptive Governance</u>

*- Enhancing responsiveness through digital tools*

In the final analysis of our collective journey through the realms of governance, we must confront the dual-edged sword of technology. When wielded with precision and foresight, technology becomes an invaluable ally in the quest for adaptive governance. Its potential to enhance the responsiveness of political systems to the needs and voices of their constituents is unparalleled in human history. Yet, we must approach this tool with caution, for its misapplication can just as easily erode the foundations of trust and equity that underpin any harmonious society.

One of the most promising avenues for technology in governance is the creation of digital platforms that facilitate real-time communication between citizens and their representatives. Such platforms can serve as virtual town halls where ideas are exchanged, feedback is gathered, and consensus is sought. They can democratize access to information, allowing for an informed citizenry that can hold their leaders accountable. The agility of digital tools enables governments to respond swiftly to emerging challenges, whether they be natural disasters, public health crises, or social unrest.

Consider the scenario in which an environmental calamity strikes a region. A robust digital governance system could instantly disseminate critical information, coordinate emergency services, and mobilize community support. Citizens could report issues, request aid, and offer resources through their connected devices, creating a synergistic response network. This is adaptive governance in action, harnessing technology to forge a resilient community capable of weathering any storm.

Moreover, the potential for artificial intelligence to predict trends and model solutions to complex societal problems is a frontier of governance that is only just being explored. By analyzing vast datasets, AI could assist policymakers in crafting legislation that preempts social issues, rather than merely reacting to them. However, we must also be vigilant of the ethical implications of such predictive governance. Ensuring transparency and safeguarding privacy are critical to maintaining the trust required for these systems to function effectively.

In the realm of economics, blockchain technology offers a transparent and secure method for transactions, which could revolutionize the management of public funds and reduce opportunities for corruption. Digital currencies could facilitate direct and efficient distribution of resources, ensuring that aid reaches those in need without the friction of bureaucracy.

Yet, for all its promise, technology alone cannot be the panacea for our governance challenges. It must be integrated thoughtfully into a broader ecosystem of policies and practices that prioritize human dignity and equity. Adaptive governance recognizes the human element at the heart of technology, channeling its transformative power to serve the greater good.

As we stand at the precipice of a new era in governance, let us embrace technology as a tool for unity and empowerment. Let us craft digital systems that are not only responsive but also inclusive, equitable, and imbued with the spirit of democratic participation. In doing so, we may yet realize the vision of a harmonious world, where governance is as dynamic and resilient as the diverse humanity it serves.


*- Safeguarding against technological risks and vulnerabilities*

In the labyrinthine digital age, technology wields the power to both uphold and undermine the pillars of governance. As we forge pathways toward adaptive governance systems, we must acknowledge the double-edged sword that technology represents. It is a catalyst for participation and transparency but also a harbinger of risks and vulnerabilities that could potentially fracture the very fabric of society.

To construct adaptive governance systems that are resilient in the face of technological change, we must first understand the nature of the risks we face. Cybersecurity threats loom large, capable of bringing the administrative machinery to a grinding halt, compromising sensitive information, and eroding public trust. The specter of misinformation campaigns can sway public opinion, disrupt elections, and stoke social unrest. Moreover, the rapid pace of technological innovation often outstrips the ability of regulatory frameworks to keep pace, leading to a governance gap where emerging technologies operate in a vacuum of oversight.

Yet, it is within our grasp to turn these formidable challenges into opportunities for strengthening the resilience of governance structures. By embracing a proactive rather than reactive stance, policymakers can anticipate potential disruptions and act to mitigate their impact. This requires a continuous process of horizon scanning, identifying emerging technologies and understanding their implications for governance systems.

One such method is the institution of robust cybersecurity protocols that protect infrastructure and data integrity. Governments must invest in state-of-the-art defense mechanisms while fostering a culture of security awareness among citizens and officials alike. In parallel, strategies to combat misinformation must be developed, leveraging technology itself to detect and counteract false narratives through fact-checking algorithms and digital literacy campaigns.

As for the governance gap, adaptive governance calls for flexible regulatory frameworks that can evolve alongside technological advancements. This necessitates a collaborative approach, engaging stakeholders from the tech industry, academia, civil society, and government to co-create guidelines that balance innovation with public interest.

Furthermore, technology offers unprecedented opportunities for scenario planning and simulation, enabling governments to model the impact of different policies before they are implemented. This predictive capacity is instrumental in crafting adaptive governance systems that can withstand the pressures of a rapidly changing world.

In safeguarding against technological risks, we must not lose sight of the profound potential technology holds for building a more inclusive, engaged, and transparent governance. By judiciously harnessing this potential, we can devise governance systems that are not only adaptive to the challenges of the present but also resilient in the face of an uncertain future. Technology, thus, becomes not just a challenge to overcome but an indispensable ally in our quest for harmonious worlds.

## 10.4 Integrating Diversity into Resilience

*- Policies that accommodate cultural complexities*

We arrive at the crux of adaptive and resilient governance: the seamless integration of diversity into the very fabric of policy-making. As we gaze upon the mosaic of our global society, the recognition of cultural complexities is not merely a courtesy—it is a cornerstone of enduring governance. The resilience of a system is not just measured by its ability to withstand shocks but also by its capacity to embrace the variegated strands of human existence.

Consider, if you will, the metaphor of the tapestry—a piece of art that derives its strength and beauty from the interlacing of different threads. Each thread represents a unique cultural narrative, a singular history, and a distinctive perspective. Governance systems that recognize these threads and weave them into the fabric of their policies do not merely pay lip service to diversity; they harness its power.

Such policies move beyond tokenism. They are crafted through the lens of cultural empathy, ensuring that decision-making processes are not homogenized but are instead reflective of the multifarious needs and values of the populace. In practice, this means engaging in a dialogue with indigenous communities when drafting environmental regulations, taking into account the festive calendars of ethnic groups in urban planning, or considering the dietary restrictions of various religions in public health initiatives.

We see the case of a Scandinavian country that has integrated Sami reindeer-herding practices into its environmental conservation efforts, ensuring the survival of both the ecosystem and the indigenous way of life. We are taken to a bustling metropolis where neighborhood councils, comprising representatives from the city's diverse inhabitants, have a say in local governance, fostering a sense of community and shared responsibility.

In these narratives, resilience is not a fortress wall against change but a dexterous dance with the dynamic rhythms of human diversity. It is the recognition that the shocks to our system—be they environmental, social, or technological—are absorbed not just by the rigidity of our structures but by the flexibility of our understanding.

Resilience is born when diversity is not just tolerated but celebrated, not just included but integrated. It is in the symphony of voices, each singing its truth, that governance finds its most robust and harmonious form, echoing through the chambers of the future with a melody as timeless as humanity itself.


*- Leveraging diversity as a strength in governance models*

In the closing pages of this exploration into the vast horizons of inclusive governance, we must anchor our thoughts on one of the most potent sources of resilience: diversity itself. It is in the polyphony of human societies that we find the melodies of adaptability and innovation. As the world hurtles towards an uncertain future, governance models must not only accommodate but actively integrate diversity into their structural framework.

We posit that the key to enduring governance lies in the very fabric that constitutes our societies. It is not merely the presence of diversity but the active engagement with it that forges systems capable of withstanding the tremors of change.

Imagine a mosaic, each piece a distinct color and shape, contributing to a coherent and beautiful whole. Similarly, governance systems should view social, cultural, and ideological differences as pieces of a larger picture, each one essential to the integrity and vibrancy of the community. When governance structures are built with the understanding that every perspective adds value, they become more than just representative; they become wise and perceptive, capable of drawing upon a wealth of experiences to navigate challenges.

Governance can leverage diversity by:

1. Encouraging inclusive policy-making processes that bring multiple voices to the table, ensuring that decisions made are not only for the people but by the people. This participatory approach serves as a bedrock for legitimacy and trust.
2. Embracing cultural diversity in problem-solving, which can lead to innovative solutions that a homogenous group might overlook. Diverse teams are shown to be more creative and to produce more sustainable outcomes.
3. Fostering a culture of continuous learning within governance institutions, where insights from different disciplines and life experiences are valued. This cultural mosaic enables governance to evolve with the times, anticipating and responding to shifts with agility.

4. Promoting intersectionality as a lens through which policy impacts are assessed, ensuring that the most vulnerable and marginalized in society are not left behind but are, in fact, central to the resilience-building process.
5. Cultivating adaptive leadership that is not only diverse in representation but is also equipped with the empathy to understand and the courage to act upon the needs of a multifaceted populace.

By embedding diversity at the core of governance models, these systems become more than just robust; they become amorphous, capable of re-shaping and re-forming in response to the ever-changing dynamics of the social landscape. They mirror the ecological resilience found in nature, where biodiversity is the cornerstone of thriving ecosystems.

As we tread the delicate path of crafting governance that is inclusive and effective, we must recognize that our differences are not a barrier but a bridge to a more resilient future. It is through the kaleidoscope of human diversity that governance systems will find the strength to endure and the wisdom to flourish.


## 10.5 Economic Flexibility for Future Challenges

*- Adapting economic policies to withstand shocks*

In the ever-shifting landscape of global economics, the ability of a governance system to adapt to sudden shocks is not just a desirable attribute—it's an absolute necessity. From financial crises to pandemics, the history of humanity is punctuated by events that have dramatically reshaped societies, often testing the resilience of their economic structures to their breaking points.

The key to economic flexibility lies not in rigid adherence to ideology, but in the pragmatic and nimble application of policies that can buffer the blow of unforeseen challenges. In this section, we explore the concept of economic plasticity—the capacity for economic systems to bend rather than break under pressure.

One of the most vital components of economic plasticity is diversification. Governance systems that encourage a wide array of industries and support a multiplicity of job sectors are better equipped to handle the collapse or decline of any single industry. Diversification acts as a safeguard, distributing the risk and ensuring that the economy as a whole can continue to function even if parts of it falter.

Another critical aspect is the establishment of robust safety nets. These systems, which range from unemployment benefits to healthcare and housing support, are crucial in maintaining the purchasing power and economic participation of citizens during crises. Safety nets also serve to stabilize demand for goods and services, providing a level of continuity for businesses in uncertain times.

Furthermore, governance systems must prioritize the accumulation and wise management of reserves. Similar to how a prudent sailor saves provisions for unforeseen storms, governments can create sovereign wealth funds and emergency budgets that can be tapped when normal economic activities are disrupted. These reserves can be used to stabilize currency, bail out critical industries, or invest in infrastructure projects that provide both immediate employment and long-term benefits to the economy.

Adaptation also extends to the regulatory framework. A governance system that promotes economic flexibility must be willing to review and revise regulations in response to changing circumstances. This doesn't imply a regulatory free-for-all, but rather the cultivation of a regulatory environment that can be quickly and effectively adjusted to facilitate recovery and growth, while still protecting the public interest.

Governance must recognize the role of technology as a driver of economic resilience. Investments in technological infrastructure can enable the rapid scaling of new industries, support remote work during times of crisis, and foster innovation that leads to new economic opportunities.

As we look to the future, our economic policies must not be carved in stone, but rather written on water—ready to flow and change shape with the currents of time. It is through this fluid approach to economic governance that we can construct systems capable of withstanding the shocks of tomorrow, safeguarding the prosperity and well-being of all citizens. The dance of governance and economy is one of perpetual motion and adaptation; it is in this dynamic embrace that the hope for a harmonious world lies.


*- Promoting sustainable growth and equitable resource distribution*

In the shifting sands of the global economy, where technological advancements and environmental imperatives reshape the landscape with a fierce urgency, the call for economic flexibility is not just prudent—it is paramount. The future challenges we face require governance systems that are both adaptive and resilient, capable of promoting sustainable growth and equitable resource distribution amidst the whirlwind of change.

This paints a vision of a world where economic policy is not a rigid structure but a fluid and responsive instrument of social justice and environmental stewardship. Here, we explore the prerequisites for such a system, emphasizing the need for innovative fiscal strategies that empower communities while safeguarding our planet's resources for generations to come.

Imagine a world where governments, in partnership with the private sector and civil society, create dynamic markets that respond to the ebbs and flows of societal needs. In this world, economic growth is decoupled from environmental degradation, where the pursuit of wealth no longer means a plundering of the earth's bounty but a harmonious exchange that benefits all.

Let's delve into the heart of adaptive economic governance, advocating for policies that are designed to evolve in lockstep with the rapid pace of innovation. Let's examine the potential of universal basic income as a safety net in the face of automation and artificial intelligence, which threaten to disrupt traditional job markets. We propose robust education and retraining programs that prepare citizens for the jobs of the future, ensuring that no one is left behind in the technological revolution.

Moreover, we argue for the implementation of green taxes and incentives that encourage businesses to prioritize sustainability, thus steering the economy toward a model where profitability and planetary health are not at odds but are inextricably linked. We envision a circular economy, where waste is minimized, resources are reused, and the life cycle of products is extended through intelligent design and policy support.

In a world beset by climate change and social inequality, it is crucial that our economic systems are equipped to handle the unforeseen. We underscore the importance of building robust social safety nets that can absorb shocks and protect the most vulnerable. Economic flexibility means not just having the capacity to adjust to new realities but also the foresight to anticipate them and the compassion to ensure that in our quest for progress, we do not trample on the rights of the marginalized or the sanctity of the environment.

We call upon leaders and citizens alike to embrace the principles of adaptive governance, to champion policies that are as diverse and dynamic as the challenges we face. In doing so, we lay the foundation for a future where economic growth is a tide that lifts all boats, where the wealth of nations is measured not just in GDP but in the health, happiness, and harmony of its people.

10.6 Environmental Stewardship as a Governance Keystone

In the heart of governance, the environment often whispers its needs in the backdrop of louder socio-economic clamors. Yet, as our world faces unprecedented ecological crises, it becomes imperative to amplify this whisper to a clarion call. Environmental stewardship must transition from a peripheral concern to a central keystone in the arch of governance.

To build resilient systems, governments must adopt a holistic approach that recognizes the interdependence of natural ecosystems and human societies. The paradigm of environmental governance requires a shift from reactive to proactive, from segmented to integrated, from exploitative to regenerative.

Imagine a governance system where environmental policy is not an addendum but the foundation. In such a system, every legislative action and policy decision is filtered through the sieve of sustainability. It is a system where the economy is reimagined as a subsidiary of the environment, not vice versa—a world where the gross domestic product (GDP) is replaced by more comprehensive measures of well-being that account for natural capital.

This vision is not utopian but attainable through the concerted efforts of policymakers, community leaders, and citizens alike. It begins with the acknowledgment that the environment is the ultimate public good, transcending borders and generations. As such, it requires collaborative governance that leverages the collective wisdom of diverse stakeholders. The inclusion of indigenous knowledge, for instance, is vital; these communities have stewarded their lands sustainably for millennia and hold invaluable insights into ecological management.

In practice, building resilient systems means embedding environmental education in the fabric of our schooling, fostering a populace that is eco-literate and empowered to act. It means investing in green technologies and infrastructure that bolster adaptation to climate change and mitigate its impacts. It also entails creating adaptive legal frameworks that can quickly respond to environmental emergencies and hold accountable those who harm the commons.

Furthermore, fostering environmental stewardship as a governance keystone involves creating incentives for conservation and restoration efforts. Policies such as carbon pricing, conservation easements, and biodiversity credits can mobilize the private sector's involvement in environmental protection.

It is imperative to establish monitoring systems that provide real-time data on ecological health, enabling swift action when thresholds of harm are approached. These systems must be transparent and accessible, cultivating trust and engagement from the public.

The governance of the future must not only be adaptive and resilient but also fundamentally green. Environmental stewardship is not a luxury but a necessity for the survival and flourishing of humanity. It is the keystone upon which a harmonious world can be built, a world where governance systems and natural ecosystems exist in symbiotic balance, supporting life in all its diversity.

*- Policy innovation for long-term sustainability*

We have traversed the contours of governance, from the digital agora to the hallowed halls of cultural heritage. Yet, as we consider the future of governance, we must underscore the centrality of environmental stewardship. It is the soil from which all policy must bloom; a keystone in the arch of sustainable governance.

Our world teeters on a delicate fulcrum. On one side lies the legacy of industrialization—its resource depletion and ecological scars. On the other side, there emerges a vision of regeneration, where governance and nature dance in symbiotic splendor. Herein lies our task: to innovate policies that not only mitigate environmental damage but actively foster ecological vitality.

Here, we explore the confluence of environmental concern and policy innovation. Governments must act as custodians of the earth, integrating environmental considerations into every legislative act and administrative decision. This holistic approach extends beyond mere conservation. It demands a reimagining of energy systems, urban design, and agricultural practices—transcending the traditional silos of governance.

Consider the prospect of "Greenprint" legislation, a policy framework that mandates environmental impact assessments for all new laws, akin to a blueprint for sustainability. Imagine a world where every new housing development is evaluated for its carbon footprint, every transportation initiative measured against its contribution to air quality, and every economic program scrutinized for its water usage efficiency.

Furthermore, fiscal innovation plays a critical role. The implementation of carbon pricing mechanisms, such as cap-and-trade systems or carbon taxes, can dynamically shift market behaviors towards lower emissions. Such economic instruments must be crafted with precision to ensure they do not disproportionately impact those least able to bear the costs, thereby upholding the principles of equity and inclusivity.

We must also seed the growth of green technology through targeted investments and subsidies. By fostering a fertile environment for clean energy startups and sustainable agriculture enterprises, governance can catalyze a wave of innovation that resonates with the rhythms of the natural world.

Education, too, is a vital strand in the web of environmental governance. Curricula at all levels should instill a sense of planetary citizenship, equipping future generations with the knowledge and passion to continue the work of environmental stewardship.

In the pursuit of long-term sustainability, governance becomes not just a structure or a system but a living entity, adaptable and resilient. It is a testament to our collective commitment to steward the earth with wisdom and care, ensuring that our harmonious worlds endure for generations to come.

Let us carry forward the message that governance, at its best, is an act of profound responsibility—a covenant with the future, a promise to the planet, and a dedication to the harmonious symphony of life.


<u>10.7 Participatory Governance for Enhanced Adaptability</u>

*- Encouraging citizen involvement in decision-making*

In the tranquil garden of democracy, the seeds of participation must be sown with care, so that the fruits of governance may be shared by all. As our journey through the intricate landscape of inclusive governance draws to a close, it is paramount to acknowledge the pivotal role of citizen engagement in enhancing the adaptability and resilience of governance systems.

Participatory governance is the fertile soil from which springs the robust tree of adaptability. It is an approach that encourages citizen involvement in decision-making processes, recognizing that the collective wisdom of a diverse populace is a reservoir of innovative solutions and perspectives. By tapping into this wellspring, governance systems can dynamically respond to changing circumstances, evolving needs, and unforeseen challenges.

The concept of participatory governance is not new, harking back to the agora of ancient Greece, where citizens gathered to discuss and decide on matters of state. In today's world, this ethos must be rekindled and recalibrated, harnessing the vast potential of digital platforms and communication networks to facilitate dialogue and deliberation on a scale never before possible.

Imagine a digital agora, a virtual space where the voices of citizens from all walks of life converge, contributing insights and ideas that shape the policies affecting their daily lives. This space is not confined by geography or limited by access; it is a ubiquitous forum that transcends borders and barriers, empowering individuals to play an active role in the governance of their communities, nations, and indeed, the global stage.

In such a system, adaptability is not merely an abstract ideal, but a tangible reality. When faced with environmental calamities, economic upheavals, or social unrest, a governance structure rooted in participatory principles can swiftly pivot, informed by the real-time input and consensus of its constituents. It can weather storms of uncertainty with the resilience that comes from being deeply embedded in the collective consciousness of the people it serves.

Moreover, participatory governance fosters a sense of ownership and accountability among citizens. When individuals have a hand in crafting the policies that govern their lives, they are more likely to support and uphold them. This collaborative spirit is the bedrock upon which resilient societies are built, societies that not only endure but thrive amidst change.

In our quest for harmonious worlds, we must not overlook the power of the individual—each person a unique thread in the grand tapestry of humanity. By weaving these threads together through participatory governance, we create a fabric that is both strong and supple, capable of stretching to accommodate new patterns without losing its fundamental integrity.

As we stand at the crossroads of history, looking towards a future that is as daunting as it is dazzling, let us choose the path of collective engagement, where every voice is heard, and every hand can help steer the ship of state. For it is through the concerted efforts of all that we can build adaptive and resilient governance systems, ensuring that the garden of democracy continues to flourish for generations to come.


*- Utilizing grassroot feedback to refine policies*

We arrive at a pivotal intersection of ideas, where the core principles of participatory governance meet the urgent need for adaptability in our systems. As our societies continue to evolve at a pace unprecedented in human history, the ability of governance structures to remain resilient hinges on their capacity to incorporate the voices of those they serve. Grassroots feedback is not merely a supplement to policy-making; it is the lifeblood that sustains the vitality and relevance of governance.

We posit a bold proposition: that the very essence of adaptability in governance is rooted in the active engagement of its citizenry. By weaving the narrative of everyday experiences into the fabric of policy decisions, governments can create a responsive and dynamic framework that not only addresses current needs but also anticipates future challenges.

The chorus of the governed must be heard, not as disparate whispers but as a harmonious ensemble that guides the hand of policy. We must shed the antiquated notion of a one-way dialogue where governments dictate and citizens simply follow. Instead, we embrace a symphony of exchange, a continuous loop where feedback from the grassroots informs every note of the policy score.

Technology, as we have seen in previous chapters, offers unprecedented tools to facilitate this dialogue. Digital platforms can capture the pulse of the populace, providing real-time insights and fostering a spirit of collaboration. In decentralized forums, ideas can be shared, policies can be debated, and consensus can be reached, all contributing to an environment of collective intelligence that can swiftly adapt to new realities.

Consider the case study of a small coastal town facing the consequences of climate change. As sea levels rise and storms intensify, traditional governance models may struggle to respond efficiently. However, a governance system that has ingrained participatory mechanisms can quickly gather insights from affected communities, co-create solutions with local experts, and implement adaptive measures that directly address the unique circumstances of the town.

Therefore, this is not simply a conclusion but a clarion call for a transformative approach to governance. It is a vision of future systems that are not rigid and hierarchical but fluid and collaborative. Here, adaptability is not an abstract concept but a tangible outcome of policies co-created with the heartbeat of the people.

We are not at an end, but at a beginning. The principles laid out within these chapters are stepping stones to a world where governance is a shared journey, a dance between leaders and citizens that moves to the rhythm of change. We close with an invitation to all readers to step into the arena of participatory governance, to raise their voices, and help steer humanity towards a future that is not only sustainable and just but also infinitely adaptable to the winds of change.


10.8 Education as the Foundation of Adaptive Governance

*- Developing critical thinkers and informed citizens*

Education is not just the transmission of knowledge; it is the cornerstone of a society's capacity to adapt and evolve. In a world where the only constant is change, our governance systems must be built on the bedrock of education that nurtures critical thinking and informed citizenry. The task is arduous but imperative: to cultivate minds that can navigate the labyrinth of global challenges and contribute to a harmonious world.

As we stand at the confluence of tradition and innovation, our educational institutions must shoulder a dual responsibility. They must honor the wisdom of the past while equipping the youth with the foresight to shape the future. It is through this delicate balance that education becomes the foundation of adaptive governance.

In classrooms that buzz with inquiry, students learn to question, not just to answer. They engage with a curriculum that is not myopic but panoramic, one that integrates global issues into local contexts. This holistic approach produces not just learners, but thinkers—individuals who can dissect complex problems, recognize the interconnectedness of systems, and propose solutions that are equitable and sustainable.

To build governance that is resilient in the face of socio-political and environmental shifts, we must foster a culture of perpetual learning. Continuous education opportunities for citizens of all ages ensure that the electorate stays abreast of developments, both technological and ideological. Lifelong learning becomes a civic duty, a necessary engagement to participate effectively in the governance process.

Critical thinking and informed decision-making are the twin pillars upon which adaptive governance rests. By nurturing these skills, education empowers citizens to hold their leaders accountable, to demand transparency, and to participate in governance not as passive subjects, but as active architects of their society.

We take a moment to envision classrooms that double as incubators for democracy, where debates are encouraged and diverse perspectives welcomed. Here, students learn the art of compromise, the strength of empathy, and the value of diversity. They emerge as citizens who understand that their voice is a vital instrument in the symphony of governance.

As we look towards the horizon, it is clear that the path to harmonious worlds is paved with the pages of textbooks, the bytes of digital learning platforms, and the collective wisdom of empowered, educated citizens. The adaptive governance systems we yearn for will not sprout in a vacuum; they will grow from the fertile ground of an educated populace, ready and able to face the challenges of tomorrow.

The blueprint for adaptive governance is not set in stone; it is written in the minds of those who are taught to think freely and critically. It is a manuscript continuously being revised as new chapters of human history unfold, guided by the steady hands of those who have learned the true essence of governance: the harmonious symphony of a diverse humanity, united in the pursuit of learning and growth.

*- Adapting educational curricula to changing governance needs*

As the sun of knowledge rises over the horizon of our collective future, it becomes abundantly clear that the foundation of a resilient and adaptive governance system is laid upon the bedrock of education. The tapestry of our societal fabric is woven with threads of wisdom passed down through generations, and it is through the loom of education that these threads are nurtured and strengthened.

To adapt educational curricula to the ever-evolving needs of governance, we must first acknowledge that the landscape of knowledge is not static. It is a dynamic ecosystem, where the winds of change constantly reshape the contours of understanding. As such, our educational frameworks must be fluid, designed to evolve alongside the shifting paradigms of political, social, and technological advancements.

In the crucible of the classroom, we must forge a new generation of thinkers, leaders, and citizens who are not only well-versed in the history and principles of governance but are also adept at navigating the complexities of a globalized and interconnected world. This calls for an interdisciplinary approach, where political science intermingles with technology, economics dances with cultural studies, and philosophy joins hands with environmental science.

To this end, curricula must be reimagined to include simulations and case studies that mirror the real-world challenges faced by contemporary governance structures. Students should be encouraged to engage in debates, participate in mock elections, and involve themselves in community projects that echo the participatory ethos of governance we aspire to instill. This experiential learning will imbue them with a sense of civic duty and a practical understanding of how inclusive governance can be achieved.

Additionally, the nurturing of critical thinking skills is paramount. Educators must instill in their wards the ability to question, analyze, and synthesize information. In a world awash with data, the capacity to discern fact from fiction, to extract wisdom from noise, becomes an indispensable tool in the arsenal of those who will lead and govern.

The symbiosis between education and governance is undeniable. As we sculpt the curricula of tomorrow, let us infuse them with the flexibility to adapt to unknown futures, the inclusivity to embrace diverse perspectives, and the foresight to anticipate the governance needs of the coming age. By doing so, we empower our successors to not only inherit the world we leave behind but to steward it with vision, compassion, and an unyielding commitment to a harmonious world for all.

In this grand endeavor, technology shall be our ally. Digital platforms can democratize access to knowledge, ensuring that education is not a privilege of the few but a fundamental right for all. Leveraging these tools, we can create virtual classrooms that span continents, allowing ideas to flourish in a borderless academic realm. This, in turn, prepares citizens for the digital dimensions of governance, where transparency and participation are greatly enhanced by technology.

The education of our youth is the most profound investment we can make in the future of governance. It is through their enlightenment that we ensure the adaptability and resilience of our governing institutions. As they learn, so shall they lead, and as they grow, so too will the strength and harmony of our world.


10.9 Public Health and Governance Interdependency

- *Strengthening health systems through policy*

The health of a nation's citizens serves as a cornerstone for its overall stability and prosperity; thus, attention to public health is not merely a matter of policy but a fundamental pillar of governance.

Strengthening health systems through policy necessitates a holistic approach, one that transcends the boundaries of healthcare provision and permeates all aspects of governance. It is an understanding that health is a shared responsibility, not only among healthcare providers and institutions but also across various sectors of government and society.

The interdependency between public health and governance can be seen in the way policies in education, environment, urban planning, and economy can have profound effects on population health outcomes. For instance, educational policies that emphasize health literacy empower citizens to make informed decisions about their well-being, leading to a healthier populace. Similarly, environmental policies that focus on clean air and water directly affect the incidence of diseases and the overall quality of life.

We must also highlight the importance of health equity, advocating for policies that ensure all members of society have access to quality healthcare services regardless of their socioeconomic status. Inclusive governance incorporates the voices of the marginalized and disenfranchised, working to dismantle barriers to health and well-being. It is a governance that recognizes the unique health challenges faced by different community demographics and strives to tailor responses that are not one-size-fits-all but are nuanced and culturally sensitive.

The COVID-19 pandemic is presented as a case study in this section, illustrating the importance of adaptive and resilient governance systems. The pandemic shed light on the weaknesses in global and national health systems, highlighting the need for governance that can rapidly mobilize resources, coordinate across borders, and implement effective crisis management strategies. It also emphasized the value of trust between citizens and their governments, a trust that is essential for public health interventions to be successful.

In crafting policies that strengthen health systems, the book suggests that governments should embrace technology and innovation. Digital health initiatives, telemedicine, and data analytics are tools that can enhance healthcare delivery and disease surveillance. However, such technological advancements must be deployed with careful consideration of privacy and ethical implications.

Ultimately, we call for governance that is proactive, not reactive. It is a governance that invests in preventative measures, promotes healthy lifestyles, and is prepared to tackle health crises with agility and compassion. Through collaborative efforts and a shared vision for the health of humanity, governance can forge a path towards a harmonious world where public health is a testament to a society's strength and unity.


*- Preparing for health crises with adaptable governance structures*

As we navigate the complex and often turbulent waters of global health, the undeniable interplay between public health and governance structures comes into sharp relief. Now, we take a closer look at how adaptable governance can prepare societies for health crises, ensuring resilience and a swift, effective response.

We must recognize that public health is not a standalone entity but is intrinsically linked with various sectors such as economy, education, and infrastructure. When health crises emerge, they ripple through these sectors, revealing the strengths and weaknesses of governance structures. It is this interconnectedness that requires our governance systems to be inherently adaptable, capable of rapidly mobilizing resources and coordinating across different sectors.

A key component of adaptability is the capacity for real-time surveillance and data analysis. Governance systems must invest in technological infrastructures that allow for the early detection of health threats. By leveraging artificial intelligence and big data analytics, governments can predict outbreaks, understand transmission patterns, and implement targeted interventions before a crisis escalates.

Building on this technological foundation, adaptable governance must also foster robust communication channels between policymakers, health experts, and the public. Transparent communication enhances trust and compliance with health measures, while misinformation can erode the very fabric of societal cooperation. In times of health crises, clear and consistent messaging from governance bodies is paramount.

Furthermore, adaptable governance structures emphasize the importance of contingency planning and simulation exercises. These practices enable governments to test their response mechanisms and refine their strategies in a controlled environment, preparing them for real-world scenarios. By continuously learning from these exercises and past health crises, governance systems can evolve to better withstand future challenges.

Public health governance must be rooted in the principle of equity. A governance system that can adapt is one that ensures all individuals and communities, regardless of their socioeconomic status, have access to the necessary resources and healthcare during a crisis. This commitment to inclusivity not only improves health outcomes but also strengthens the social contract between governments and citizens.

The health of the public is a direct reflection of the efficacy and adaptability of our governance structures. As we look to the future, let us strive to build governance systems that are prepared to face health crises, not as isolated shocks but as integral parts of the complex ecosystems they serve. By doing so, we create a harmonious world where the health and well-being of every individual is a shared responsibility and a collective triumph.

*- Blueprint for creating adaptable and resilient governance frameworks*

We gather the threads of discourse from earlier chapters to weave a coherent blueprint for governance that can stand the test of time and the turbulence of change. To chart the way forward, we must recognize that the foundations of governance rest on the bedrock of societal values and aspirations. As we cast our eyes towards the horizon, we see a landscape marked by the convergence of technology, environmental stewardship, economic fluidity, and cultural vibrancy—a world where governance is not just a mechanism of rule but an expression of collective human endeavor.

To build governance frameworks that are both adaptable and resilient, we must first embrace a principle of structured flexibility. This means creating systems that allow for rapid response and policy iteration without losing sight of long-term goals and stability. It requires an intricate balance of strong, yet malleable institutions that can evolve with societal shifts while providing a steady hand during crises.

Next, we must foster inclusive dialogue and decision-making processes, ensuring that the voices of the marginalized and underrepresented are amplified and heeded. This inclusivity should not be a token gesture but woven into the very fabric of governance, ensuring that policies are not only made for the people but by the people.

In the digital age, we must leverage technology to enhance transparency and accountability, building trust between the governed and those who govern. Digital platforms can facilitate broader participation and enable real-time feedback loops, turning governance into a dynamic, interactive process.

Environmental governance calls for a paradigm shift, recognizing that our fates are inextricably linked to the health of our planet. Policies must transcend borders and generations, embedding sustainability into every decision and action. This means prioritizing renewable resources, protecting biodiversity, and incentivizing behaviors that contribute to ecological balance.

Economic governance should strive for systems that are equitable and just, recognizing that true resilience comes from shared prosperity. Alternative economic models that emphasize community, cooperation, and the common good should be explored and supported.

Cultural heritage and the arts must be preserved and promoted, ensuring that the tapestry of human expression remains vibrant and serves as a source of inspiration and identity for future generations.

In the realm of education, governance systems must commit to nurturing critical, compassionate, and creative thinkers who can navigate the complexities of a diverse world. Education must be viewed not as a commodity but as a public good, essential for the flourishing of democracy and the cultivation of informed citizens.

Public health governance must be proactive, not reactive, building infrastructures that can withstand pandemics and ensure access to quality care for all.

The blueprint for resilient and adaptable governance is one that anticipates change, values diversity, and commits to the common good. It is a governance that is not rigid but learns, adapts, and grows. It is a governance that listens, responds, and acts with foresight and empathy. As we close this volume, let us remember that governance is an art as much as a science, and it is through our collective imagination, will, and spirit that we can bring about harmonious worlds.


*- Engaging the international community in collaborative governance evolution*

The quest for harmonious worlds is not a solitary journey but a collective voyage. As we stand at the precipice of a new era, we must envision a system of governance that is not only adaptive and resilient but one that is intricately woven with the threads of international collaboration and mutual respect.

Our global society is a mosaic, rich with diversity, yet challenged by the complexities of unifying a myriad of beliefs, values, and systems. The future of governance, therefore, lies in our ability to engage the international community in a dialogue of collaborative evolution—a conversation that transcends borders, cultures, and ideologies.

To initiate this transformative journey, we must first acknowledge that no single approach to governance can be universally applied. Instead, we must embrace a pluralistic methodology, one that is flexible and capable of accommodating the distinctive needs of different societies. Such a system would not impose, but rather propose; it would not dictate, but facilitate.

In this spirit, the international community must come together to create a platform for shared learning and exchange. This platform would serve as a fertile ground for the cross-pollination of ideas, where successful governance strategies from one nation can inspire and inform the policies of another. Governments, civil society, and international organizations must work in concert to foster an ecosystem of governance innovation that values both local wisdom and global insights.

Moreover, the participation of citizens in this evolutionary process is paramount. By leveraging digital democracy, we can cultivate a more engaged and informed citizenry, capable of contributing to the governance dialogue with their unique perspectives and experiences. In this way, each individual becomes a vital architect of the adaptive governance framework, ensuring that it remains grounded in the realities and aspirations of the people it serves.

As we look to the future, it is imperative that we also consider the role of education in preparing the next generation for the challenges of governance in a diverse world. By instilling the principles of empathy, collaboration, and critical thinking, we can nurture a cadre of future leaders who are equipped to build bridges where walls once stood.

The path to harmonious worlds is paved with the stepping stones of collective effort and open-mindedness. By engaging the international community in the continuous evolution of collaborative governance, we can forge a future that is not only adaptive and resilient but also equitable and just. It is a future where every voice is heard, every culture is honored, and every society thrives. Together, we can turn the page and begin writing a new chapter in the story of humanity—one that celebrates our differences and unites us in our common pursuit of a harmonious world.

# About The Author

Abraham Chaffin is a conduit of the transformative power of AI for societal good. With a MS in Software Development and a background in artificial intelligence, he has dedicated his career to leveraging advanced technology to address some of the world's most pressing issues.

His work to harness the insights of AI on many critical topics has resulted in an array of books that not only highlight the potential of AI in various sectors but also delve into the philosophical and ethical dimensions of this rapidly evolving technology. His unique approach combines deep technical expertise with a profound understanding of human values, aiming to bridge the gap between diverse ideological backgrounds and promote a more unified, empathetic world.

His titles such as "The Four Horsemen of Peace: An AI Prophecy of Peace" and "AI's Insight Into Empathy: Cultivating Compassion in a Divided World" reflect his commitment to using AI as a tool for peace and understanding. In "AI Contemplates Morality in a Complex World," he explores the necessity of ethical innovation, while "AI's Insight Into the Future of Work" offers pragmatic solutions for the AI and automation revolution.